WHEN AMERICA

BECAME

SUBURBAN

WHEN

AMERICA

BECAME

SUBURBAN

ROBERT A. BEAUREGARD

university of minnesota press
minneapolis ▪ london

Every effort was made to obtain permission to reproduce the illustrations in this book. If any proper acknowledgment has not been made, we encourage copyright holders to notify us.

Published by the University of Minnesota Press
111 Third Avenue South, Suite 290
Minneapolis, MN 55401-2520
http://www.upress.umn.edu

Library of Congress Cataloging-in-Publication Data

Beauregard, Robert A.
    When America became suburban / Robert A. Beauregard.
        p.   cm.
    Includes bibliographical references and index.
    ISBN-13: 978-0-8166-4884-9 (hc : alk. paper)
    ISBN-10: 0-8166-4884-0 (hc : alk. paper)
    ISBN-13: 978-0-8166-4885-6 (pb : alk. paper)
    ISBN-10: 0-8166-4885-9 (pb : alk. paper)
    1. Suburbs—United States—History. 2. Urbanization—United
States—History. I. Title.
    HT352.U6B43 2006
    307.760973—dc22

                                                2006013891

Printed in the United States of America on acid-free paper

The University of Minnesota is an equal-opportunity educator and employer.

12 11 10 09 08 07 06   10 9 8 7 6 5 4 3 2 1

Whatever may be the good or evil tendencies of populous cities, they are the result to which all countries, that are once fertile, free, and intelligent, inevitably lead.

—George Tucker, *Progress of the United States in Population and Wealth in Fifty Years* (1855)

Contents

Preface

In the decades after World War II, America's identity was radically altered. Spurred by the return of economic prosperity, the extension of the nation's global dominance, and—most importantly for the story I will tell—the simultaneous decline of the industrial cities and the rise of the suburbs, Americans reimagined their country and what it meant to be an American.

The United States and the world had changed. In the process of disengaging from its industrial past, manual work was becoming less valued. Office buildings displaced factories as the era's dominant urban image; consumption surpassed production. The industrial landscape receded from view as people abandoned the large, central cities and small towns for new bedroom communities, embraced more leisure-oriented lifestyles, and rearranged their daily existence around a conspicuous and status-conscious consumption. Living differently, Americans began to think differently of themselves.

In that special period between the end of World War II and the recession of the mid-1970s, what I call the short American Century, the United States became the most prosperous of nations, the first suburban society, and a global power. It also discarded its industrial cities. At the root of these changes was a rupture in previous patterns of urbanization. This rupture triggered consequences that redefined the dominant way of life and eventually changed the nation's global image. The decline of the industrial city set in motion a series of events that led eventually to a reimagining of the national identity.

A reinvented America, now anchored in the postwar suburbs, was projected globally. Domestic prosperity and suburbanization figured prominently in the ideological contest known as the Cold War. The United States mobilized its suburban lifestyle and consumer culture to tout the superiority of capitalist democracy over communist dictatorship and thereby widen the ideological divide between itself and the Soviet Union. Less often noted is that this narrative enabled the country to distinguish itself from its European origins. Rejecting the old-world culture associated with European cities, Americans forged a unique identity out of the suburbs, the consumption that made suburban life both desirable and possible, and the abandonment of the industrial centers.

Positioned in relationship to Cold War rhetoric and juxtaposed against the country's European heritage, the new national narrative added another argument to the cultural artifact of American exceptionalism. In the seventeenth and eighteenth centuries, freedom from religious persecution and feudal autocracy had set the United States apart from the societies of Europe. In the late nineteenth century, with industrialization rampant, opportunity and the absence of socialism were the ostensible markers of its uniqueness. In the twentieth century, a reluctant "welfare state," persistent racism, and an "American way of life" separated the nation from its European counterparts.[1]

These many claims to exceptionalism are all rooted in the vastness of the nation's territory and the riches it contains. The great size of the United States has acted as a political safety valve and a spur to waves of investment and economic growth; it has also enabled the country's inhabitants to discover frontiers on a regular basis. Westward expansion, industrialization, rural depopulation, and mass suburbanization are only a few of the innumerable ways in which geography has shaped the country's politics, served its economy, and harbored its social diversity. The frequent reconfiguration of human settlements strengthened the conviction that America was different from other nations.

Yet in certain ways the industrial cities were unexceptional. Other countries—England, Germany, France—had similar experiences in the mid-to-late nineteenth century, experiences that often preceded analogous developments in the United States. And their industrial cities faltered after World War II, though the scale of their plight was not as great. What they did not suffer was the mass suburbanization that occurred as industrial cities declined after World War II or the challenge that such wrenching events posed to national identity.[2]

The industrial cities had brought the United States to commanding heights. After World War II, the global economy had little use for them. Novel forms of real estate investment and new types of suburban communities further contributed to their redundancy. Developers, households, retailers, and commercial investors turned their attention to the bedroom suburbs. There, on the peripheries of the older cities, they created a unique way of life, one independent of the constraints but also devoid of the opportunities of large cities. The fact that suburbanization diffused across all but the poorest social strata and stopped well short of welcoming African Americans hardly detracts from its significance; in fact, it is an integral part of it. These two events—the decline of the industrial city and mass suburbanization—fueled a remarkable economic prosperity as well. The entire transition, deeply rooted in American society, was made possible by the switch from a distributive to a parasitic urbanization.

For centuries, and with few exceptions, the country's cities had grown simultaneously, all benefiting from an ever-expanding economy and a burgeoning population. Yet urbanization turned parasitic beginning in the 1930s. When World War II ended, the suburbs and the cities of the Sunbelt prospered by drawing population and investment from the older metropolitan cores. No longer were just a few places left behind as the country grew; massive disinvestment from the industrial cities became a requirement for national growth.

The simultaneous decline of the industrial cities, the growth of the suburbs, unprecedented domestic prosperity, and a reinvigorated global dominance were all related. Together, they defined the short American Century. Even more important for understanding the early postwar period, these events triggered a profound transformation of the American way of life. The country's identity was about to be reimagined.

This book originated in my long-standing fascination with the industrial cities of the United States and, more specifically, with their near collapse after World War II.[3] For almost a century, the cities on which the country had built its economic prosperity and military might were a ruling presence in national affairs. Even during the peak of the urban crisis in the late 1960s, their decline was of widespread concern and a persistent object of media attention and government programs. Subsequently, public commentators, academic observers, and national policy makers lost interest. In the throes of what seemed then to be a deathwatch for these cities, commentators searched for more optimistic scenarios. Sunbelt cities, the booming suburbs, and, later, edge cities drew their attention and fulfilled their needs. Amply documented and extensively—even neurotically—probed, the historical dynamics underlying these phenomena nonetheless eluded academic scrutiny. Though unacknowledged, a rupture in urbanization had taken place.

My initial goal was to document and interpret this rupture. I quickly realized, though, that the "normal science" of urban studies, at least as practiced in the United States, was unduly restrictive.[4] While the field had embraced the "spatial turn" and globalization has become a dominant theme, the field has maintained a myopic attitude toward the rest of the world. Few U.S. urban scholars consider transnational influences on U.S. urban development, the ways that developments in the United States influence developments elsewhere, or the role of empire in the shaping of American society.[5] My investigations had led me to the realization that industrial cities in other advanced economies had met similar postwar fates and to a greater appreciation of the role played by immigration—a trickle during the short American Century—in the growth of U.S. cities. Given the colonial heritage of the country, its international economy, the centrality of immigration, and relentless projections of U.S. culture from film to clothing, the transnational character of U.S. cities had to be addressed. A global sensibility—an immersion in the "web of global interdependencies"— seemed unavoidable.[6]

I also sought to bridge the divide between writings that cast cities as cultural realms and those that view them as political economies. Over the past three decades or so, numerous efforts have been made to merge the two approaches, many of them quite admirable.[7] However, I did not want to study the usual themes connecting culture and the city: popular entertainment, memorials, architecture, urban planning and design, colonialism, shopping behavior, museums. I wanted to connect with larger cultural debates. What really interested me was the question of how changes in the way people lived affected how they thought about themselves and the nation. More simply, the issue is the relation between place and identity, an issue I view as central to any investigation of urban culture. The twin themes of national identity and American exceptionalism seemed ideal for this purpose, while having the additional benefit of setting cities and suburbs in both national and global arenas.

At the same time, I hoped to overcome the ahistoricism of writings in political economy and their cultural offspring. Although space had been fervently embraced, most urban scholars (with the obvious exception of historians) had yet to take seriously the necessity for a historical point of view. Even when included, such a point of view has been rudimentary at best.[8] Urbanization cannot be understood otherwise, and national identity and American exceptionalism are always historically specific constructions.

Although this book is historical, it is not a history book. A loose chronology of postwar U.S. urbanization lurks below the surface of the text, but my argument is less about generative sequences than about the confluence of events previously treated as autonomous. The book's claim to being historical stems from its focus on a specific time period, the years from the late 1940s to the mid-1970s. It was then that the rupture in the processes of urbanization became most consequential. This rupture produced events whose effects continue to reverberate throughout American society. The text, though, relies on historical events—the Cold War, the Marshall Plan, the 1930s Depression, the postwar "golden age" of the economy—for its flow, not for its historical meaning. That meaning, I thought, could best be found in how these events influenced both the portrayal of national identity and the ideological positioning of the nation in the global arena.

This led me to the "short American Century," the era when four momentous events collided: the decline of the industrial cities, the rise of the mass-produced suburbs and Sunbelt cities, unprecedented domestic prosperity, and a global dominance militarily challenged by the Soviet Union but otherwise ascendant. This was a unique period in U.S. history. Numerous historians and social scientists have commented on the mutual dynamics of suburbanization and domestic prosperity or of domestic prosperity and global dominance. Rarer are the scholars who have explored the global dimensions of suburbanization.[9] And while almost every observer of the postwar scene has placed the decline of the industrial cities in the suburban equation, and vice versa, no significant effort has been made to connect these events to national identity and then weave them into the postwar global projections of the nation.

Many readers, I suspect, will find my attention to national identity and the related theme of American exceptionalism disconcerting. How, they might ask, can one write about a reputed national identity for such a large, culturally diverse society? Is it not the case that American exceptionalism has been soundly dismissed either as a specious quest—many countries and peoples view themselves as "different," even "exceptional"—or as inherently flawed? And what about the global arrogance that such a claim encourages?

In my defense, national identities "are to be distinguished, not by their falsity/genuineness, but by the style in which they are imagined." While they are certainly "invented" and contain numerous contradictions, this does not preclude them from acting as a wedge for prying open the meaning of national events.[10]

As for American exceptionalism, it continues to occupy the energies of scholars and popular commentators, despite the many pitfalls inherent to its claim. Debates about who Americans are and how they are different from, say, Japanese or Germans, Chinese or Canadians, are ubiquitous, even if implicit, in public deliberations on a variety of issues. National identity and exceptionalism pervade debates around immigration and the ethnic transition of neighborhoods. They have arisen in foreign affairs; for example, in the relationship of the U.S. economy to that of the European Union or as regards military interventions in the Middle East. And they persist in academic circles as U.S. scholars weigh the value of one or another European social theory. As contemporary and resilient as patriotism and individualism, national identity and American exceptionalism endure.[11]

American exceptionalism is, for me, an issue of representation and ideology, not fact; it is a form of collective rumination produced out of the myriad encounters among collective experiences, imagined possibilities, and individual yearnings. Additionally, American exceptionalism and national identity confer a moral tone on the text; they are concerns that bring values to the surface of the debate.[12] (Not to be overlooked in this regard is the moral tone embedded in my thinly veiled disappointment with the decline of the industrial cities and my suspicion of the suburbs.) Of utmost importance here is the fact that my discussion of national identity and American exceptionalism is confined to the short American Century, a period in which these issues were widely debated—naively so, critics might note. Once the period ended, these issues became even more problematic and much less alluring—they did not disappear.[13]

At its core, this is a book about postwar urbanization and its consequences. My interest is in the implications that the rupture in urbanization had for the way Americans understood "America" and for the ideals they displayed to the world. Dominant ways of living have a tendency to seep into the identity of a country. They bind the nation together ideologically and project its values and accomplishments beyond its borders. For a specific historical period and a specific country, this book explores the complex ways in which how people lived affected who they were, or at least who they believed they were, and how they represented themselves to the world.

Two final comments—about cognitive style and about perspective— need to be made before briefly describing the organization of the book.

First, by design, this is a text focused on interpretation, not explanation. My goal is not to produce an abstract rendition of events and conditions that isolates causes and consequences and values parsimony in doing so. My search is for meaning. Thus, the approach is one of accumulating facts and ideas in order to create layers of complexity that enable the reader to grasp what happened in this short American Century. No attempt is made to subtract detail—and knowledge—to reveal reality's essence.[14]

Second, my interpretive scheme is made up of social forces, rather than of people and organizations making decisions and shaping the world. The key "actors" are suburbanization, job loss, immigration, capital disinvestment, ideological conflicts, obsolescence, consumption, and a host of similar phenomena. Developers, government officials, middle-class households, and others appear in the text, but they remain faceless and are less actors than categories of influence and response. While committed to this approach, I am also ambivalent. What haunts me is that the book pays too little attention to the "who" of these postwar transformations, the active voice of social theory. Not to be forgotten is that urbanization is a consequence of "the underlying struggles between various groups and . . . the economic, political, and ideological solutions to such struggles."[15]

Chapter 1 elaborates the argument sketched at the beginning of the preface. In addition, it sets the political context through a brief description of the short American Century and touches, albeit lightly, on national identity and American exceptionalism. The next three chapters explore the material basis for the rupture in urbanization that replaced distributive processes with parasitic ones. In chapter 2, I review the decline of the country's large industrial cities, the rise of the mass-produced suburbs, and the emergence of cities in the Sunbelt in order to suggest the extent to which this tectonic shift influenced how people live in the United States. Chapter 3 documents the rupture and frames it historically in terms of long waves of development that cross national borders. That chapter also situates parasitic urbanization globally. Then, in chapter 4, I offer an argument for why parasitic urbanization, despite its costs, took hold and was encouraged. The emphasis is on cultural predispositions and the biases inherent to the institutions of the U.S. political economy.

The next three chapters extend the rupture into the economic and cultural realms of postwar American society. Chapter 5 couples the proliferation of the suburbs with the domestic prosperity of the period.

These were mutually constituting events that exacerbated urban decline even as they fed on it. In making this case, I also reflect on the economic contribution made by the shrinkage of the industrial cities. Chapter 6 discusses the transformation, from urban to suburban, of the country's dominant way of life, and chapter 7 shows how these changes became part of the nation's global project, particularly in Europe and particularly as regards the Cold War. In the final chapter, chapter 8, I tie together the various strands of my argument around national identity, urbanity, exceptionalism, and the ever-present American frontier. The book concludes with a brief discussion of the demise of the short American Century and the purported resurgence of America's older cities.

The Short American Century

From the end of World War II in 1945 to the recession of the early 1970s, the United States was the most affluent and the most influential of nations. During those years, the United States realized the destiny that Henry R. Luce, one of the country's most outspoken publishers, had famously foreshadowed in 1941. Luce had urged Americans "to accommodate themselves spiritually and practically to the fact" that "their nation became in the 20th century the most powerful and vital nation in the world." The mantle of world leadership, he challenged, could no longer be avoided; isolationism would have to be abandoned. The subsequent projection of a U.S. presence promoted democracy, abundance, and American ideals across the globe. The American Century had ostensibly begun.[1]

These years were among the most prosperous in American history. Jobs were plentiful and wages were on the rise. Young married couples were confident enough of the future to flee apartments in the cities for homes with mortgages in the suburbs. There, they started families in unprecedented numbers. The gains from high productivity and a favorable balance of international trade were spread throughout the economy. The United States was a bountiful society admired throughout the world for its vast array of consumer goods and comfortable way of life.

Americans celebrated the wealth of consumer products, their scientific achievements, the stability and openness of their government, and the myriad opportunities available to them for personal advancement. The national mood was buoyant; a shared sense of accomplishment nurtured a federal government sure of its ability to overcome all obstacles, whether domestic or foreign. Except for paranoia about communism and the persistent challenge of race relations, Americans were satisfied with who they had become and with their prospects for the future. America, they believed, was the envy of the world. Throughout what would turn out to be a shorter American Century than Luce had envisioned, the formidable combination of prosperity, democracy, and military strength repelled all challenges to U.S. global supremacy.[2]

While the nation was basking in prosperity and international glory, the industrial cities were undergoing precipitous decline. Urban economies were collapsing, and residents were leaving for the suburbs in ever-rising numbers. Once-robust manufacturing firms closed their operations or moved to more favorable locations. The ripple effects produced job loss and business closings. Racial tensions, poverty, and physical decay became urban problems of seemingly overwhelming magnitude. Riots erupted in African American inner-city neighborhoods in the 1960s, and numerous city governments faced bankruptcy during the economic downturn of the early 1970s.

The consequences were devastating. The remaining residents suffered, businesses from department stores to textile factories closed their doors, slums spread, and city governments were burdened with shrinking revenues and an unrelenting demand for services. Metropolitan economies dependent on these cities stagnated and demands for federal assistance increased in intensity. The country's image was being tarnished as the consequences of decline reverberated throughout society. The nation's cities, about which its citizens have always been ambivalent, became (to many observers) an embarrassment. A less stressful time, one beyond the urban crisis, was difficult to imagine.[3]

The industrial cities of the United States had enjoyed uninterrupted growth prior to World War II. Decade after decade, more and more people had taken up residence in them. Growth seemed inevitable. The belief in a never-ending expansion survived even the short-lived population declines that a few industrial cities had experienced in the 1930s. The massive loss of people and hemorrhaging of jobs and investment after the war was an abrupt departure from normality. Almost half of the fifty largest cities—places like New York City, Philadelphia, Detroit, Michigan, and St. Louis, Missouri—lost population between 1950 and 1970, with that number increasing in the 1970s. Cities such as Buffalo, New York; Pittsburgh, Pennsylvania; Youngstown, Ohio; Gary, Indiana; Camden, New Jersey; and East St. Louis, Illinois, shed from one-third to one-half their residents. Medium-size and small cities were similarly afflicted. A few decades earlier, only the most aberrant of cities had experienced a shrinkage in population. But postwar urban decline was more than a temporary deviation from unrelenting expansion, more than an "optical illusion."[4] Here was a sharp and possibly permanent shift in the country's pattern of urbanization.

The whole process of urbanization seems, in retrospect, to have ruptured.[5] Whereas cities in the United States had enjoyed nearly continuous growth since their founding, and all cities together had shared in national growth, in the short American Century some cities declined while others prospered. The underlying cause was a restructuring of the core urban processes that had operated since European colonization in the seventeenth century. For 200 years, the distribution of human settlements in the United States had been governed by a form of urbanization in which the forces of concentration were strong and the forces of deconcentration and decentralization comparatively weak. As a result, cities grew to relatively high densities. Moreover, very few cities failed to expand, even though new cities emerged to compete with existing ones and the country's population migrated relentlessly westward. National growth was shared.

Beginning sometime in the twentieth century, this *distributive* urbanization was replaced by a more *parasitic* variety. National expansion

Figure 1. Skyline of Minneapolis, 1948. Photograph by Gordon Ray. Courtesy of Minnesota Historical Society.

was no longer shared. Instead, population growth in emerging cities and suburbs was inextricably tied to population loss in aging ones. The forces of agglomeration had weakened in the postwar period, while those of dispersal had gained strength. Parasitic urbanization thereby produced the trauma that devastated older, industrial cities, created a crisis of national consequences, and undermined the way of life that had defined achievement in the United States for hundreds of years. The dominance of the center—the industrial cities had been the nuclei of the emerging metropolitan areas—was replaced by a fragmentation of the periphery brought about by suburban development. Urbanization had jumped to the metropolitan scale.

The transition from distributive to parasitic urbanization was the product of a number of forces. Of prime importance was a rearrangement of the global division of labor that decimated manufacturing and subsequently weakened the trade status of the advanced industrial countries. This industrial restructuring worked in combination with innovations in transportation, a robust market in suburban land, and the maturation of the real estate industry to spur investment in the metropolitan periphery. Government failures to maximize the use of existing infrastructure or to subsidize private-sector housing in the cities contributed to the propulsion of people to the suburban fringe and to regions beyond the industrial heartland. Racial antagonisms fueled by African American migration from the South also played a role by discouraging white households from moving to, and encouraging white flight from, those cities in which African Americans were congregating.

Population dispersion put older cities at a demographic disadvantage. It took away young and relatively affluent families and left behind older households. In-migrating racial minorities only partially compensated numerically. And with immigration at historically low levels, the older cities were unable to neutralize their population loss as they had done in the past, much less to grow. Moreover, the disparity in incomes between those who left and those who arrived worked to the further disadvantage of these central cities. A lowering of aggregate disposable incomes dampened rents, house values, retail sales, and local tax revenues.

Surprisingly, in retrospect, the cities had the attention of the national government, and political and business leaders organized to resist the forces of decay. However, whatever financial assistance and political support the cities received seemed to have a perverse effect. Urban renewal intensified slums and devastated small businesses.

Highways disrupted neighborhoods and allowed downtown office workers to commute to work from the suburbs. The expansion of social services contributed to higher taxes, and antidiscrimination laws allowed the black middle-class to flee their old neighborhoods, leaving behind deepening poverty.[6]

The end result was not only the decline of the industrial cities but regional decline as well. The industrialized regions of the Northeast and the Midwest grew more slowly and became less prosperous relative to the West and the South. Cities in the Sunbelt boomed while those in the Rustbelt became weaker and weaker. In all regions, the suburbs expanded at astounding rates, initially drawing residents from the older central cities.

Except that it was so tragic, the sudden decline of cities after World War II amid unprecedented domestic prosperity and global dominance might be taken as ironic. The manufacturing cities had enabled the United States to emerge victorious from two world wars and to establish itself as an industrial giant. The country had become the source of much of the world's finance, an undefeatable military power, and the command center of international diplomacy. Yet in that quarter century from the late 1940s to the early 1970s, when prosperity and global ascendance were the twin axes of American identity, the country's cities were literally being abandoned. In a sense, their success contributed to their demise.

The United States was hardly an exception to global trends. Cities in other industrialized countries were experiencing a similar, if less dramatic, turn of fate. The advanced economies of the world were casting off goods production and remaking their economies. Suggestive of the global forces in operation, the predicament of U.S. industrial cities occurred almost simultaneously with the rapid growth of Third World cities; both were fueled by the exporting of low-wage manufacturing jobs. Worldwide, urbanization was undergoing dramatic change.

The cognitive dissonance of widespread and deeply troubling urban decline coexisting with domestic affluence and global supremacy was resolved by the promise of mass suburbanization. New, predominately residential suburbs flourished around the older industrial cities and in the emerging metropolitan areas of California, Arizona, Texas, Florida, and other Sunbelt states. Suburban development was celebrated while urban decline was explained away as inevitable—the industrial cities' obsolescence as a sign of progress rather than as a national defect—and even necessary for economic growth.

Suburbanization provided the investment in new construction

and the purchase of consumer goods that, along with rising exports to Europe, anchored national prosperity. Suburbanization and economic growth complemented each other.[7] The suburban lifestyle required massive new investments and unending household purchases ranging from automobiles and refrigerators to backyard barbecue grills. These new goods and communities changed how people commuted to work and spent their leisure time, when they visited their relatives, the ways they interacted with neighbors, and even the dreams they had for their children.

Of course, suburban prosperity was not available to all people; African Americans in particular were denied access. Suburbanization, whether draining residents from Chicago or driving the growth of Houston, was mainly for white households. "Urban ghettos were reserved for African Americans and other minorities; suburbs were to remain lily white."[8] The fruits of national growth, just as with the burdens of industrial-city decline, fell unevenly across the racial divide. The white majority benefited and, not surprisingly, the suburban image came to dominate the history of the period.

Quintessentially American, the suburban lifestyle also provided symbolic allure for U.S. exports. Awash in consumer goods, enjoying nearly full employment, and blessed with high wages, the daily life of the "average" American became a model for people around the globe. Suburban life anchored a standard of living commensurate with the nation's status as the leader of the "free world" and established the country's economy and form of government as the best hope for affluence, democracy, and world peace. Life in the suburbs was a mark of American exceptionalism and a model to which all nations could aspire. Not so praiseworthy, and more of an embarrassment than an accomplishment, was the trauma of the industrial cities. Deterioration and decay did not engender pride. These cities could be admired for their past but not for their present state, while the future looked bleak. Consequently, they were of little use ideologically in bolstering the nation's international stature.

Neglect of the cities has deep roots in the American consciousness. From the country's initial European settlement, a sense of destiny has encouraged a selective perception, and centuries of growth and acclaim have inured the nation to the costs of its accomplishments. It is as if Americans have struck a Faustian bargain in which progress has been traded for self-reflection, compassion, and a sense of history. The result is a moral imagination incapable of registering the destruction that accompanies advance.[9]

Figure 2. Suburban housing development, Torrance, California, 1963. Courtesy Herald Examiner Collection/Los Angeles Public Library.

One makes such claims, of course, in the face of an American character that is relentlessly elusive. What it means to be an American resists generalization, and not just because the United States is a country of immigrants with diverse cultural inclinations, skills, and possessions. Americans are, in historian Michael Kammen's felicitous phrase, a "people of paradox." They attempt to balance individualism with collectivism, mobility with community, consensus with freedom, majority rule with minority rights. "Americans more than most," Kammen wrote, "have historically tended to ignore their [anomalies], for they feel that inconsistency is a bad thing." Consequently, Americans are blinded to "the larger and internalized tensions within the society."[10]

These paradoxes contribute not just to the American ambivalence toward cities but also to a moral indifference that has left cities to fend for themselves with only minimal aid from the larger society. The "shame of the cities" was too anemic to induce the guilt necessary for resisting and reversing postwar urban decline.[11] Popular outrage was weakened by flight; households and businesses opted to leave the cities rather than fight for their survival. Political will materialized only briefly beyond the confines of city governments, and even this moment of attention paled in comparison with the overwhelming support for suburbanization. In the early postwar period, Americans believed in the efficacy of the national government to win wars, manage the economy, and fight communism, but not in its ability to resolve, or even take full responsibility for, the plight of the cities.

The decline of the industrial cities eroded civic culture and heightened national cynicism. Consumption displaced the collective resolve that had characterized the war effort, and suburban migration weakened identification with the cities and the people who hoped to use them as a stepping-stone to middle-class status. These cities had done more than position the country at the top of the global hierarchy. They also had anchored the national character and provided the crucibles within which differences in culture, politics, and economic position were negotiated. In combination with the unending reinvention of frontiers, the central cities had held the country together for nearly a century. Their abandonment precipitated the loss of the country's urbanity, its ability to make a common culture out of diversity. With it went the belief in a singular national character.

The reader might reject such an interpretation out of hand. One can hardly commit to cultural paradox and at the same time put forth a singular and dominant rationale for this indifference to troubled cities. To be fair, not all urban commentators have viewed the juxtaposition of urban decline with domestic affluence and global dominance as either ironic or embarrassing. A society committed to growth since its inception, voraciously consuming more and more land throughout the nineteenth century and expanding its frontiers well into the twentieth century, cannot but have a convincing rationale for the peoples and places that are inevitably left behind.

The banner of progress has served well those who treat man-made misfortunes as a small price to pay for unfettered individualism or the elevation of the human condition.[12] Whether or not it was inevitable or necessary, the decline of the industrial cities enabled the United States to maintain its trajectory of growth. Ostensibly, these cities had become obsolete, a drag on the constant change that characterizes a dynamic and innovative society. The flight of households and businesses, the argument continues, was a rational response to this obsolescence and enabled a successful adjustment to changing technology and consumer demand. Necessarily, the industrial cities had to be "downsized" if the country were to make the transition from a goods-producing society to a postindustrial service society. Failing to do so would be to lag behind in the global competition for growth and dominance.

Even though such an argument hints at urban decline's contribution to growth, it casts this contribution as a cost whose reasonableness is beyond question. That people and investors fled the industrial cities is no more and no less than one event on a progressive journey of accomplishment and prosperity for which the United States seemingly holds the patent. Rather than lament this state of affairs, observers were encouraged to rejoice in the ability and prescience of the institution—not government but the mythical market—that made it happen.

From this point of view, the decline of the industrial cities was part of the unrelenting restlessness of capitalism as it roamed the landscape picking up and discarding investment opportunities. In order to maintain rising levels of profitability, capitalism destroys past investments, with some of the costs of that destruction borne by other capitalists, some by government, and the remainder by those unlucky enough to be in the path of progress. Progress is always, in that much-used Schumpetarian phrase, a matter of "creative destruction."[13]

Growth, though, always threatens to undermine itself as emergent economic sectors and more powerful investors build their wealth on the economic trendsetters of an earlier era. And governments, because they are democratic, cannot wholly ignore such immoderate consequences. Their responses often involve stricter regulations, higher taxes, or both in combination, each of which depletes the profits that are understood as the incentive and the reward for bringing about growth. Consequently, to avoid total collapse—economic, political, and cultural—of the dominant social order, it is best to mitigate the destruction, sweeping it beyond the borders of unavoidable guilt even if not wholly out of sight.

Capitalism is destined to destroy what it has previously built. Growth with decline is unavoidable in a political economy always flirting with internal contradictions. The shame of the postwar cities, then, is hardly ironic. Rather, it is an outcome of institutions enmeshed in their own logics. In the short American Century, a country of great wealth and global influence ignored its cities because it seemed the only path to growth.

That the decline of the industrial cities, mass suburbanization, domestic prosperity, and global dominance were inextricably linked during these years deserves greater attention. The foregoing synopsis only hints at the complexity of these relationships. Anchoring those intricacies is the mid-twentieth-century rupture in the core urbanization processes that had governed settlement patterns for the previous hundred years. This rupture produced the geographical consequences that set the national identity in flux. Central-city decline, suburbanization, and Sunbelt-city growth, however, were not the only contributors to the reimagination of America. The affluence and internationalism of the period engendered a pervasive sense of accomplishment and invulnerability. Celebrated and yet also condemned for its arrogance, the proclamation of an American Century symbolized this ideological exuberance.

American Exceptionalism

The story of postwar urbanization and the corresponding American way of life is incomplete in the absence of a global perspective and, specifically, of reference to the nation's "Cold War triumphalism."[14] This plotline leads to the celebration of an American Century, its first cousin, American exceptionalism, and to the latter claim's disconcerting underside—persistent racism and enduring poverty in the cities.

World War II had propelled the United States to the pinnacle of military power and elevated it to the top of the world's ranking of wealthiest nations. Before the war, the U.S. armed services were small and had limited geographical reach. The country had a large and dynamic economy, but fervent isolationism stifled its global potential. Despite its involvement in World War I and President Woodrow Wilson's efforts to create a League of Nations, the United States preferred to leave world leadership to others. On the economic side, protectionism was the foreign policy of choice.

A successful war against Japan, Germany, and their allies changed all of this. No longer could the United States ignore its global responsibilities. National political leaders, corporate executives, and financiers recognized the benefits of a world presence and the importance of international bodies (such as the International Monetary Fund) and agreements (such as the Bretton Woods Agreement on currency) for managing conflict and regulating trade and foreign investment. World War II had generated massive amounts of new plants and equipment, numerous technological advances, and a wealth of industrial know-how—the foundation for a robust economy. The early postwar years became ones of expansion and prosperity, spurred by the Marshall Plan that helped rebuild Europe, and did so in ways that favored U.S. investors. From the end of World War II to the mid-1970s, the United States enjoyed a "golden age of affluence and hope."[15]

Given this scenario, many urban commentators of the 1940s,

little suspecting what actually was to occur, predicted a new round of expansion for the country's large cities. With exports flowing abundantly to Europe, worker productivity high, labor well paid, marriages and birthrates on the rise, and capital readily available, the further growth of the industrial cities seemed preordained. Prosperity and industrial agglomeration would drive the concentration of investments and households, and the cities would rebound from the slow growth they had experienced over the past fifteen years. Regrettably, this urban scenario was not to be.

Prosperity did follow the war. Workers enjoyed rising wages. Consumption increased dramatically, and capital investment was robust. National population growth was fueled by a baby boom. Notwithstanding, and with a slight delay, the large and medium-size cities, particularly those for whom manufacturing was a core function, failed to thrive. Instead, many lost population, were racked by abnormally high levels of disinvestment, and experienced the litany of social, economic, and fiscal problems that attended urban population loss in the early postwar decades. The trauma of these cities was experienced throughout the country. Yet this was a period that many people praised—the American Century.

The American Century might or might not refer to the whole of the twentieth century, might or might not have ended, and might or might not be cast as American except by the most chauvinistic or myopic of commentators.[16] The phrase itself is the product of an enthusiastic booster, Henry Luce, whose magazines played a pivotal role in interpreting and defining postwar American culture. Luce wrote in 1941 that the United States had become rich, accomplished, and powerful but had eluded the obligations conferred by its unique status. America, he urged, must take on the responsibility "to herself as well as to history for the world environment in which she lives." The failure to do so would be to embrace "the moral bankruptcy of isolationism." Luce believed in a "truly American internationalism" that would bring freedom, growth, and satisfaction to peoples across the globe. To do so would be "to create the first great American Century."[17]

Luce's argument repeated the core ideas that Walter Lippman, a famous political commentator of this period, had voiced two years earlier in *Life* magazine. Lippman also lamented the reluctance of Americans to end their isolationism, "the general refusal to accept the American Destiny in the post-War world." America's confidence, he argued, had been eroded by the failure of peace to survive after World War I, the Depression, and the lack of success of President Franklin D.

Roosevelt's New Deal reforms. National withdrawal had to be replaced by international engagement. Announcing the nation's destiny, Lippman wrote, "What Rome was to the ancient world, what Great Britain has been to the modern world, America is to be to the world of tomorrow." It was a time of national self-congratulation.[18]

The idea of the American Century had its critics. One commentator on the left deemed it "smug, self-righteous, superior, and fatuously lacking in a decent regard for the susceptibilities of the rest of mankind." It was even likened to imperialism, or at least to a justification for it. Decades later, American historians would react in a less alarmist fashion. Sean Wilentz glibly labeled it "a loose and baggy conceit dreamed up by a journalist," and David White treated it as a myth, one of many imaginative traditions urged upon the public by leaders and intellectuals.[19] Whether the idea was conceit, myth, or reality, the United States nonetheless positioned itself differently in the postwar period, taking on the mantle of superpower, leader of the "free world," and exemplar of technological and economic accomplishment.

Critics could not be faulted for comparing the call for an American Century to the earlier fascination with Manifest Destiny.[20] In the late nineteenth century, the United States was hardly a singular world power. Yet it was entering a period when its investments overseas would grow, its military forays would extend outside the region, and its international political influence would spread. The United States was not Great Britain; it lacked a comparable navy and army, and its imperial pretensions had not created a vast web of colonies and protectorates. Nor was it at the center of international trade. Still, neither was it so far behind on these measures as to be uncompetitive. As two world wars would show, the United States had the industrial and organizational capacity to quickly close the gap. That it would become dominant in the twentieth century was predictable, particularly in hindsight, but, nevertheless, hardly guaranteed.

From World War II until the early 1970s, the United States was irrefutably the dominant global power and the most prosperous of nations. Just after World War II ended, the nation stood alone as the world's military master, challenged only by a more insular and economically weaker Soviet Union that lacked the much-feared atomic bomb. The U.S. Army was uncontested on land, as were the Navy on the seas and the Air Force high above both. The economy was intact; the country had not suffered the physical devastation that had been visited on England, Germany, Japan, and Russia. Of all the combatants, only the United States approached peace stronger and more dominant diplomatically than when it had entered the conflict.

This global dominance was matched by domestic prosperity. For the next twenty-five years, from roughly 1948 to 1973, the economy experienced unprecedented growth. Productivity exceeded that attained in any other country, the gross national product increased fivefold, median income more than doubled in constant dollars, and home ownership (a good indicator of the level of personal consumption) rose by 50 percent. Americans were generally affluent, and capital was abundant; overseas investment was four times greater in 1970 than it had been in 1945. The country was blessed with a wealth of consumer products, and consumers were blessed with the purchasing power to obtain them. The American Dream was spreading; more and more people thought of themselves as middle-class.[21]

Not simply a transparent label, the term "American Century" was also a veiled reference to American exceptionalism. Americans were not the first or the only people to think of themselves as unique or as divinely ordained. Early in the twentieth century, the historian Charles A. Beard had noted that "American politicians believed . . . that the United States lived under a special economic dispensation and that the grave social problems which had menaced Europe for more than a generation when the Civil War broke out could never arise on American soil."[22] Less than a half century later, Luce reworked this belief to argue that the country was destined for greatness in ways that other nations were not. Together, the American Century and American exceptionalism sited "world progress in the American nation." The origins of this exceptionalism included the weakness of working-class radicalism, two centuries of democracy, and the general stability of the government.[23]

American exceptionalism was built in part on the *embourgeoisement* of the working class. The establishment of high-wage jobs—what came to be called the family wage—in the postwar period and the economy's shift to primarily consumer goods meant that most people, despite economic disparities, had roughly similar access to basic commodities and to many luxuries. Socialist inclinations were also vitiated by the lack of a parliamentary democracy, an entrenched two-party system at the national level, and a culture of individualism and upward mobility.

National claims to being exceptional are always ideological; they are intended to construct a worldview that symbolizes and elevates the nation. As statements of fact, such assertions are held "in ill-repute among contemporary historians" and other scholars. Critics are uncomfortable with the hubris inherent in such claims, the unproblematized appropriation of the nation-state as a basis of comparison, and the rigidity and parochialism that American exceptionalism confers on any international perspective. Yet this ideological trope remains resilient in the same way that national identities remain potent. This was particularly the case during the short American Century when the ideological battles of the Cold War raged.[24]

The notion of American exceptionalism is inextricably tied to England and western Europe. This "greater" Europe has been the basis of comparison for the United States since the latter's initial colonization. As Lewis Mumford wrote, "The settlement of America had its origins in the unsettlement of Europe."[25] Later, the thirteen colonies broke from Europe politically, but economic ties remained unsevered. And rather than forging a culture in opposition to the European Enlightenment, the country's leaders initially embraced it. Through the early twentieth century, Europe served as an important source of intellectual engagement and artistic accomplishment. Only in about the 1920s did American cultural independence become pronounced.

This transition was completed during the short American Century when American exceptionalism, at least along its cultural dimension, could be most convincingly argued. Diplomatic and economic ties remained significant, however. And European cities still lingered as the touchstone against which U.S. cities were judged. In fact, the comparison of cities had its roots in colonial times, extended through the brash commercialism and unbridled industrialization from 1850 to 1950, and continued with the anonymity and conformity attributed to the postwar suburbs.[26] Overall, the United States has never fully separated itself from Europe. Even as late as the mid-1990s, one noted historian commented that as regards comparisons between the United States and the rest of the world, Europe still "serve[d] as the standard from which all deviations are measured."[27]

During the early postwar period, the United States added another argument to its case for exceptionalism. Americans developed a distinctive way of life, one based on rising incomes, a vast array of consumer goods, broadening educational opportunities, rising levels of home ownership, and access to a style of living heretofore unimagined. That way of life was a suburban way of life. Other countries—Germany and Japan, Sweden and Denmark, for example—eventually did as well economically, but it was the United States, not Europe, that pioneered the new social and spatial order known as suburbanization. Sweden and Finland built new towns and England also had suburbs, but no country had a settlement pattern of this type or suburbanization to this extent. America was exceptional both in the opportunities it held forth and in the lifestyle many of its people were about to adopt.[28]

These promised opportunities were inextricably tied to the land. The vast territory of the country, coupled with population growth, allowed the development of a large national market for goods and offered an ever-receding frontier on whose other side—the undeveloped side—freedom and riches beckoned. Made famous by Frederick Jackson Turner's announcement of its closure in 1890 and the subject of much rumination among intellectuals concerned with establishing an American culture, America's frontier has never been wholly erased. Even after the national territory had been fully settled, it was constantly being reinvented.[29]

This reinvention has occurred in the realms of culture and ideology and in parallel with the restlessness of U.S. capitalism, thereby connecting American exceptionalism to domestic prosperity. In the period of the short American Century, the country's frontier was created anew in the form of the "crabgrass frontier" of suburbanization for the masses.[30] Here, the United States was truly exceptional. It was the first country to embrace this settlement pattern across much of its population, and also the first country to abandon its industrial cities.

The dark side to American exceptionalism is less often acknowledged. The postwar decline of the industrial cities is one such embarrassment. Although industrial cities in other countries—England, France, Germany, Italy, Canada—lost population during the Great Depression and World War II, only those of the United States and the United Kingdom witnessed additional and severe decline after the war. The troubles experienced by European cities hardly rivaled the flight of residents and businesses or the concentration of poverty and juvenile delinquency, among other social problems, experienced in the United States.

This exception did not exist in isolation from two other social conditions that distinguished, and continue to distinguish, the United States from comparable advanced societies: the persistence of racial discrimination and widespread poverty. One of the last countries to abolish slavery, the United States has never fully integrated African Americans. Segregated in the military, channeled to low-paying and low-status jobs, and, after World War II, concentrated in separate residential areas, African Americans have yet to achieve parity with the dominant Anglo population. They are more likely to be poor and unemployed, to lag behind in educational attainment, or to be impris-oned or plagued by health problems, and they are less wealthy than their white counterparts.[31]

This "American dilemma," as Swedish sociologist Gunnar Myrdal characterized it in his influential study of 1944, lingers.[32] African Americans have made advances—the middle class has grown and the educational gap has narrowed—but even though overt institutional dis-crimination has been greatly diminished, the living conditions for many are acceptable only relative to the poor of less developed countries. Police brutality against African Americans and other minorities con-tinues. Except in a strictly legal sense, African Americans are second-class citizens.

The scope and persistence of poverty in one of the world's most affluent and powerful countries also sets the United States apart. No other advanced economy has maintained the levels of poverty that exist in the United States. During the short American Century, the percentage of the population struggling below the official poverty line declined. As the economy weakened in the 1970s and the federal gov-ernment tempered its activism, poverty expanded once again. From the onset of industrialization in the mid-nineteenth century, the coun-try has maintained a sizable population of poor people. Other coun-tries, particularly those with robust welfare states, virtually eliminated poverty after World War II. On measures of poverty and the income inequality associated with it, the United States has performed less ad-mirably than other industrialized societies.[33]

Racial discrimination and poverty, of course, are integral com-ponents of urban decline. African Americans and poor people—overlapping categories—are concentrated in the cities. And poverty and racial segregation are mutually reinforcing, thereby making it even more difficult for African Americans to escape their predicament. Indicative of this dilemma was "the slum," one of the most powerful urban symbols from the late 1940s to the 1970s. The slum was not imagined in race-neutral terms. In popular perception and in academic circles it meant African Americans mired in poverty, prone to crime, and dependent on welfare.[34] "Ghetto," a more precise characterization and a frequent synonym for "slum," was the term of choice for cities during most of the short American Century.

African Americans do live outside the cities, though many sub-urbs are closed to them. When they have suburbanized, they have often ended up in segregated communities and neighborhoods, the oldest of the postwar communities, or the industrial satellites that collapsed in the postwar decades. Nonetheless, the enduring perception of African Americans is as city dwellers, a perception based on their migration from southern farms to northern factories in the early to mid-twentieth century. A combination of geographical concentration and media stereotyping, not to mention the well-known anxiety that middle-class and white suburbanites have about minorities, has stamped the cities with the stigma of race.

Racial discrimination and poverty existed prior to the decline of the country's large industrial cities. The flight from the cities intensified these conditions and further concentrated them geographically. Race, poor people, and the cities were forged into a single symbol of American fear and ambivalence.

Throughout the short American Century, these exceptions to American accomplishment lingered as deep flaws in the image that the United States wished to convey to the world. They also revealed other problems, muddled political decision making, and imposed economic costs on those who had not disinvested quickly enough from the declining cities. Claims to American exceptionalism, awash in Cold War ideology in the 1950s and 1960s, suppressed these less desirable conditions.[35] Threatened by communism, critical portrayals suffered. Into this ideological fray came the new suburban way of life. If not an antidote, it was at least a distraction from these embarrassments. Mass suburbanization strengthened claims to an American exceptionalism.

Reprise

That domestic prosperity, global dominance, industrial-city decline, and mass suburbanization erupted and subsided in unison is no mere coincidence. Their historical juxtaposition in the short American Century was momentous. Both U.S. global dominance and U.S. urban decline had their roots in the domestic affluence of the postwar period. Economic prosperity at home subsequently provided the financial and ideological basis for the nation's global ambitions, while its defense spending, aggressive export policies, foreign aid, and, most importantly, mass suburbanization expanded the national economy.

The decline of the older, industrial cities also contributed to postwar prosperity. The out-migration of households and investment fueled suburbanization as well as the regional shift of the country's wealth and population from the Northeast to the West and the Southwest. These great movements of people and business further boosted the demand for a wide variety of goods and services, thereby generating additional rounds of investment, job growth, and wage increases.

In this and other ways, the short American Century and the urban crisis were inextricably linked. To achieve prosperity and dominance, the United States had to sacrifice its industrial cities. Precipitous urban decline in the quarter century after World War II, an event unprecedented in the country's history, was the price America paid to be the most powerful and most affluent nation in the world.[36]

With city living once again desirable and with many of the once-industrial cities enjoying renewed investment and even population growth through the 1980s and 1990s, it was easy to forget the urban trauma that had transpired a few decades earlier. Of course, Americans have never been wedded to the past; the future is more beguiling. Nevertheless, a sense of history, a sense of the unavoidable and myriad ways in which the past implicates the present, is essential if Americans are to grasp who they have become and how they arrived there. These are the raw materials of a national identity.

Just as the consequences of the urban crisis spread beyond municipal and national boundaries, so its relevance extends beyond the short American Century. During this historical period, the decline of the industrial cities and the growth of the suburbs redefined the American way of life and reshaped the nation's destiny. To say more now, however, would be to jump ahead in the story. Before we can piece together the puzzle of this historical period, we must know more about urban decline, mass suburbanization, and the rupture in urbanization that gave rise to them.

2

Urbanization's Consequences

Just before the midpoint of the twentieth century, the processes of urbanization that had governed the country's growth for almost 100 years were fundamentally altered. Whereas most cities and towns had benefited from steady increases in population and geographical expansion prior to these years, this was no longer the case by the early postwar period. Growth turned from distributive to parasitic. Despite a booming national economy and an ever-expanding national population, in order for some cities and the emerging suburbs to grow, other cities had to decline.

This new type of urbanization involved a wrenching loss of residents from the industrial cities, a loss that was accompanied by a host of social, economic, and political ills. It also included a surge of population from older cities into rapidly growing bedroom suburbs and, a bit later, a parallel growth of cities in the western and southern states. Not surprisingly, one result was expansion in the size and number of metropolitan areas. These effects of the rupture in urbanization anchored numerous changes during the short American Century and established the basis for a corresponding transformation of the country's identity.[1]

Of these three consequences—industrial city decline, mass suburbanization, and Sunbelt-city growth—suburbanization had been underway in various forms prior to and during World War II. Its roots extended to the late nineteenth century, and although weak then, they were significantly strengthened in the 1920s. A few large cities existed in the West and South, but for the most part, urban growth was concentrated in the northeastern region of the country. The big surprise was the sudden collapse of the industrial cities, many of which were quite large and seemingly invincible. Large cities in the nineteenth century or the first half of the twentieth century had not experienced sustained losses of residents and jobs or such relentless disinvestment. And although industrial-city decline also played a significant though unacknowledged role in spurring national economic growth, suburbanization dominated the general perception of the period's prosperity.

Through negative images projected in the mass media and the collective anxiety engendered by the urban crisis, the decline of the cities challenged the growth of the suburbs for prominence or, more accurately, notoriety. The nation celebrated its suburban lifestyle, consumer products, and high wages. It also had to contend with pictures of boarded-up buildings, rioting African Americans, looted stores, burnt-out automobiles discarded on inner-city highways, and idle and abandoned factories. U.S. cities were perceived at home and abroad as free-falling into inescapable chaos.[2] Consequently, the urban crisis spurred additional waves of suburbanization. For these reasons, the plight of the industrial cities, one of the major consequences of urbanization's rupture after World War II, takes narrative and historical precedence.[3]

Shrinking Cities

The decline of the country's industrial cities was not just an ironic counterweight to the short American Century; it was also an affront to a history of nearly seamless growth. From 1790, when the federal government first began collecting population data, until the end of World War II, the big cities of the United States had grown without interruption. Decade after decade, with rare exceptions, the cities at the top of the urban hierarchy—Chicago; Cleveland, Ohio; Detroit; Baltimore, Maryland; Philadelphia; and New York—that had made the country into an economic leviathan expanded in population. Only the Depression of the 1930s deflected them from this path.

Beginning in the 1950s, these cities experienced an unrelenting flight of households. Voting with their feet, large numbers of residents rejected the urban way of life. Take one exemplary city: St. Louis. Between 1950 and 1960, more than one of every four residents—230,000 people—left the city. Another 180,000 departed between 1960 and 1970. Much of the exodus consisted of white households. And even though people were moving into the city, many had little education and

| *Urbanization's Consequences*

faced poor job prospects. As one commentator alarmingly remarked, the resultant neighborhood transition "was accompanied by [housing] vacancies, widespread vandalism, a sharp increase in crime, and deterioration of city services."[4] By the end of the century, St. Louis had yet to recover; it continued to lose residents and investors to other places. This story, albeit told in less dire tones, was repeated across all of the cities where manufacturing had been the engine of growth.

The loss of residents was only part of the trauma. Employment fell as factories closed, fled to the suburbs, or laid off workers. Slums expanded, blight spread across central business districts, and industrial areas witnessed large-scale abandonment. Urban tax bases shrank, and local governments entered into years of chronic fiscal stress.

New groups moved into these cities, particularly African Americans from the rural South. They arrived just as manufacturing jobs were leaving. Discriminated against in both labor markets and housing markets, African American and Puerto Rican households suffered from high levels of unemployment in comparison to whites. They became disproportionately poor and were locked into older neighborhoods and channeled into public housing projects. Racial tensions increased. The confluence of race, poverty, and segregation exacerbated white flight.

Prior to the 1930s, observers paid scant attention to even the possibility of urban population loss. No compelling reason existed to do so. Here and there, once in a while, a few cities cast off residents. Except for catastrophes (such as epidemics) in the late 1800s, the losses were small, and the cities quickly regained their prosperity.[5]

In retrospect, as early as the turn of the nineteenth century to the twentieth, evidence pointed to a slackening in urban expansion. In 1901, Adna Weber, one of the country's first urban demographers, noted that the growth rate of cities had slowed. This was hardly surprising, given the economic slump of the mid-1890s and the diminution in the rate at which the labor force was being industrialized and thus urbanized. From 1870 to 1880, the 159 cities of 25,000 or more residents grew by 50 percent, but in the following decade they increased by only 33 percent. Weber interpreted the relative decline as a temporary "check to the concentration of population" and a response to the evils of congestion. As explanation, he posited a rhythmical movement in which "the rate of concentration rises and falls in each alternate decade."[6] Weber was unconcerned.

Not until the 1930s did cities attract attention for actually losing population rather than simply growing more slowly. Even then, caution in regard to dire predictions and a degree of disbelief prevailed; the country was experiencing a deep and unexpected economic depression. A report published in 1937 by the Urbanism Committee of the federal government's National Resources Board, *Our Cities: Their Role in the National Economy,* documented the deceleration of urban population growth in the 1920s. During that time, growth had dropped to 26 percent, well below the 130 percent average for the prior three decades. The rate fell further—to 3 percent—in the 1930s. The report's authors argued that "the national urban pattern [was] becoming fixed" as the country established a "roughly stable rural-urban equilibrium."[7] Rural-to-urban migration, along with the expansion in industrial activity and jobs, had been major contributors to the previous expansion of cities. Now, both had slackened. The data caused one sociologist, William F. Ogburn, to write that "cities that are losing population have a touch of sadness about them."[8]

The level of urbanization in the country—that is, the distribution of population between urban and nonurban places—seemed to be stabilizing. Consequently, few observers expected large cities to become more numerous, though rare was the commentator who believed that cities would experience absolute population loss, even against the background of Depression-era gloom. Two scenarios were formulated by contemporary pundits. In one, the cities would grow rapidly "only at the expense of each other." In the other, the central cities of metropolitan areas would experience decentralization; that is, the population of surrounding areas would expand more rapidly than that in the center, while the central cities would still add residents. Only if decentralization continued too long or was "uncontrolled" would the central cities actually be threatened. Such predictions suggested neither panic nor alarm.[9]

By the 1940s, the decline of cities was widely acknowledged. One-quarter of the large cities and over one-third of the medium-size and small cities had lost residents in the 1930s.[10] Akron, Ohio; Cleveland; Grand Rapids, Michigan; and Newark, New Jersey, were four of the most prominent cities that became smaller during the Depression. With the economy slowed, people were less likely to move into new homes, investors were less likely to expand factories or build homes in new areas, and local governments were less inclined to extend roads and sewers onto unimproved land. Commentators were clearly divided in their assessments. They either optimistically believed in the combined powers of postwar expansion and urban redevelopment to reverse the trend or pessimistically claimed that the city had become obsolete.[11]

In 1943, Homer Hoyt, one of the nation's most influential real estate economists, offered cautious optimism. He noted that three of every ten cities with more than 100,000 residents had lost population in the 1930s. From this, he concluded that "the failure of cities to expand employment opportunities in their trade and industries" sufficient to attract rural migrants indicated a "waning power." Nonetheless, he believed that the cities would rebound if high-quality urban housing was built and if economic advantage or government programs directed peacetime industries to them.[12]

Four years later, the economist Mabel Walker, drawing from the same census data, bluntly provided the bleak perspective. She wrote that "the cities are not growing. They are shrinking. The process of urbanization has reversed itself." Her claim was based on the demographic facts: Between 1910 and 1920, none of the ninety-two largest cities had cast off residents, four did so in the 1920s, and twenty-eight declined in size between 1930 and 1940. The cities with more than 25,000 inhabitants exhibited corresponding numbers, with one-quarter of the total having a net population loss in the 1930s. The population decline in rural areas had ceased, she argued, and the large and medium-size cities were now decentralizing. This decentralization was a direct consequence of households and industry taking advantage of new forms of transportation, the automobile and the truck in particular.[13]

By the 1950s, urban commentators had become obsessed with population loss from the cities and the associated social and economic decline. Times had changed, and the processes of urbanization no longer favored the concentration of population and industry in the country's traditional urban centers. Moreover, housing and employment opportunities outside the cities, coupled with recognition of spreading blight, rising minority presence, and the deepening fiscal difficulties of city governments, further inflamed public ambivalence toward living in cities.

Urban population decline in the decades after World War II was unprecedented, not only in its incidence and intensity but also in its duration. For many cities, the flight of residents continued well beyond the 1950s. A hard core of fourteen large cities—places like Cleveland, St. Louis, Buffalo, and Philadelphia—shed population for each of the next four decades.[14] At the end of the twentieth century, and for these cities, the prospects for a return to years of uninterrupted prosperity were dim. This sudden reversal in the fortunes of the nation's industrial cities, for it is these cities that suffered the most, was one of the most momentous events of the latter half of the twentieth century.

The pattern of population growth for U.S. cities took on a whole new character sometime between 1930 and 1950. By midcentury, the continuous expansion of the country's cities had suffered a breach that was not only sudden but also doggedly persistent. Regardless of size, all industrial cities (and a number of others) cast off residents. This historical rupture, though, did not occur just in the United States. In the United Kingdom, western Europe, and even Canada, industrial cities sustained often-precipitous and certainly unexpected population losses. Postwar urban decline was a global phenomenon. And as befits a phenomenon of such stature, its domestic consequences were profound.[15]

The surge in the number of large cities experiencing population loss began in 1930, receded in the 1940s, and then returned with a vengeance in the following decade. (See Figure 3.) Prior to that, on average, fewer than two large cities lost residents in any ten-year period. From 1950 to 1990, and by contrast, twenty-five was the norm.[16] Here was evidence of a profound rupture in urbanization.

Before 1930, only one decade (1830–1839) witnessed more than a handful of large cities shedding residents. Of the five cities that cast off residents then, three had losses of less than 5 percent, a percentage change hardly significant given the rudimentary enumerative techniques in use at the time. Three decades (1880–1889, 1910–1919, and 1920–1929) had no large cities with such losses. All of this changed during the 1930s, when fifteen large cities suffered population declines. The likelihood that the country would eventually emerge from that decade's depression and return to prosperity suggested to observers that the population loss was only temporary—a condition that would disappear when the economy recovered.

This did not happen. Persistent decline took root in the 1950s, and although it eventually abated, it continued into the twenty-first century. The worst decade was the 1970s, when two-thirds of the large cities shrank. In that decade, after the widespread riots of the 1960s and in the midst of the worst recession since the Great Depression of the 1930s, the country's anxiety over urban decline arguably peaked. That anxiety exacerbated the flight of white households.

The defining characteristic of cities with persistent population losses was their reliance on manufacturing as their core economic function. Goods production was the force that had attracted and retained businesses and households as these cities grew. On average, over one-third of the workers in these cities were employed in factories in 1950, compared to just over one-quarter of workers for the country as a whole. Nearly one-half of the employed residents of Detroit and Rochester labored in manufacturing, and four in ten did so in Cleveland

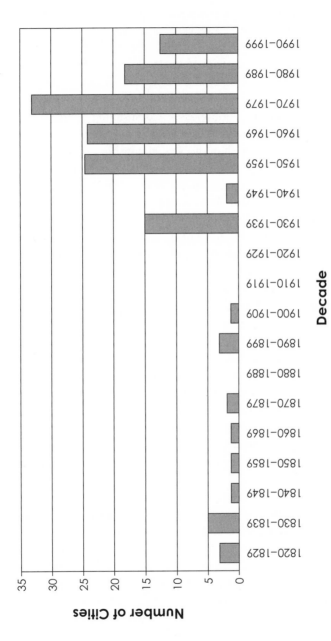

Figure 3. Large cities with population loss, 1820–2000. For actual numbers and sources, see Appendix A.

and Buffalo. In Baltimore, the number of high-wage, full-time manufacturing jobs fell by one-fifth between 1953 and 1959, grew in the early 1960s, and then descended once again. From 1948 to 1974, nearly 40,000 manufacturing jobs disappeared from that city's labor market. Across the country, factories dispersed into the metropolitan periphery and beyond, and such industries as steelmaking, television and radio production, and tire making were severely downsized.[17] Each job that was lost represented a household disinclined to remain in the city.

The size of the population losses was stunning. Before 1930, if a large city shed population, it was likely that only a few thousand people were involved. Portsmouth, New Hampshire, in the 1830s declined by approximately 140 residents, and Troy, New York, lost just over twice that number in the 1890s, hardly significant given their sizes then. After World War II, the magnitude of these losses expanded fortyfold. In the 1950s and 1960s, the average large city with a population decline shed nearly 50,000 residents in each decade. Over the next ten years, that number doubled. Only in the 1980s did this upward trend slacken, though the average loss still approximated that of the 1950s. At this level, the average large city was casting off nearly 5,000 residents—more than 1,500 households—each year. This absent population became visible in empty houses, closed stores, and less busy sidewalks.

Among the large cities, and in any given decade, the size of these decrements varied widely. At the onset of postwar decline in the 1950s, New York City, St. Louis, and Boston each became smaller by over 100,000 people. At the other extreme, the population decline was not as great and the consequences were not as dire. Cincinnati; Portland, Oregon; and Syracuse experienced shortfalls of less than one-twentieth of that amount. In a growing national economy, though, any loss was cause for concern.

Pegging a major ten-year loss at 100,000 people no longer made sense in the 1970s. For this decade, the criterion for a major loss had to be doubled, and New York City, Chicago, Detroit, and Philadelphia all exceeded that new benchmark. New York City, true to its status as the nation's largest city, posted the biggest reduction. It had over 800,000 fewer residents in 1980 than ten years earlier. Even the "small" losses were bigger: Fort Worth, Texas, had a decrease of just fewer than 10,000 residents, Portland, just over 16,000, and Denver, Colorado, and Louisville, Kentucky, slightly more than 22,000.

From 1950 to 1980, a time that roughly overlapped the short American Century, 62 percent of the largest cities experienced at least a decade or more of population loss.[18] The cities with the largest absolute losses were New York, Detroit, Chicago, and St. Louis, all of whose populations fell by over 400,000 during this time.

Locally, of course, the issue is not the total number of people who leave but the relative proportion. A drop of 50,000 people has a different impact on a city of 3 million than on a city of one-quarter million. St. Louis led the race to the bottom on this dimension, losing nearly half its residents. Buffalo; Pittsburgh; Cleveland; Providence, Rhode Island; and Detroit followed, with their populations becoming more than one-third smaller.

Surprisingly, and tempering one's sense of the magnitude of these shifts, the proportionate change of cities losing population in the late twentieth century was not that much different from the changes that occurred in the mid-nineteenth century. For the three decades after 1950, the average percentage population losses for the declining large cities was roughly similar to that which cities with population declines experienced from 1830 to 1870. Only the decade of the 1970s was an anomaly; it was the ten-year period that most distinguished the twentieth-century cities from their nineteenth-century counterparts on this measure. If, instead, the postwar period is compared to the first half of the twentieth century, a much different picture emerges. For the four decades between 1910 and 1950, the average population loss was nearly zero for two decades and was less than 2 percent for two others. Postwar population declines were significantly higher.[19] Unlike urbanization in the early twentieth century, that of the late twentieth century harbored an unprecedented rejection of the large, industrial cities by both households and investors.

The comparative magnitude of the postwar losses is partly a function of the fact that the largest cities had simply become bigger. In 1880, the average large city had a population of about 150,000 people. By 1920, that number had increased more than threefold, and thirty years later it was larger by half again. Indicative of this trend to bigger and bigger cities was the population change of the fiftieth largest city: Denver at 36,000 in 1880, Youngstown at 132,000 in 1920, and Worcester, Massachusetts, at 203,000 in 1950.

More to the point, the rupture in the underlying dynamics of urbanization was primarily an issue of persistence and pervasiveness. Beginning in 1950, twenty large cities lost population in each successive decade to 1980; this did not happen to any large city prior to 1930 and only one large city—Jersey City, New Jersey—prior to 1950. Moreover, the shrinkage of the cities changed from being abnormal to being common. Population loss struck the large cities and reached down the urban hierarchy to numerous medium-size and small central cities. With the exception of small cities in the 1950s, over 50 percent of the cities in these three size categories—small, medium, and large—lost population in each of the three postwar decades. The greatest losses were in the 1970s, when almost nine of every ten large cities and seven of every ten medium-size and small cities lost residents. The absolute losses, of course, declined as the size of the city decreased.[20]

Nevertheless, the large industrial cities carried the weight of this shift in the country's pattern of urbanization. A greater proportion lost population, their losses far exceeded (by orders of magnitude) those from medium-size and small cities, and their losses persisted. Big cities had been the source of the country's economic prowess and the symbols of its energy and genius. Now, it seemed, as one prominent economist noted, that "the central city is no longer able to function as a general-purpose economic system."[21] Unable to do so, it could not retain residents.

Sunbelt Cities and Suburbanization

What gives the sudden and striking reversal of city growth even more salience is that during this time numerous other cities in the country were experiencing rapid growth. In addition, suburbanization was accelerating at a dizzying pace. And at least in the early postwar years, the good fortunes of the emerging cities and suburbs were based, parasitically, on the miseries of the industrial cities.

The cities that grew were not those in the industrial heartland—roughly the northeastern quadrant of the country—but those in the South and West. Most cities in these latter regions drew their wealth from commerce, agriculture, and natural resources such as oil and gas rather than from goods production. Manufacturing was an important part of the local economy in only a few of these cities—Birmingham, Alabama, and Omaha, Nebraska, for example. Although large cities, for instance, Los Angeles, Houston, and New Orleans, did exist in the South and West, for the most part, and prior to World War II, cities there were less dependent on manufacturing and were fewer and smaller than those in the industrial Northeast.[22]

World War II had a unique impact in these regions. Because the country was fighting a war in the Pacific against Japan, military installations had to be built and defense industries located on the West Coast. This triggered migration to these states and to the Gulf Coast and the southern states as well. Many of the migrants stayed after the war to enjoy the sun, year-round recreation, and inexpensive housing. Throughout the 1960s and 1970s, these regions prospered, and more and more people arrived. Investors took advantage of the favorable business climate, lack of unionization, and low costs. During this time, they became known as the Sunbelt and garnered a reputation as "the new frontier of economic development and political power."[23]

Subsequently, the Sunbelt experienced strong job growth and even more households from the declining industrial Northeast—now nicknamed the Rustbelt—flocked to these rim states. While the Sunbelt economy had a manufacturing component, particularly in aerospace and semiconductors, it was also diversified in agribusiness, oil, real estate, and leisure activities. And it benefited greatly from defense spending and other federal outlays such as highway funds. Much of the growth took place in and around existing cities and involved not only relocatees from within the country but Mexicans from south of the border. From 1935 to 1960, the western region received more migrants and immigrants than all the other regions of the country combined. Only in 1970 did it lose its dominance, and then it did so to the South.[24] With the possibility of easily annexing growth in peripheral areas, the Sunbelt cities became the antithesis of their Rustbelt counterparts.

To provide just a few examples: San Diego, California, grew from 150,000 residents in 1930 to 876,000 in 1980; San Antonio, Texas, and Miami, Florida, were three times bigger in 1980 than in 1930. Among the small cities in 1930, San Jose, California, experienced a tenfold population increase, Fresno, California, had a sevenfold increase, and Montgomery, Alabama, tripled in size. The number of Sunbelt cities among the country's fifty largest cities predictably rose, from eighteen to twenty-five between 1930 and 1980. Moreover, of all the cities that grew enough to make this list, all were from the West and South, places like Tucson, Arizona, and Austin, Texas. Not one city from the Northeast joined them.[25]

If growth is a valued criterion, Phoenix, Arizona, is a true urban success story. It was one of the fastest-growing cities in the country over the second half of the twentieth century, and in 1980, it became the country's ninth-largest city, with a population of just over three-quarters of a million residents. (By 2000, it had 1.3 million residents.)[26] Yet in 1930, Phoenix had had fewer than 50,000 residents, and in 1900 it had been a mere village of 5,544 people on the dry Arizona landscape. Its rise to the top was phenomenal, and its trajectory of growth was unchallenged by any contemporary city of comparable size.

The rise of Sunbelt cities to the top of the urban hierarchy was part of a larger regional shift of people and investment from the older, industrial cities in the Northeast and Midwest to the metropolitan areas of the South, Southwest, and West. Cities were the vehicles by which economic activity was spread across the states and through which the national economy was integrated. By the early twentieth century, a person no longer had to travel to Boston for medical specialists or a university education or to New York City for financial advice. These and other functions were increasingly available west of the Mississippi River and south of Washington, D.C. The Sunbelt, which once lagged behind the Rustbelt, was catching up.

Sixteen of the country's largest central cities grew in each of the three decades after World War II. Only one of them—Columbus, Ohio—was located in the country's traditional industrial region. Included in these "cities of relentless growth" was San Jose, a city that increased nearly sixfold in population: In 1950, it had fewer than 100,000 residents; by 1980 it had over 625,000. El Paso, Texas, tripled in size, while San Diego and Austin more than doubled. Columbus was a mere laggard, increasing by only 50 percent.[27] From the early postwar years onward, the fastest-growing cities were predominantly located in the Sunbelt. This pattern continued into the 1980s, when all of the twenty-five fastest-growing small cities were in the South and Southwest. Twelve were in California, four in Texas, and three in Arizona. The leader was Mesa, Arizona.[28]

Central cities in the Northeast and Midwest either stagnated or shed residents. Population growth was almost the exclusive domain of cities of the West and South. Of the twelve cities that dropped out of the top-fifty category between 1950 and 1980, only four—Jacksonville; Norfolk, Virginia; Richmond, Virginia; and Tampa, Florida—were from outside the industrial heartland. Of those four, Jacksonville later returned. The twelve cities that replaced them were all from the Sunbelt. Some of them made huge leaps in rank; in the 1950s, Phoenix went from ninety-eighth to twenty-ninth and El Paso from seventy-fifth to forty-sixth.

Metropolitan growth was also concentrated in the Sunbelt, though to a lesser extent than central-city growth. In the South and West, metropolitan growth rates were double and triple those in the Northeast and Midwest. People were moving from one side of the country to the other, and at the same time, they were continuing to shift from nonmetropolitan to metropolitan areas. In 1950, four of every ten individuals lived outside of metropolitan areas; in 1980, only two of ten did so.[29] Notably, the "new" cities were being built at much lower densities than older ones. Since 1900, central-city population densities have been lower in the South and West than in the Northeast and Midwest. And although densities rose slightly in the cities of the Northeast and West through the mid-1970s, they fell in the Midwest and South.

A comparison of the South and the Midwest reveals both the impact of suburbanization on Rustbelt central cities and the formation of new metropolises in the Sunbelt. Midwestern central cities declined in population density, a consequence that cannot be attributed either to an expansion in municipal boundaries or to a rise in the number of new central cities in the region. Rather, these cities became less dense as households abandoned them. Southern central cities also declined in density. This, though, was mainly a result of the rise of new, low-density cities that were growing there. The lower densities of the newer metropolitan areas diluted the higher densities of the older metropolitan areas.[30]

Along with the emerging cities of the South and West, the suburbs dominated the expansion of metropolitan areas and even enabled metropolitan areas with declining central cities to experience overall population growth. This was the case for Buffalo, Detroit, and St. Louis, whose central cities had deep and sustained population losses in the early postwar period but whose metropolitan areas expanded without interruption. Newly built suburbs were proliferating on the peripheries of declining and growing central cities alike. With this, the country was being drawn toward a new way of life. In 1960, one major business publication claimed that "no one can doubt that a fundamental change has come over the U.S. Once a rural country, it turned urban in the 1910s; now it has turned suburban."[31]

Of course, population had been moving away from the cities as early as the seventeenth century, and had been moving westward as well. The first European colonists settled along the coasts—Plymouth Colony, Jamestown—and only later pushed inland to Augusta, Buffalo, and Pittsburgh. The eastern seaboard and, to a lesser extent, the Gulf of Mexico were the entry points. Still later did Omaha, Chicago, and St. Louis grow into cities through the relentless flows of domestic migrants and European immigrants. New settlements were established in the interior of the country as the population pushed the frontier westward. Although settlers eventually established towns, villages, and trading posts on the Pacific coast, urbanization there lagged behind that in the East.

In the eighteenth century, the settlements that grew into cities, places like Boston and Philadelphia, became surrounded by villages and small towns along with a scattering of farms. Since they were generally self-sufficient, many of these settlements had little to do with the nearby city. Industrialization and the development of railroads and streetcars in the nineteenth century made it possible, and necessary, for these outlying communities to establish more-enduring ties to the larger cities, particularly as these cities grew bigger and their needs for food and markets expanded.

The inhabitants of the first suburbs of the early nineteenth century were mainly an affluent class of businesspeople and their families; they could afford country estates and used ferry services and early horse-drawn-streetcar lines and railroads to travel to and from the city. They lived in such places as Brooklyn Heights across the East River from Manhattan, West Roxbury near Boston, and Germantown and Chestnut Hill outside Philadelphia. As the streetcar lines were extended, more land was made accessible and available for development, and more households resided outside the cities.[32]

The early railroad and streetcar suburbs were unlike the later postwar suburbs; they were more like villages. Predominantly residential and mainly comprising single-family detached homes, they also had small commercial areas, usually near a train station or along a trolley line. Moreover, they were adjacent to farmland and open space, though many abutted the growing cities that had given rise to them. A few industrial suburbs, such as West Allis outside of Milwaukee, Wisconsin, and East St. Louis across the Mississippi River from its namesake, were scattered about in the periphery of these nascent metropolitan areas. That their growth was compatible with distributive urbanization also made them different from the postwar suburbs.[33]

Not until the 1920s did the suburbs begin to take an embryonic postwar form. With the introduction of the automobile, development was less confined to land near streetcar lines or railway stations. Weblike rather than linear and nodal, road networks, unlike rail lines, allowed more land to become accessible. Consequently, development spread at lower densities than was characteristic either of the cities or of the street-car and railroad suburbs of the time. Central cities occupied a rapidly declining proportion of metropolitan space; the land area in the suburban peripheries was two and one-half times greater in 1970 than in 1950.[34]

Automobiles were relatively expensive before World War II, though, and this limited suburbanization to the more affluent households. Nevertheless, as industry left the city, population followed. But whereas in 1920 less than 9 percent of the country's population was living in suburbs, by 1930 that portion had increased to just over 14 percent.[35]

When World War II ended, the outlying areas of cities consisted mostly of a scattering of relatively independent villages and towns, farms and forests, industrial suburbs, and residential communities of various sizes. As a result, the suburban periphery contained a range of social classes. Not one of these communities, nor all of them together, as yet challenged the economic, cultural, demographic, and political dominance of the central city. By 1940, the suburbs had barely increased their share of the national population to 15 percent, mainly owing to the slowdown in economic growth brought on by the previous decade's depression. The cities still claimed twice that amount. In the average metropolitan district, the central city had more than half of the population with the remainder divided among a large number of municipalities and unincorporated areas. Pittsburgh, for example, contained nearly 48 percent of the district's population in 1940, with the next largest municipality (McKeesport, a mill town that manufactured steel) having a mere 4 percent.

The country entered a period of mass suburbanization after World War II. Marriage and child rearing had been postponed during the economic slowdown and the war, when people, for the most part, had saved rather than consumed. The end of the war released a pent-up demand for starting families and buying consumer goods. A housing shortage in the central cities, the availability of low-cost mortgage financing for new home buying, rising incomes that made home ownership and automobile purchases possible, and mass production techniques in the housing industry that kept costs relatively affordable contributed to a rapid expansion of new home construction in the suburbs and a flight from the older, industrial cities.

In the early postwar years, the industrial centers of the northeastern and north-central regions of the country were particularly hard-hit by suburbanization. A significant fraction of suburban growth was a result of the out-migration of white and middle-class households from the central cities. In the 1970s alone, 13 million more residents left the central cities than moved there, a major increase over the previous decade. More than 26 million people moved to the suburbs.[36]

Not everyone fled, of course. Most of those who initially went to the suburbs were white. Racial discrimination in suburban housing markets was widespread and virtually unimpeded. Minorities, mainly

African Americans, were also discriminated against in the cities, but they were not wholly excluded, as was the case in new suburban developments. And even though it was possible for people of below-average incomes to buy homes in the suburbs, the suburbs were still primarily middle-class. Being almost exclusively middle-class and mostly white, they diverged in social makeup from the central cities.[37]

During the short American Century, suburban areas enjoyed phenomenal growth and transformed the country's settlement pattern. Once, the central cities had been surrounded by small towns and rural hamlets. In 1900, less than 6 percent of the country's population resided adjacent to central cities, and only one-quarter of the nation's residents lived in metropolitan areas, an indicator of its still-rural character. By the late 1970s, the cities were enmeshed in a web of suburban communities. Almost one of every two residents of the country lived in the suburbs, and three-quarters of the nation's population resided in metropolitan areas. (See Figure 4.) This realignment was driven

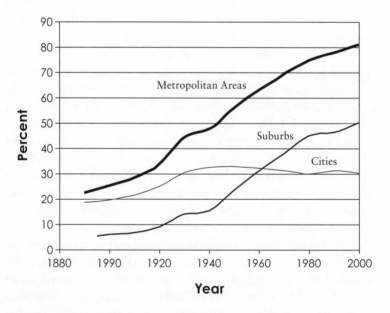

Figure 4. Percent of U.S. population living in metropolitan areas, central cities, and suburbs, 1890–2000. Data are from Donald J. Bogue, Population Growth in Standard Metropolitan Areas, 1900–1950 *(Washington, D.C.: Government Printing Office, 1954); U.S. Bureau of the Census,* 1990 Census Profile *(Washington, D.C.: U.S. Department of Commerce, 1991), number 3, figure 1; and U.S. Department of Commerce,* Metropolitan Districts: Population and Area *(Washington, D.C.: U.S. Superintendent of Documents, 1932).*

mainly by suburbanization; the growth in the central cities' share of the nation's population was anemic by comparison.[38]

These changes are reflected in the differential growth rates for the central cities and the suburbs; for the first two decades of the twentieth century, the central cities grew faster. During the 1920s, as part of the nascent transition from distributive to parasitic urbanization, the relationship was reversed. From then until 1980, the suburbs grew faster than the central cities—five times faster in the 1950s, over four times faster in the next ten years, and nearly five times faster in the 1970s. These differences are even more impressive when one considers that new central cities were being created as part of the increasing metropolitanization of the population and thus are also included in the central-city growth rates. Only in the 1980s did central city growth exceed that of the suburbs, and then just barely. This reversal, though, is due more to statistics than to any rebound in the fortunes of the once-industrial cities; new central cities added to the metropolitan category were the primary reason for aggregate central-city growth.[39]

Suburban growth was robust around the older central cities in the northeastern and north-central regions of the country, that is, the cities that were suffering the most serious population loss. Out-migration from the central cities, specifically the flight of white households, was a major contributor to early postwar suburban expansion. This internal migration connected central-city decline to suburban prosperity. The centrifugal movement of the central-city population also engendered a further out-migration of businesses and eventually eroded central-city dominance. Previously, the peripheries of these cities had been relatively insignificant; by the 1970s, they had become pivotal in the social, economic, and political life of the metropolitan region.[40]

Consider that the central cities had once had most of the metropolitan population. By 1980, the majority of those residents lived in the suburbs. Moreover, the larger the city, the greater the loss of its demographic dominance. Among the large-city metropolitan areas of 1950, nearly six of every ten residents lived in the central city. In 1980, only four of them did. For the cities with the worst population loss, and after thirty years of relentless decline, fewer than three of every ten metropolitan residents still made their homes in the urban core. This population shift had numerous negative consequences, including the loss of representation in state legislatures and Congress and of the symbolic claim to defining the identity of the region.[41]

The out-migration of central-city households was both numerically important and symbolically meaningful prior to the 1970s. After that time, its contribution to suburbanization waned. The jump in the birthrate in the 1950s had much to do with suburban growth once households left the cities. Thereafter, the formation of new households, additional births, and migration from nonmetropolitan areas made a greater contribution. By the 1970s, most people moving to the suburbs came from other suburbs or from nonmetropolitan areas.[42] During these decades, out-migration from many of the central cities exceeded in-migration while natural increase was insufficient to prevent a net loss. The in-migration of African Americans hardly compensated for the deficit of white households. Further reflecting the weaknesses of the older central cities, their suburbs experienced a net out-migration in the 1970s, although in many instances natural increase prevented a population decline.[43]

The flight of population and of retail and manufacturing jobs from the industrial cities, with many white-collar jobs initially remaining behind, established commuting as a significant metropolitan phenomenon. At its core was the automobile. During the early postwar years, most commuters traveled from their suburban homes to downtown places of work. As the deconcentration of employment and the dispersal of job sites fueled low-density development, commuting patterns changed. Throughout most of the twentieth century until the 1970s, only a small number of central-city residents commuted to jobs in the suburbs.[44] When job growth in the suburbs accelerated in the 1980s, reverse commuting (from central city to suburbs) increased, as did suburb-to-suburb commuting. These flows eventually overwhelmed the traditional commuting pattern in many metropolitan areas.

With the geographical spread of the postwar metropolis, commuting distances and commuting times rose also. In the larger metropolises, they became so great as to discourage workers from taking jobs in the central city. Dispersing the central city was the solution. Establishing business and financial services in office parks or adjacent to suburban shopping malls effectively reconstituted core functions outside the central cities and made cross-commuting more prevalent. While only a few suburbs were becoming "urban places in their own right," contrary to what one commentator had predicted in 1975, the multinodal metropolis was a major change in how the suburbs were organized.[45]

The multiplicity of multifunctional commercial and residential nodes in the suburban periphery was mainly a post-1980s phenomenon, though it had roots in the 1970s.[46] Places like Tyson's Corner, Virginia, outside Washington, D.C.; Stamford, Connecticut, northeast of New York City; and Irvine, just south of Los Angeles, came to be known as edge cities. They engendered additional low-density development, made it possible for sprawl and agglomeration to coexist, and enabled metropolitan areas to grew even larger.

Edge cities, sprawling suburban peripheries, and robust Sunbelt cities were the second major consequence of the postwar rupture in urbanization processes. Mass suburbanization dominated. It shaped how the Sunbelt developed—automobile-centric, with low-density and anemic central cities—and it gave rise to the edge cities without which suburban development would have been stymied. Nevertheless, neither the Sunbelt cities nor the suburbs prospered independently of the central cities. Of particular importance is the devastation that visited the large, industrial cities as residents fled.

Urban Decline

The growth of the suburbs was inseparable from the decline of the large, industrial cities. The older, central cities provided residents for the burgeoning, peripheral housing developments and later spun off the businesses that anchored shopping malls and industrial parks. With the loss of population, jobs, consumer expenditures, and tax revenues, decline struck these cities with a vengeance. As the cities shrank, their problems multiplied. One newspaper columnist noted in 1970, a bit belatedly, that "the conclusion is inescapable . . . cities are losing population; . . . the population that remains is largely poor; . . . [and] jobs and industry are locating elsewhere."[47]

Rapid population growth might bring traffic congestion, escalating land values and home prices, and overcrowded schools, but growth is far more desirable than decline. With rare exceptions, cities add residents when their economies are expanding. An expanding economy, moreover, most often means that jobs are plentiful, incomes are rising, and tax bases are growing. In growing cities, people can be optimistic about the future.

Postwar population loss from the industrial cities, on the other hand, was associated with numerous economic, fiscal, and social problems.[48] Investors and households became pessimistic, and this further weakened the propensity to stay and invest. Elected officials and a few business leaders were optimistic, but their optimism rang false in the face of so much dire and contradictory evidence.

Central to these many urban ills were weak and shrinking city economies. When jobs disappear, residents often leave a city, a condition that frequently leads to a drop in the aggregate disposable income available for buying clothes, going to the movies, renovating houses, and contributing to local charities. Resident flight spurs additional job loss through the withdrawal of demand for public and private services and for such goods as housing and groceries. Because there are fewer home owners and businesses to tax and because property values are falling, the local government also suffers as revenues fall. In addition, the number of poor residents usually increases as less affluent households move to the city to take advantage of lower rents. Their presence burdens local governments with a rising need for social services. Consequently, local tax rates are often raised, making the city less desirable in another way. As social problems deepen and government revenues decline, city governments frequently find themselves suffering chronic fiscal stress and perhaps even facing bankruptcy.[49]

Although numerous cities could be selected, Philadelphia will do to illustrate the fact that population loss is often, even if not invariably, accompanied by other losses that diminish the city economically, fiscally, and socially. As one of the postwar cities suffering prolonged decline, by 1980 Philadelphia's population had dropped by almost 20 percent from what it had been at the end of World War II. Nearly 400,000 fewer people lived there than had done so thirty years previously.

The flight of residents was triggered by a loss of jobs, down by one-fifth over this period, and by the closure of business establishments, one-half as numerous as they had been in 1950. Retail stores, movie theaters, and restaurants, diners, and taverns followed; of every ten of these in 1950, only six were still operating in 1980. And while the number of homes and apartments in the city increased to match the heightened demand caused by falling household size, the number of vacant housing units grew fourfold, to more than 65,000, as people fled decaying neighborhoods. These changes produced a drop in real property values—over $1 billion in constant dollars—pushing the government into fiscal stress. Balancing the city's budget proved difficult, and debt increased by almost 40 percent in real terms. Per capita incomes rose, but they lagged well behind incomes in the suburbs and increased against a background of deepening poverty.[50]

Population loss did not cause all of these unpleasant conditions. While job loss usually precedes resident flight, the lure of suburbia, the disinvestment in housing and neighborhoods that occurred throughout the 1930s and 1940s, and the influx of African Americans also contributed to the out-migration of (mostly white) residents. Whether cause or effect, population loss is inevitably associated with a host of urban ills.

In fact, population growth is such a significant aspect of urban development that cities can become less desirable even when they are simply growing relatively slowly rather than actually losing residents. Slow growth is a sign of impending problems; it indicates a city "at risk." Cities compete with each other for residents, investment, and reputation. Even if a city is still adding residents, lagging behind its peers diminishes its competitive advantages. Having a net loss of population is bad, but slow growth or no growth is almost equally disconcerting.[51]

Amid what was a stunning and undeniable period of affluence and influence between the late 1940s and mid-1970s, the country's large cities went into a tailspin. Urban decline seemed unavoidable. And while widely reported in the media, debated in legislatures, and lamented in certain corporate boardrooms, it was mediated ideologically by the growth of the suburbs and Sunbelt cities and by the domestic prosperity that seemed to extend to all Americans. Consequently, the decay of the industrial cities was bothersome but hardly indicative of national decline. Nonetheless, the consequences of urban population loss were momentous and extensive.

One of the most important consequences of postwar urbanization involved how people lived, worked, and played with others. To better understand these changes, we need to look more closely at the dynamics underlying industrial-city decline and suburban expansion. In chapter 3, we turn specifically to the interconnected processes that governed the growth and decline of cities and suburbs, small towns, and rural areas and the shift from distributive to parasitic urbanization.

3

Parasitic Urbanization

The sudden loss of population from the industrial cities coupled with mass suburbanization and Sunbelt-city growth constituted a sharp break in the country's developmental trajectory. They were the consequences of a profound rupture in the underlying dynamics of urbanization. After 1945, the distributive urbanization that had prevailed from the mid-1800s to the early 1940s gave way to parasitic urbanization. This was a turning point. No longer would national growth be shared; cities of the West and South along with suburbs throughout the country would prosper by draining people and investments from the older, industrial cities.[1]

Of course, turning points are never abrupt, and historical periods rarely have crisp boundaries. Yet the two periods are substantially different. The degree to which people clustered in cities, the frequency at which new cities came into existence, and the processes by which cities developed are hardly comparable. Moreover, postwar city growth took place in a different part of the country than did urban decline. The demographic realities and the workings of the national economy were also distinct. After midcentury, the environment for the large, industrial cities—cities that had dominated their metropolitan areas and made the United States into a prosperous nation and a global power—turned inhospitable.

The decades after World War II brought forth novel institutional and social relationships that spurred a new round of economic expansion. From the stock market crash of 1929 that triggered a worldwide economic depression to the recovery years of the early 1940s, the United

States had stagnated economically and demographically. During the war, the decentralization of military installations and defense industries had presaged the suburbanization and regional shifts that soon followed. It was the cessation of the war and the return of prosperity, though, that released blockages to real estate investment, domestic consumption, residential mobility, marriage, and the raising of children. Into existence came a new set of social realities averse to simply expanding existing cities. Parasitic urbanization—a "breakup of the old urban form," as Lewis Mumford put it—was the response.[2]

Distributive and parasitic urbanization are part of a larger historical dynamic in which societies grow and decline, expand and contract, in response to novel technologies and social arrangements. Development unfolds in long waves of institutional change. Driven by innovations that reshape the economy, these waves undergo qualitative transformations as the consequences of those innovations are depleted and new technologies and institutional relations are launched. Each wave creates, even as it is sustained by, unique patterns of urbanization.

These long waves, moreover, are not confined to national boundaries. Development ebbs and flows in many countries simultaneously. This fact directs our attention to the transnational dimension of these transformations. The full meaning of American postwar central-city decline, mass suburbanization, and their cultural consequences can only be grasped by looking outside the United States. The country has never been isolated from international commerce, immigration, the flow of ideas, or regional conflicts. Nor has it, through either size or the sheer fact of its great wealth and power, managed to sequester itself from the predatory forces that rack other countries. In those fateful postwar years, its cities, weakened and vulnerable, were defenseless against such global influences.

Urbanization's Rupture

An astute observer tracking urbanization in the early twentieth century—the growing population in cities, the expansion in the number of urban places—would not have predicted the reversal that first appeared during the 1930s and became virulent thereafter. Nor would that person have grasped the subsequent importance of incipient suburbanization. The initial loss of central-city population was easily explained away as a result of the economic depression; the population loss that followed as the 1940s waned and the 1950s unfolded was more perplexing. Commentators viewed the latter with cautious concern and with an optimism that held that appropriate government interventions could reverse the trend. Even now, a contemporary of our earlier observer might interpret the aggregate data as suggesting a slowing-down of urbanization and a geographical adjustment, but certainly not a radical break in past trends. Looking more closely, we find a relentless and serious population loss that extended to the smallest of the central cities and that involved a radical rearrangement of the country's population. This was not just the normal waxing and waning of demographic growth. The pattern of urbanization of the late nineteenth and early twentieth centuries had been broken.

Standing back from individual cities and taking into view the century-long trajectory of urban expansion, deceleration is obvious; the sharp reversal is not. (See Figure 5.) The sudden rupture of the central cities and the precipitous rise of the suburbs after World War II are imperceptible. The sole hint lies in the 1930s, when a slight dampening in these trends occurred. That same decade also witnessed a slowing-down—to a miniscule one-half of 1 percent—in the movement of people to urban areas. The central cities saw their share of the total population drop, but only by a small amount. The aggregate quality of these trends and the pervasive background of growth masked a tectonic shift.

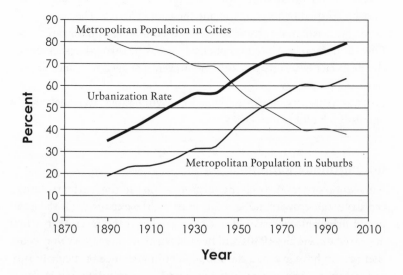

Figure 5. Urbanization and metropolitanization, 1890–2000. The data for this figure are from Alan Altshuler, William Morrill, Harold Wolman, and Faith Mitchell, eds., Governance and Opportunity in Metropolitan America (Washington, D.C.: National Academy Press, 1999), 25, table 2.2.

The relevant story is not decade-by-decade variations but the overall differences between the time prior to the Great Depression of the 1930s and the years after World War II. In both periods, the country added residents in roughly the same numbers. In both periods, the country became more urban. What was sharply different was the way it urbanized: primarily in high-density central cities in the first period and mainly in low-density suburbs and sprawling cities in the second.[3] From 1930 onward, the central cities maintained their share of the country's population through the addition of new central cities and the expansion of smaller cities in the South and West. However, the older manufacturing cities no longer functioned as the motor of rising urbanization. Instead, it was the suburbs that were pulling in residents, and they were doing so at a rate much faster than the central cities.

The decline of the industrial cities in the 1960s and 1970s and their subsequent stagnation, combined with the dampening of suburban growth thereafter, eventually brought urbanization to a virtual halt. Population losses in the United States and abroad were offered as hard evidence that counterurbanization was underway.[4] Deconcentration seemed to be taking hold. Even though short-lived, it contributed to the sense that the United States had reached a demographic plateau at roughly three-quarters of the population living in urbanized areas. By the end of the twentieth century, urban stasis had become an accurate characterization of the nation's demographic fate.

The rupture in urbanization is clearer when we compare the earlier period of central-city expansion with the postwar period of central-city decline. The first begins in 1893 and ends in 1929; the second goes from 1948 to 1973.

The last decade of the nineteenth century, like the 1930s, was a turning point in the country's history. Well beyond the devastation of the Civil War, this decade was both the end of one long wave of development and the beginning of another. In 1890, the superintendent of the census declared that a frontier no longer existed, and Frederick Jackson Turner, the famous geographer, responded by declaring this the end of "the first period of American history."[5] The dividing line was an economic slump in 1893–1894. After that, the central cities surged, and the national economy prospered. By the 1930s, the population living in urban places had more than tripled, and the number of central cities had quadrupled. The country went from a primarily agricultural to a primarily industrial nation. It developed the "largest economy" in the world, industrialization matured, corporate capitalism took hold, immigration was robust, and the industrial cities experienced significant growth. Over one-half of its residents lived in urban communities by 1920. The seeds of the postwar metropolis had been planted.[6]

The second period began in 1948 and ended in 1973. These were decades of devastating population loss from the cities, a shift from an industrial economy to one based on personal, business, and financial services, and the emergence of a dominant suburban way of life. Immigration, a major contributor to urban growth prior to the 1920s, was far below its earlier levels. A major depression and World War II had stifled expansion. These were years of contraction and quiescence, and they left urban deterioration in their wake. In doing so, they established the conditions for a peculiar form of postwar recovery.

The differences between the period of city growth and that of central-city decline and mass suburbanization are quite pronounced. Three core urban processes distinguished the latter from the former and explain the parasitic urbanization that ensued. First, a severe drop-off in immigration and rural-to-urban migration coupled with a regional shift in households and investment had a severe impact on population growth in the industrial cities. Second, a shrinking of household size coupled with widespread adoption of the automobile brought about a low-density pattern of urbanization that lessened commitment to high-density cities. And third, the ability of suburbs in the Northeast to resist annexation and of cities in the Sunbelt to expand their boundaries by using laws allowing the annexation of peripheral areas enabled growing cities to avoid the pitfalls of stagnation. All of this took place amid a demographic slowdown.[7]

After 1945, the United States became demographically lethargic. The population continued to expand but at a lessened rate. Natural increase—the excess of births over deaths—slowed, and immigration failed to compensate. For the older, industrial cities, the precipitous decline in immigration and the virtual cessation of rural-to-urban migration were particularly unfortunate.

Immigrants to the United States have generally settled in cities, at least initially, and boosted populations through their numbers, their higher birthrates, and their larger families. In 1920, during the earlier period, more than one-half of all recent immigrants lived in urban areas; among Irish and Russian immigrants almost nine in ten did so. In the postwar period, immigration was lower than it had been even in the 1920s, when new federal laws severely restricted new entrants.[8] Without a flow of immigrants to compensate for declining birthrates and households lost to suburbanization, the central cities failed to grow. The importance of immigration was made even clearer when the numbers of immigrants began to increase in the late 1970s. Cities that had been experiencing population loss actually grew. Many of the new immigrants gravitated to metropolitan areas; just over one-half of all immigrants relocated to central cities. Another one-third went directly to the suburbs. The metropolitan areas of Los Angeles and New York City were the destinations of two of every five immigrants.[9]

Not only did the manufacturing cities of the Northeast and Midwest suffer from a constricted flow of foreign immigrants in the early postwar decades, but they also lacked the demographic benefit of migration from the countryside. Rural-to-urban migration to the central cities, with the exception of African Americans coming from the South, dampened considerably after World War II. In the earlier period, the industrialization of urban and rural economies drew rural inhabitants to the cities in large numbers. Agriculture had become mechanized, and numerous rural occupations were disappearing. And even though the number of farms had increased, agricultural employment declined.

Nearly 500,000 people per year moved from farms to cities and towns during the late nineteenth century. By 1870, the rural population had peaked numerically, even though it had been shrinking relative to the urban population since 1790. And while it subsequently grew by one-third between 1890 and 1930, the urban population more than doubled. During the 1880s, rural-to-urban migration reached its highest point. After 1930, it decelerated to one-half the rate it had achieved in the earlier period.[10] Slack rural migration and more choices of where to live meant population woes for central cities. By 1950, fewer than four of every ten U.S. residents lived in the countryside, and when they migrated to urban areas, central cities were not necessarily where they went.[11] Suburbs were the more desirable destination. Cities did grow through internal migration, but they were not the same cities that had grown previously. The most attractive were those in the South and West.

Black migration from the South rose significantly, going from less than 900,000 in the 1920s to nearly 1.5 million in the three postwar decades. Forty years later, "two-thirds of all black Americans living outside the South could be found inside the city limits of the twelve largest cities." For New York City, Puerto Rican in-migration was also a major factor, and nearly 500,000 Puerto Ricans had settled there by 1960. Neither blacks nor Puerto Ricans were numerous enough to slacken the overall population loss from the central cities, however.[12]

Further compounding the weaknesses of the industrial cities in the second period was the regional shift in population. From the beginnings of European colonization, the mean center of the U.S. population had moved progressively westward. In 1790, it was near Baltimore. A century later, it was southeast of Indianapolis, Indiana. After that, it took a southerly turn, and by 1980, the center was south and slightly west of St. Louis.[13] Americans have continually pushed the frontier in the direction of the Pacific Ocean and the Gulf of Mexico.

Consequently, the northeastern and north-central regions, where most of the postwar urban decline occurred, saw their national shares of the population shrink. Surprisingly, this shrinkage occurred in both periods. And while their shares actually increased during the Depression and World War II, it was the Northeast that grew across these two decades, not the Midwest. The latter continued its demographic slide, to be joined by the Northeast only after the war. Comparatively, the West had the best performance. It doubled its national share of the population in the first period, from 5 percent to 10 percent, and ended the second period with almost one-quarter of the country's residents. The South was stable earlier and grew later, though more slowly than the western states. The big picture here is one of regional population shifts away from the parts of the country where industrialization and urban concentration had thrived.[14]

In terms of urbanization, the postwar decades are much less impressive than their 1890–1930 counterparts.[15] A smaller proportion of residents became urban, the urbanization rate slowed, and the central cities became much less attractive as places of residence. While the population continued to urbanize, the growth shifted to the suburbs and away from the metropolitan cores. As a consequence, relatively fewer large urban places were created even though smaller cities continued to proliferate. Given that no country can be more than 100 percent urban, one cannot but wonder if this slowdown is not simply a matter of statistical limits or even of the rising friction of progressive urbanization, which is easier when the country is mostly rural than when it is mostly urban. Yet other countries in the late twentieth century were much more urbanized: Belgium at 96 percent, the United Kingdom at 89 percent, the Netherlands at 87 percent, and Germany at 85 percent.[16] The greater land area of the United States and the country's bias for low-density development suggest that it will not soon match these numbers.

An equally plausible explanation for the slowdown of urbanization is the possibility that with the demise of an industrialization that thrived on high concentrations of manufacturing and supportive activities, and thus on high densities, the country simply no longer needed to create large cities. The forces of agglomeration had weakened. Yet the nation was still spawning new central cities and increasing the size of existing ones. (Suburbs and metropolitan areas were also expanding in number.) More precisely, while the rate at which new central cities originated fell relative to the earlier period, the actual number of new central cities rose; there were many more cities in 1950 than in 1890. Growth, though, was higher in the smaller than in the larger urban places.

Counteracting the flight of households and the paltry flows of immigrants was the continued decline in the size of households, a factor that anchors the second broad dimension that separates the earlier period of urbanization from its postwar counterpart. Households were not as big in comparison to those of the early twentieth century, and more people were living alone or in childless couples. In the older cities, these changes tempered the falling demand for local goods and services, especially housing, and slowed the loss of retailers. Smaller households also meant different types of living arrangements. The cities came to be widely perceived as the places of residence for the elderly, young singles, childless couples, and people living alternative lifestyles. Traditional families—husband, wife, children—were prevalent in the suburbs. Race, of course, confounds these distinctions.

Smaller households were feasible in part because the postwar housing industry had much greater capacity. Home builders developed mass-production techniques and became bigger. Supply could keep pace with demand, and even lead it. By contrast, there were only a few large-scale residential developers prior to the 1920s. For this reason, and because most developer-built housing before 1945 was in the cities on expensive land, home construction tracked population growth; it was mainly demand driven. With numerous new families clamoring for housing after World War II and with the housing stock in the cities overcrowded and obsolete, builders responded with massive suburban development. New housing construction on a yearly basis increased almost fourfold, while the total population barely doubled. With automobile usage also rising, suburban housing became more and more accessible, and the siphoning of households from the central cities accelerated.[17]

One consequence of these events was that the postwar suburbs and Sunbelt cities had much lower densities than the industrial cities. The average density of the twenty-five largest cities, while increasing slightly from 1910 to 1950, dropped precipitously in the next forty years. The falloff occurred mainly among the largest of the cities. New York maintained its supremacy and even increased its density to 24,000 people per square mile. Large cities that were persistently losing population, however—such as Detroit, whose density declined from just over 11,000 to 7,000 people per square mile—pulled down the average. The growth of the low-density cities of the South and West—Dallas and Los Angeles, for example—also diluted the aggregate numbers. In 1910, all of the ten largest cities had densities exceeding 10,000 people per square mile. In 1980, only three of the ten largest cities were this crowded. Houston, Dallas, San Diego, and Phoenix fell below 3,000.[18]

Sunbelt cities simply occupied much more land than the Rustbelt cities of the earlier period. During the post–World War II years, the land area of the largest cities more than doubled. The older, industrial cities contributed little to this expansion compared to the rapidly growing southern and western cities with their vast land areas. St. Louis, Boston, Cleveland, and Pittsburgh in 1950 each covered less than 100 square miles, whereas thirty years later the Sunbelt cities were three and four times bigger. Among the top twenty-five cities in population size in 1980, Houston stretched over 550 square miles, and Los Angeles was nearly as large. The phenomenon is not just historical; it is also regional, with the constraints on local government expansion being less in the southern and western than in the northeastern and north-central regions. Cities of the Sunbelt were better able to do something that was no longer available to cities in the Rustbelt: They could annex adjacent land and consolidate with adjacent municipalities, the third, broad difference between distributive and parasitic urbanization.

As ways of capturing growth or vacant land on the periphery, annexation and consolidation have always been important for enabling central cities to maintain their metropolitan dominance. Like cities generally, those in the United States have grown by attracting new residents and retaining existing ones. They have also taken possession of surrounding areas that already had people in them or where new migrants might move. Land for expansion is crucial.

Probably the most striking example of this involves the statistical disappearance of two of the country's large cities: Brooklyn, New York, and Allegheny, Pennsylvania. Brooklyn was the fourth-largest city in the country in 1890 but was consolidated with New York City in 1898. Only a few years earlier, ironically, Brooklyn had annexed four towns in order to increase its size. Threatened by the growth of Chicago, New York City's elites wanted to expand; they wanted "a city so large, rich, and important that its preeminence could never be challenged."[19] Allegheny was a prosperous city of German immigrants and numerous industries just across the Allegheny River from Pittsburgh.

In 1900, Allegheny was the twenty-seventh-largest city, and Pittsburgh was the eleventh largest. Despite resistance, annexation was forced in 1906. Territorial expansion made it possible for cities to prosper.[20]

While many cities grew through annexation prior to the 1920s, after World War II this avenue was no longer open to them, and was less available for cities in the northeastern and north-central regions than for those in other parts of the country. Annexation was primarily a nineteenth-century mechanism. The twenty largest cities that lost population between 1950 and 1970 added only 83 square miles to their land areas after 1930. In the preceding eighty years, they had added 1,602 square miles.[21] During the mid-1800s, many peripheral areas had been unincorporated. This made them unable to levy taxes or provide public services (such as police protection, water, and sewer connections) and thus vulnerable to annexation. Moreover, those that were incorporated were sparsely developed, with small tax bases that limited growth. Becoming annexed to a larger municipality solved these problems.

Between roughly 1850 and 1910, peripheral areas became more populated, and state legislatures made incorporation and local self-rule easier. These legislatures also surrendered power over annexations and consolidations to the voters. Many suburban communities took advantage of this to establish separate identities, improve services, or evade the high taxes of the central cities. Others incorporated as industrial suburbs or as entertainment communities, with amusement parks at their center. Over the next few decades, the laws supporting suburban autonomy and the ability to remain fiscally independent of the central cities were strengthened. Under these conditions, it was nearly impossible for the older central cities to achieve significant growth through territorial expansion after World War II.[22]

In addition, three other obstacles stymied the outward movement of the municipal boundaries of the older, industrial cities.[23] One was the growth of non-Anglo communities in the central cities and their perceived association with vice and destitution. This repulsed middle-class, white suburbanites. A second was the rise of special service districts to address metropolis-wide public service needs, thereby weakening one of the arguments for annexation and consolidation. The last was a change in attitude toward expansion. In the nineteenth century, city and state officials believed that it was inevitable that cities would add to their land areas. In the late twentieth century, few city officials thought in these terms.

Older cities did annex land after World War II. In fact, the number of cities over 5,000 population that engaged in annexation rose each year from the end of the war to 1955. However, the average size of an annexation was a relatively miniscule 0.7 square miles.[24] Only cities in the South and West retained this ability to any noteworthy degree. The twenty largest cities that grew in population size after 1950 doubled their land area between 1930 and 1970; the twenty largest cities that lost population were only 5 percent bigger. Only four of the former—Indianapolis, Columbus, Milwaukee, and Toledo, Ohio—were not in the southern or western regions. All but San Francisco; Oakland, California; and Birmingham among the latter were in the northeastern and north-central regions. State legislatures in the South and West looked more favorably on annexation and consolidation. Consequently, cities like Oklahoma City and Phoenix were able to increase greatly in land area. Houston, which occupied 25 square miles in 1940, sprawled to over 550 square miles forty years later.

Clearly, annexation is only one factor in the decline of the industrial cities in the Northeast and Midwest and in the rapid growth of the suburbs and cities of the Sunbelt. In fact, the allure of territorial expansion—the lingering American fascination with the frontier—persisted after World War II in another form: metropolitan consolidation.[25] Even so, few metropolitan governments were realized. Regional needs, though, were unavoidable, and numerous metropolis-wide service districts were established to deliver public transportation and water or to manage ports. In rare instances, municipalities adjacent to a central city agreed to share tax bases.

Proponents of metropolitanization argued that in order for a city to grow, it must be able to absorb peripheral growth. Its boundaries, to use a more contemporary term, must be elastic. Elastic cities in contrast to inelastic ones are ostensibly less racially segregated, the income gap between the central city and suburbs is smaller, public schools are less racially divided, bond ratings are higher, and poverty rates are lower. Elasticity, however, was not and is not easily achieved for the cities that most need it.[26]

In numerous other ways, the cities of the postwar period faced a much different set of economic, social, and political conditions than did the cities of the early twentieth century. Depleted immigration, slack rural-to-urban migration, low-density patterns of land development, and constraints on annexation were the major factors around which these dynamics were organized. Two distinct periods are thus evident: one of distributive urbanization, in which national growth was more or less shared, and the other of parasitic urbanization, in which national growth was dependent on the decline of the older, industrial cities. Parasitic urbanization favored suburban expansion and low-density Sunbelt cities. A century-long pattern of urbanization had been ruptured.

Waves of Development

The shift from distributive to parasitic urbanization seems even more anomalous, though probably not permanent, when set in its historical context. Across the long waves of development extending back to the late eighteenth century, urbanization was distributive. As national population growth and economic prosperity waxed and waned, cities expanded in size and number. A few cities lost residents as technologies changed and economies restructured, but the relationship between decline there and growth elsewhere was tenuous at best. Only in the most recent long wave, beginning after World War II, did urbanization become parasitic. Profoundly historical, parasitic urbanization emerged from a unique constellation of social conditions. And to the degree that distributive urbanization seemed to have strengthened in the late 1970s, its replacement might well have only been temporary—a historical anomaly.

Urbanization is both cause and consequence of the wavelike rhythms of development that follow technological advances, bursts of investment, the geographical extension of markets, and population growth. Urbanization processes thus exhibit significant historical variation. This is the case despite the fact that urbanization is most often conceived as a single and continuous process by which societies become more and more urbanized as the forces of concentration produce more and larger cities.[27] That development brings with it urbanization, and vice versa, is a claim that has achieved the status of common wisdom.

However, the sources of economic wealth, the types of people who live in cities (for example, lawyers and computer programmers rather than apparel workers), the functions of local governments, and even the city's physical form have shifted from one period of development to the next.[28] In the United States, the industrial city was not the colonial city, and a traveler back in time would have been endlessly confused by the particulars of daily life and appalled by the prevailing standards, or lack thereof, of public sanitation. The geographical mixing of activities—homes, businesses, and workshops literally on top of each other—in the colonial city disappeared in the late industrial city, the result of changing technology, new social arrangements, and the reformist zeal for order and efficiency.

As an example, consider what Eric Lampard has called industrial urbanization.[29] A cumulative and dynamic process, it generated sharply rising concentrations of human activity and highly differentiated systems of cities in the countries where it occurred. Beginning in the later decades of the eighteenth century, the absorption of the labor force in manufacturing spurred an upsurge in the urban population that exceeded overall population growth. Industrial technology and specialization enabled higher and higher levels of concentration, and the "specialization of functions [made] inevitably for specialization of areas."[30] External economies reinforced these tendencies in an upward spiral of agglomeration. This process waned only when tertiary functions (for example, services) replaced manufacturing as the propulsive force in the economy and as growth in personal incomes and technological advances disengaged from urbanization, events dated in the mid-twentieth century.[31]

The point here is that urbanization takes different forms in different periods. Urban historians recognize this when they contrast colonial, industrial, and corporate, or postindustrial, cities. And when late-twentieth-century urban theorists announced a radical break between a modern and postmodern urbanism, they too acknowledged the importance of thinking in terms of historical eras. Precise temporal distinctions are elusive, though, and one form of urbanization fades into another rather than abruptly displacing its predecessor.[32]

One way to specify these periods of urbanization is to use and extend the long waves of development identified by the Russian economist N. D. Kondratieff in the 1920s. Drawing mainly on commodity price fluctuations for the United States, England, and France, he determined that these waves normally span approximately forty to sixty years and are divided roughly equally between periods of expansion and of contraction. His first wave went from 1789 to 1849 and his second from 1849 to 1896. He did not date the turning point of the third wave, since, when he wrote, the contraction phase (begun in 1930) had yet to be completed. If congruent with the length of previous contractions, it and the third wave would have ended roughly in 1945.[33]

Kondratieff situated long waves in the cyclical nature of capitalist economies as they adjusted both to price changes and to technological inventions discovered during downswings and applied during upswings. To these factors he later added investments in basic capital goods, such as infrastructure and factories, with the cyclical phases depending on the type and useful productive life of these commodities.[34] Drawing on this perspective, other analysts have verified the existence of construction or building cycles whose length falls between that of long waves of development and the short duration (seven to ten years) of business cycles.[35] These cycles last between fifteen and twenty years and have been documented for numerous countries, cities, and regions and traced as far back as the eighteenth century. For the United States, these long swings, as they are often called, first appeared in the early nineteenth century.

Two long swings followed the Civil War, with the second ending in the 1890s. The subsequent cycle lasted until just after World War I, and the next two went, respectively, to 1933 at the depth of the Depression, and the end of World War II. Although the postwar period is less easily cast in this framework, a point to be considered below, it does seem that the first postwar swing extended to the early 1960s, another went to the mid-1970s, and the third to the late 1980s. In most instances, these long swings end with a recession.

To ask what drives long swings is to question why investment flows into buildings and infrastructure. Here is where the surges and contractions of urbanization become part of the story. Population growth, household formation, and immigration certainly play a role, along with changes in the size of the labor force. Because these are crude measures of demand, though, and because the real estate and construction sectors are also driven by the availability of capital, the organizational capacities of developers, and the interest of investors, they are weakly connected to long swings. More appropriate as drivers of long swings are long-term investments in basic infrastructure (for example, highway systems and electricity grids) and productive fixed capital such as factories. Technological change and industry formation and decline are also major inducements and have an impact on construction investment, particularly in regional economies dependent on a single industry, as, for example, Akron was on rubber, Pittsburgh was on steel, and Detroit was on automobile assembly.[36]

Historically, and for the United States, long swings of building activity have been associated with transportation innovations.[37] Canal construction that began in the mid-1820s roughly corresponded with the earliest (1830–1843) U.S. building cycle. Later, the railroad replaced the canal as the major form of long-distance freight transport and spurred two long swings, one between 1843 and 1862 and the second beginning after the Civil War. The latter was anchored in the consolidation and integration of a national railroad network. A fourth transport-building cycle (1878–1900) emerged from another surge in railroad activity; a fifth, from street and electric railway development;

and a final cycle (1918–1933), from the automobile. Each transport innovation created a demand not just for vehicles, repair shops, and storage facilities but also for the businesses that sold supplies to users and operators. In addition, each innovation opened new land for development and extended the range for commuting to jobs in the city.

The automobile has had a unique impact on the geography of urbanization. The railroad reinforced the forces of centralization and concentration; the automobile weakened them. Unlike rail networks or canals, roads and highways are more flexible and ubiquitous in their location. Stores, factories, and homes can be dispersed and still have access to places where jobs and services are abundant. Moreover, the automobile is a highly individualistic mode of transportation and one that requires a great deal of redundant infrastructure, from parking spaces and garages to roads and highways and gasoline stations. It is a space-consuming innovation. The automobile thus changed the form of the metropolis while introducing new types of buildings and forcing modification of existing ones. Stables gave way to garages, and streets needed to be widened to allow on-street parking.[38]

Transportation innovations, of course, depend for their existence and diffusion on cultural and institutional forces. Without the rise in personal disposable income and government subsidies for roads and highways, for example, widespread automobile ownership after World War II would have been less likely. Social factors (for example, high rates of household formation, racial discrimination) also mediate settlement patterns. Immigration waxes and wanes, new industries have greater or lesser demands for physical plant than the industries they replace (compare, for example, computer software with tire production), and the real estate industry becomes better organized to undertake large projects.

The land economist Homer Hoyt argued in the 1930s that past building cycles in cities, Chicago specifically, were "generated largely by a sudden and unexpected increase in population which was in turn due to a rush to take advantage of economic opportunities."[39] According to his research, when the number of residents increased precipitously, housing became overcrowded, public facilities were used at capacity, and industrial and commercial buildings became fully occupied. Soon thereafter, and in response to unmet demand, land sales increased, lots were subdivided, and new construction ensued. Not until eight to ten years had passed did land values reach their peak. As real estate investment persisted without a corresponding expansion in population, the stage was set for the land boom to end. As long as industrial opportunities continued to attract new residents, though, the city would experience another building boom.

Prior to the twentieth century, cities were mainly able to expand laterally onto vacant land. When the technology became available to build skyscrapers, cities extended themselves vertically into office towers and apartment buildings. The density of development rose. As the 1930s approached, the rate of population increase and the ratio of buildings to inhabitants slackened, indicators of the disappearance of vacant land and the limits to densification. By inference, these relations between job expansion, population growth, building activity, and land values did not hold for the older, industrial cities in the early postwar period. With their dominant yet diminishing manufacturing bases, built-up areas, inability to annex, and already densely developed downtowns, lateral expansion was not generally an option, and vertical extension was hardly sufficient to maintain overall growth.[40]

Fracturing the relentless repetition of these long swings was World War II. The years between 1945 and 1975 were a time of continuous secular expansion that greatly exceeded the normal duration of building cycles. (See Figure 6.) During these years, cycles seemed absent. After 1975, the cycles returned.[41] This anomaly was directly related to the shift from distributive to parasitic urbanization.

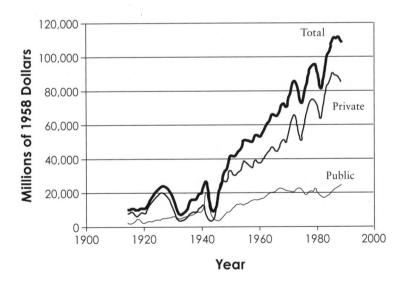

Figure 6. *New construction in the United States, 1915–1989. The data for this figure are from U.S. Department of Commerce,* Value of New Construction Put in Place *(Washington, D.C.: Government Printing Office, various years).*

Building activity in the postwar period became disengaged from a number of underlying forces to which it had traditionally responded. Demand no longer led supply. For example, between the end of World War II and the early 1960s, housing starts lost their connection to the formation of new households. These two phenomena had always increased and decreased together. New homes were built either by their owners or by builders in response to newly formed households. Beginning in the 1950s, housing construction and household formation drifted apart. Only once before, in the 1920s, had the number of housing starts exceeded the number of new households. After the 1940s, this was common, a finding that points to the early postwar prosperity, the rejection of the central cities, and the embrace of the suburbs.[42]

We can further explore these themes and bring the dynamics of postwar urbanization back to the center of the discussion by reflecting on an extended series of Kondratieff cycles. (See Figure 7.) The cycles that Kondratieff originally identified ended in 1929, the turning point from expansion to contraction of his third long wave. These waves can be projected forward with some certainty to 1975. Framing the period of parasitic urbanization in this fashion makes its deviation from historical trends even more obvious. It also brings together a number of conditions and events whose conjuncture is central to an understanding of why parasitic urbanization occurred.

In the first two waves, extending from 1789 to 1896, the nation continually extended its territory until it had reached the West Coast and established its northern and southern continental boundaries. Throughout these years, immigrants entered the United States in relatively large numbers. They settled first along the Atlantic coast and then

Development Cycles	Urbanization Dynamics
First Wave (1789–1814–1849)	
Mercantile and petty commodity production	Distributive urbanization:
Nascent industrialization	Predominately rural society
Early state-building period	Small town growth along
Canal construction	Atlantic coast and rivers
War of 1812	Steady westward expansion
Louisiana Purchase (1803)	
Greater Florida purchased from Spain (1819)	
Northwest annexed (1846)	
Mexican Accession (1848)	

Second Wave (1849–1873–1896)

Fordist industrialization
Three railroad-building cycles (1843–1900)
Civil War (1860–1864)
Mechanization of agriculture
Growth of state and local governments
"Classic" era of immigration
Major business slump (1893–1894)
Gadsden Purchase (1853)
Alaska Purchase (1867)
Hawaiian Annexation (1898)
End of U.S. land expansion

Distributive urbanization:
Rise of large industrial cities
Nascent suburbanization
(1890s)
Steady westward expansion
"Closing" of the frontier

Third Wave (1896–1929–1948)

Maturing of Fordist mass production
Expansion of national government
Rise of local government service functions
Street railway–building cycle (early)
First automobile-building cycle
World War I (1914–1917)
Dampening of immigration
Great Depression (1929–1937)
World War II (1941–1945)

Distributive urbanization:
Slowing of urbanization
Central city growth
Early automobile-driven
suburbanization
"Filling-in" of the West
Building boom of the 1920s

Fourth Wave (1948–1975–?)

Collapse of heavy manufacturing and
dominance of business, financial,
and leisure services
Local governments turn to economic development
Keynesian national government
Major automobile-building cycle
Surge in air travel
Major recession (1973–1975)
Finance-driven investment, post-1973
Minor recessions (1982–1983, 1991–1992)
Korean conflict (1950–1953)
Vietnam conflict (1965–1975)
Globalization
Renewed immigration (late)

Parasitic urbanization:
Collapse of industrial city
Mass suburbanization
Racial transition in cities
Regional shifts to the West
and South
Rise of the Sunbelt cities
Emergence of edge cities
(1980s)
Era of global cities

Figure 7. Long waves of urban development in the United States. The three dates indicated for each wave are the beginning of the expansion phase, the turning point to the contraction phase, and the end of the contraction phase; all dates are approximate. Based on N. D. Kondratieff, "Long Waves in Economic Life," Review of Economic Statistics *17, no. 6 (1935): 105–115 for waves to 1920; J. J. van Duijn,* The Long Wave in Economic Life *(London: George Allen and Unwin, 1983); John Short,* The New Urban Order *(Oxford: Blackwell, 1996), 71–78; Richard A. Walker, "The Transformation of Urban Structure in the Nineteenth Century and the Beginning of Suburbanization," in* Urbanization and Conflict, *ed. K. R. Cox, 165–205 (Chicago: Maaroufa Press, 1978), as well as numerous urban and U.S. histories.*

migrated westward. As the first wave ebbed, small-scale manufacturing appeared, and by the end of the second wave, Fordist industrialization involving large factories and mass production began to dominate the economy. The second wave thus witnessed the rise of the large industrial cities and the establishment of towns that would later grow to be major metropolises. Both these waves were times of distributive urbanization. By the 1890s, land expansion had ceased, and the geographical "frontier," in a statistical claim offered by the Bureau of the Census, had closed.

Urbanization and the flow of population to the West continued throughout the rise and fall of the third wave. The country was filling in its empty spaces along the two coasts and, less expansively, populating the middle of the country. Cities, particularly those reliant on manufacturing, experienced rapid growth, and the Northeast became highly urbanized. By the early twentieth century, though, observers were commenting on the slowdown in city growth. Later, this concern would be dispelled by the boom of the 1920s and the nascent suburbanization brought about by the country's first automobile-driven building cycle. Nonetheless, it lingered as a premonition of central-city decline.

Underway just after a major panic (recession) in 1893, the third wave included two world wars, the second of which defines its end. Between the wars, the country experienced the devastating Depression. These years, and the years of war mobilization that followed, would later be significant in the fate of the industrial cities. The Depression brought widespread disinvestment that weakened the public infrastructure of the cities and prevented new investment that would have staved off obsolescence and kept pace with the demand for factories, housing, stores, and office buildings. The war spurred investment, but mostly outside the cities and in the South and West. While central cities as a whole continued to expand in size and number, although quite modestly, through the 1930s and World War II, they also experienced spreading blight and physical decay. The disinvestment consequent to the Depression and World War II was a major element in the postwar fortunes of the industrial cities, their suburbs, and the Sunbelt cities. In hindsight, signs of a transition from distributive to parasitic urbanization were visible.

Parasitic urbanization occurred in the expansion phase of the fourth wave. Most new construction activity during these years took place in the outlying areas of central cities. Investment shifted from the metropolitan cores to the metropolitan peripheries and rested on the widespread adoption of the automobile and on the domestic prosperity

that had taken hold of the economy. The collapse of heavy manufacturing depleted jobs in the cities and exacerbated the flight of households to the suburbs. White flight, in turn, was further fueled by the
in-migration of poor blacks from the South and their concentration
in slum neighborhoods. With immigration in a slump, no mechanism
existed for compensating the cities for their loss of white, middle-class
households.[43]

Bolstering the expansion that encased and enabled parasitic urbanization was a governance regime dedicated to economic growth.
Tolerant of suburbanization and the regional realignments that generated large investments and high levels of consumer expenditures,
Keynesian governmental policies and Fordist production regimes were
mutually supportive during these years. Compensatory regional and
urban policies were passed, and the federal government mounted a
major initiative to confront poverty and discrimination in the 1960s,
but these efforts paled in comparison with the support that national,
state, and local governments provided for the decentralization of households and businesses. The governance regime and the regime of accumulation were one.[44]

After this time, parasitic urbanization ebbed. Automobile ownership was pervasive by the mid-1970s, and most of the highways linking central cities to their suburbs and to one another had been built.
Black migration to the cities dropped off significantly, job loss slowed,
and immigration rose once again. A number of cities experienced gentrification, and a few pundits proclaimed a move back to the cities.
Suburbs and Sunbelt cities grew and grew, although suburbs were also
beginning to reach the limits of a tolerable commuting range. This
begot edge cities and further weakened the centrality of the metropolitan cores. A post-Keynesian governance regime maintained its bias
for low-density, developer-driven urbanization, and new initiatives for
older cities were scarce. Local governments were forced to be more
competitive, and many were able to lure investors and begin rebuilding
their downtowns. But no positive change is without undesirable consequences, and social polarization deepened.

As the fourth wave entered its contraction phase, a number of the
cities that were losing population benefited. The slowdown in suburbanization and regional realignments, the aging of the country's population
and the diminution in national growth, and the rise in new immigrants
dampened the negative impacts of parasitic urbanization. The country
began to return to its earlier distributive pattern.

Parasitic urbanization, then, stands as an anomaly in the history of urban development in the United States. Of the eight phases of the country's four long waves, only one—the expansion phase of the fourth wave—deviated from the traditional, distributive path of urbanization. Yet despite such distinctiveness, its causes are elusive. This is what a long-wave perspective suggests: Complex events are conjunctural. Many factors come into play at any particular moment. It was not just the automobile, a pro-growth governance regime, deteriorated city environments, racial tensions, the cessation of territorial expansion, the drop-off in immigration, or a diminution in the forces of agglomeration attendant to deindustrialization that produced parasitic urbanization, but all of them together and simultaneously.

The forces behind this transition, moreover, were not confined to the United States. Parasitic urbanization took place at the same time that a worldwide restructuring of manufacturing was undermining the industrial base on which the country had built its international dominance. Transnational migration was moribund and urbanization on the rise elsewhere. Older cities in other industrialized countries also experienced decline, if not full-blown parasitic urbanization. Exceptional in some ways, what happened in the United States in the short American Century was part of a global transformation.

Global Parallels

Kondratieff never meant his long waves to apply to single countries. The fates of nations unfold along parallel and interdependent paths. Countries that have analogous political economies and cultures are very likely to encounter global forces and respond to internal challenges in similar ways.

The assumption that countries are isolated from what is happening outside their territories ignores too much contrary evidence. National boundaries are more or less permeable. Government policies are imitated, practices from city planning to building technologies are shared, mechanisms for financing development are adopted and adapted, and the fortunes of industries are transformed as international trade restructures local employment opportunities, housing markets, and migratory flows. In a world crisscrossed by transnational relations, no country develops in isolation.[45] This suggests that the cities of other urbanized and advanced industrial countries, such as England and Canada, might have also experienced the consequences associated with parasitic urbanization. In fact, this was the case. Industrial-city decline and decentralization were common. Moreover, they were influenced, as they were in the United States, by a changing global landscape of world urbanization, immigrant flows, and industrial change.

Like their U.S. counterparts, numerous industrial cities shed residents after World War II. These cities had also known only growth. The timing was slightly different from one country to the next, and the scale of population loss did not match that which occurred in the United States, but the rough simultaneity of large-city shrinkage in multiple countries points to urban decline as an international, though hardly a fully global, phenomenon.[46]

The large cities of the United Kingdom and western Europe followed a path of population change that reflected, even if it did not fully mimic, that of U.S. industrial cities. (See Table 1.) The postwar shift was less abrupt, but population loss was clearly evident and was neither slight nor temporary. From 1800 to 1930, only a few large cities in the United Kingdom and western Europe lost population. This number jumped in the 1930s, rose again in the 1940s, ebbed, and then increased again in the 1960s. In the subsequent two decades, more and more of these cities cast off residents.

The timing was clearly different from that which occurred in the United States. The beginning of population loss in the Depression of the 1930s was similar, but the historical trajectory had a much different shape. First, the percentage of large European cities losing population in the 1940s was greater than it was in the previous ten years. This was very much unlike U.S. cities. The reason seems to lie in World War II. Of the large cities that lost population in the 1940s, fourteen were in

Table 1. Population Loss in Cities of the United Kingdom and Western Europe, 1800–1990

	Pre-1930	1930–1940	1940–1950	1950–1960	1960–1970	1970–1980	1980–1990
Number of cities with a decade loss	19	11	21	11	28	37	39
Percent	4.5	17.7	33.9	17.7	45.2	60.0	62.9

Note: Included here are sixty-two cities that had populations of 500,000 or more in 1960–1961 or populations of 250,000 or more in 1900–1901. The percent shown is the ratio of the number of cities that lost population in a decade to the total number of cities. For the pre-1930 period, the denominator was the total number of cities times the number of time periods (nine) between 1800 and 1930 in the original table.

Sources: B. R. Mitchell, ed., *European Historical Statistics, 1750–1975* (New York: Facts on File, 1981), and B. B. Mitchell, ed., *International Historical Statistics: Europe, 1750–1993*, 4th ed. (London: Macmillan, 1992).

Germany, six were in the United Kingdom, and one (Vienna) was in Austria. The expansion of the armed forces, war casualties, and bombing raids all contributed to the smaller number of residents. The last factor was particularly important and was absent in the United States.

Second, the percentage of large cities losing population in the 1950s declined significantly from what it had been in a decade earlier. Again, this was a deviation from the U.S. pattern. The underlying processes of urbanization seemed to have remained in effect, with many cities rebounding from the problems of the previous decade. The number of German and U.K. cities losing population dropped by half. The Depression and the war had passed.

Third, the onset of chronic urban population loss in U.K. and western European cities appeared in the 1960s rather than in the 1950s, that is, later than it did in the United States. Slow growth induced by wartime recovery dampened population movements, and the result was that these cities did relatively well after the war. In the United States, by contrast, the 1950s were a time of accelerating collapse for the cities.

Fourth, for thirty-five years after World War II, the cities of these countries followed a similar path, a trend in which more and more cities shed residents. Whereas U.S. cities rebounded in the late 1970s, U.K. and western European cities did not. Rather, they continued to cast off inhabitants. Despite this, the percentage of cities with population losses later began to stabilize. In the United States, the United Kingdom, and the western European countries alike, the late 1970s and the early 1980s were the tail end of severe urban population decline.[47]

As for which cities sustained the biggest losses, the large cities of the United Kingdom and western Europe cannot compete for this dubious honor with their U.S. counterparts. The western European cities experienced the smallest declines, with the cities of the United Kingdom suffering losses closer to those of the United States. In the 1960s, for example, Rotterdam, The Hague, and Amsterdam had the highest absolute losses for western European cities, hovering around 50,000. By comparison, Hamburg had a decrease of 40,000 residents and Stockholm of just over 20,000. These are small numbers when compared to those of cities in the United Kingdom. Glasgow had 158,000 fewer inhabitants, and Manchester shrank by 118,000 residents.[48] These numbers approach but neither match nor exceed the average loss of 50,000 for all large cities in the United States in the 1960s and losses of over 200,000 in the 1970s for New York City, Chicago, Detroit, and Philadelphia. Moreover, none of the cities in the United Kingdom, with the exception of London, can equal in either absolute or percentage terms the flight of residents from St. Louis, Detroit, Cleveland, Buffalo, and Pittsburgh across the postwar decades. Only London exceeded their losses in absolute terms, while Liverpool, Glasgow, and Manchester—cities with major population declines—fared much better percentage-wise.[49]

Many of these cities continued to shrink after the postwar period had come to a close. Between 1971 and 1981, the population of the main cities of the metropolitan counties dropped by 10 percent, and that of large towns (over 175,000) by 5 percent. With only two exceptions, Dudley and Plymouth, all the urban administrative areas in Great Britain were smaller in population size at the end than at the beginning of this period. Still, the losses were not as great as those that occurred in the United States. The exception was London, which shed approximately 800,000 residents, 11 percent of its total, over these ten years.[50]

In Germany, the populations of both West Berlin and East Berlin shrank after World War II.[51] Admittedly, this is a unique case; Berlin had been divided after the war with the western portion ceded to the Federal Republic of Germany and the eastern given to the socialist German Democratic Republic. Neither escaped the forces that drove out residents and expanded the population in the periphery. West Berlin's population fell until the mid-1980s but then grew. The population in the surrounding areas also increased after 1950 but peaked in 1975 and then fell again in the next decade. After that, it rose once again. By contrast, East Berlin lost residents continuously from 1950 to the early 1990s, while its peripheral areas expanded.

Finally, the Canadian cities deserve mention. They also experienced a loss of residents, but the declines were less severe than for western European cities, and the timing was closer to that of the United Kingdom and western Europe than to that of the United States. Growth rates were high just after World War II and fell thereafter, with the largest urban areas leading the way. In the 1970s, when the cities of Canada seemed to have been least able to retain population, Montreal and Toronto had the biggest losses. During the mid-1970s, Montreal shed almost 135,000 residents, and Toronto nearly 80,000. Even then, only one-third of the central cities in Canada's metropolitan areas declined in population, and their losses were relatively small.[52] Population depletion diminished in the 1980s, and a number of cities even began to add new residents over and above out-migration.

Canada's inner cities (that is, the central business districts of the central cities plus the surrounding mixed-used districts and neighborhoods) seem to have fared the worst. Many of them were losing residents as far back as the 1950s and persisted in doing so until the 1980s. Their fortunes then reversed, and they began to add inhabitants.[53] To this extent, large Canadian cities were more like the large cities of western Europe than those of the United States. In all of these countries, the central urban cores lost population after World War II.

Like major cities in the United States, most European and Canadian cities had achieved their large size and built their early-twentieth-century prosperity on industrialization and port functions. London is a good example. It was one of the premier manufacturing cities of the nineteenth and early twentieth centuries (particularly in textiles) and one of the world's great ports.[54] Manchester, Birmingham, and Sheffield were even more dependent on manufacturing. In Germany, Essen and Dortmund were industrial centers, and they shed residents from 1960 onward. So too did Rotterdam and Montreal (also seaports). These cities were all in countries highly industrialized in the twentieth century, and their cities contained the manufacturing that made them so. Although they continued to urbanize, the global restructuring of manufacturing worked against their industrial cities.

Suburbanization also took place around cities in Canada, western Europe, the United Kingdom, and Australia during the postwar decades. Prior to the 1980s, though, no other country sustained the mass suburbanization that occurred in the United States or experienced suburbanization in conjunction with the widespread adoption of the automobile, a vast network of highways, and low-density sprawl. Rather, suburbanization took the form of new towns—as in Finland, England, and Sweden—that were either relatively self-sufficient or connected to employment centers in the cities via mass transit. In western Europe, cultural predispositions, the supply of middle-class residences in central areas, and the low investment potential of single-family homes discouraged U.S.-style suburbanization. Sprawl was not a condition prevalent outside the United States.[55]

Incipient suburbanization existed in many countries—including the United States—as far back as the late nineteenth century. For example, middle-class estates, places like Clapham and Hampstead, had been established outside the city of London during the late 1800s. Social distinctions were being expressed as physical segregation, the bourgeois family was redefining the home and daily life, and the middle class was fleeing the social and economic problems of the industrial city.[56]

Relative decentralization, with the periphery growing faster than the urban cores, began in the 1950s and 1960s. Not until the 1970s did "vigorous growth in the suburbs" exceed growth in the cities.[57] Cities in the United Kingdom, Germany, France, and Italy all underwent this decentralization without deconcentration. Only in the 1970s and 1980s did deconcentration occur. This caused one commentator to note that for western Europe, "the counterpoint to suburbanization is inner-city decline," a story familiar to students of postwar U.S. urbanization.[58] In the 1970s, almost all major cities in the advanced industrial countries—Lisbon being the exception—lost population. And all of these cities, except for London and Manchester, had peripheral population growth. By the 1980s, suburbanization had become ubiquitous and pronounced in Europe, with the largest percentage increases outside Helsinki and Lisbon.[59]

In Canada, suburban areas were being settled as early as the first quarter of the twentieth century. The suburban population steadily increased until the 1950s, but not to the same extent as occurred in the United States. Decentralization quickened in the 1970s as the number of central city residents fell. Later, while suburbanization maintained its trajectory, the central cities were repopulated.[60]

The cities of South Africa also have a suburban history. Suburbanization occurred prior to World War II, and there was a surge in U.S.-style suburbs in the 1980s and thereafter.[61] In the first half of the twentieth century, suburbs—such as Westdene, Albertville, Rosebank, and Parktown—were built around Johannesburg's urban core. Peripheral development also included the apartheid-based townships designated exclusively for blacks, the most prominent and infamous being the communities that make up Soweto just southwest of the city. In the 1980s, lower-density suburbs, places like Sandton and Randburg, with gated communities and political autonomy, appeared to the north. After the political dispensation in 1994, the pace of construction of these developments accelerated.

Consequently, although suburbanization was not confined to the United States, the mass suburbanization of single-family detached homes, shopping malls, an automobile-dependent lifestyle, and low-density sprawl was peculiar to it. Cities in other advanced industrial countries experienced decentralization and, in the 1970s, central-city deconcentration. Only after the 1980s—after the short American century had ended—did they begin to mimic U.S. suburbs. Espoo and Vantaa outside Helsinki, the gated communities of São Paulo, and Bangsar on the periphery of Kuala Lumpur are striking examples of this late-twentieth-century phenomenon.[62]

Suburbanization and urban decline in the United States and other industrialized countries unfolded against a backdrop of rapid urbanization across the globe and the rise of megacities in Asia, Africa, and South America. While population growth slowed in the United States beginning in 1960, it was increasing worldwide. In the 1950s, the U.S. population had grown at roughly the same rate as that for the world. During the next decade, U.S. population growth began to lag. By the 1980s, the world population was expanding twice as fast as the U.S. population, and in developing countries, urban places were growing "three times as fast as those in advanced nations."[63] North America and Europe fell behind Asia, Africa, and South America, while India and China became the world's most populous countries. By 1990, the world population had reached 5.3 billion people, with the industrialized countries having 23 percent of the total, down from 33 percent forty years previously.[64]

In addition, just when the level of urbanization in the United States began to reach a plateau, urbanization accelerated worldwide. Across the three immediate-postwar decades, the urbanization rate went from 52 percent to 71 percent in the more developed countries and from 16 percent to 31 percent in the less developed countries. Although the latter had much lower levels of urbanization than the former, the gap was narrowing.[65] Europe maintained the highest levels of urbanization, with Australia, New Zealand, a number of South American countries (for example, Argentina), Canada, and the United States close behind.

Whereas New York, London, and Paris were once the biggest cities in the world, by the late twentieth century they had been eclipsed by cities outside North America and Europe. For example, using the category of city-region rather than central city, the largest "city" in the world in the late 1990s was Tokyo, with more than 27 million people, followed by Mexico City, São Paulo, Seoul, and then New York, at nearly 15 million people. None of the other top ten largest metropolitan areas were in North America or Europe.[66] The United States did place four urban areas in the top fifty: Los Angeles at sixteenth, Chicago at twenty-seventh, Philadelphia at twenty-ninth, and San Francisco at forty-sixth. São Paulo and Buenos Aires in South America and Calcutta, Bombay, Seoul, Tokyo, and Beijing in Asia have far surpassed their North American and western European counterparts in population growth.[67] Central-city decline and suburbanization thus unfolded within a national demographic slowdown for industrial countries but within a global demographic expansion and rising worldwide levels of urbanization.

Linking the rise of parasitic urbanization in the United States to global population growth is immigration. More precisely, the connection is the paucity of immigration during the period of parasitic urbanization. Two major waves of immigration took place in the country during the twentieth century, one between 1901 and 1930 and the other after 1971. The first is often considered the "classic" era of immigration, when over 18 million foreigners entered the United States. From then until the 1970s, immigration slackened to one-third the annual average; only 7.5 million newcomers established residence in the country. The hiatus was a function of restrictive immigration laws passed in the 1920s, the Depression, and World War II. To the extent that immigration flows were too meager in the early postwar decades to counter the loss of residents from the central cities, both central-city decline and suburbanization were amplified. In the 1970s, urban transnational migration revived, and immigration once again become a major factor in national and central-city population growth.[68]

Suburbanization and urban decline in the United States were also affected by another global phenomenon: the deindustrialization of the global North and the rise of manufacturing in the global South. Manufacturing growth (measured by output) grew worldwide from 1953 to 1980. In North America and western Europe, however, the expansion of manufacturing slowed even as value added in production continued to rise.[69] The industrial countries lost heavy manufacturing, such as steelworking and shipbuilding, to places like Korea, Brazil, and Japan.

More generally, the number of high-wage manufacturing jobs fell while low-wage manufacturing jobs grew in newly industrializing countries such as Malaysia. From 1960 to 1980, manufacturing employment increased by 20 percent in the United States. Outside the country, it went up by 170 percent, and in the underdeveloped countries, by over 500 percent. Manufacturing jobs surged in Brazil, Mexico, and Venezuela as well as in Egypt, Nigeria, and Kenya and throughout East and Southeast Asia. Exports rose as well, with newly industrialized countries almost doubling their shipments of manufactured goods while manufactured exports from the United States dropped by more than 20 percent. Value added also increased in these countries, though only in a few of them did productivity improve significantly. Overall, and between 1960 and 1976, labor productivity rose faster in developed market economies than in developing economies.[70]

The simultaneous decentralization of manufacturing activity from the early postwar U.S. cities and the dispersion of manufacturing to less developed countries were important factors in parasitic urbanization.

For the cities, the closing of large factories severed many households' residential ties to the cities and contributed to blight and decay. For the suburbs, the early decentralization of light manufacturing anchored local tax bases and attracted households. Later, as the economy shifted to advanced services, educated suburbanites were poised to benefit while less educated city residents were not. The new international division of labor amplified these conditions by weakening city-based, low-wage manufacturing. The result was shrinking employment prospects, especially among minorities, and a lessened attractiveness to skilled migrants.

Of the major forces acting on U.S. cities in the postwar period, many were international in scope.[71] They included the slackening of population growth and urbanization in industrialized countries, the dampening of immigration, and the global restructuring of manufacturing. The United States was different, not exceptional, in the population loss suffered by its industrial cities and in the centrifugal nature of metropolitan development. Moreover, the turn to parasitic urbanization occurred as the United States and other advanced industrial countries began a demographic slowdown. Urbanization ebbed in the United States, whereas in the global South and in Asia it was robust. The country eventually benefited from heightened immigration, but this came after the short American Century and after the most intense period of parasitic urbanization had passed.

Conclusion

From the perspective of the industrial cities of the global North, and in an era of parasitic urbanization, the world had radically changed. No longer were they the largest cities on the planet. No longer were their countries the leaders in population growth and their ports the prime nodes of world trade. They were urbanizing much more slowly than countries in the global South, though many of their cities remained the destinations for immigrants. And even though these cities had developed strengths in advanced business and financial services and dominated politically and militarily, their countries no longer controlled goods production as they once did.

The fourth wave brought forces inhospitable to the industrial cities of the global North and ruptured the prevailing dynamics of urbanization. The automobile and, later, low-cost air travel, a shift away from heavy manufacturing to nondurable consumer goods, and the rise of easily dispersed service functions eroded the agglomerative tendencies that made it possible for these cities to become big and to thrive. Population loss soon followed as parasitic urbanization took root. Not just the United States was affected; cities in all countries that had built their prosperity on manufacturing and shipping suffered.

In the United States, the demise of these industrial sectors hurt the older cities of the Northeast, as did the spread of automobile ownership (which occurred much faster than in other countries), the construction of highways connecting centers to peripheries, and the emergence of builders and developers able to mass-produce housing. With annexation and consolidation denied, these cities could not defend themselves against suburbanization. Without immigration to replace households lost to suburbs and other regions, the industrial cities went into decline, and the country began its journey from an urban to a suburban nation.

4

Culture and Institutions

The desire to make sense of the world often triggers a search for a previously hidden logic. When the industrial cities grew large and congested, could households have done other than move to the periphery, factories other than to relocate to less crowded sites, and retail activities other than to follow? And, since prosperity seems to be the key to suburbanization, what else would one have expected from the economic expansion of the 1950s and 1960s? As one historian has written, "Suburban growth would have occurred . . . with or without [government housing subsidies] or entrepreneurs like the Levitts. This is because people who can afford to—and many more could in the postwar era—seem naturally to desire lots of space around them."[1]

Loss, though, does not have to be followed by loss, decline by more of the same, or demographic growth by the emptying out of the cities. San Francisco and New York City managed to avoid the fates of St. Louis and Detroit, while Montreal and Dortmund escaped collapse despite experiencing shrinking populations.

To assert that the consequences of parasitic urbanization were contingent is different from declaring them avoidable. During these years, city officials and local property owners attempted to stanch the outflow of businesses and residents, replace slums with new housing, boost downtown property values, improve city schools, and build the highways and airports that would maintain the cities' centrality in their regions. At the same time, other elected officials and investors made decisions that harmed the cities. Governments divided neighborhoods with limited-access highways and forced numerous small businesses out of the downtowns in order to create land for urban-renewal projects. Businesses financed inexpensive tract housing, moved department-store branches to the suburbs, and relocated manufacturing operations. Unscrupulous real estate agents and bankers encouraged the racial transition of inner-city neighborhoods. Efforts were made to save the industrial cities; more effort was expended to enable Sunbelt cities to grow and urban peripheries to suburbanize. So much would have had to change for postwar urbanization to have unfolded other than the way it did.

Notwithstanding, this is not a book about postwar growth coalitions and boosters, suburban real estate developers, financiers, or political leaders. Nor is it a book so bold as to propose how the forces of parasitic urbanization could have been deflected. My concern is with the fundamental relationships that constrain and direct developmental possibilities and thus with the broad trends of urban change. The actions of individuals and organizations are moved to the background.[2]

Trends appear when individuals, groups, and institutions make mutually supportive decisions at roughly the same time and in multiple places. People adopt similar worldviews and act accordingly. Consequently, cultural attitudes and institutional tendencies that underlie these trends play an important role in the dynamics of growth and decline.[3] They point to why the United States mounted only token resistance to the deterioration of its industrial cities and why suburbanization triumphed. Parasitic urbanization was anchored in supportive institutions and in a culture that amplified its core logic. Three factors were most prominent: the ambivalence toward cities that has prevailed since the country was first colonized, the reluctance of state and federal governments to regulate suburbanization and redirect development to faltering cities, and the lack of interest that investors and developers had in the city compared to their infatuation with the suburban frontier.

The confluence of these factors distinguished the trajectory of urbanization in the United States from its counterparts in western Europe and elsewhere. An aversion to cities, governments inclined to pursue growth and indifferent to preserving past investments, and investors prejudiced against high-risk ventures combined to turn distributive urbanization parasitic. What transformed these necessary conditions into sufficient ones was the expanding postwar economy. Before turning to the role of domestic prosperity, however, the cultural and institutional conditions of the time must be addressed.

Urban Ambivalence

During the depths of the postwar urban crisis, commentators were fond of pointing out how much Americans disliked and even hated the cities. They not only noted the flight to the suburbs but also admitted into evidence polling data that found that numerous city residents would prefer to avoid the city's congestion, noise, crime, and high prices. One critic offered the observation that "only 22 percent of the American people—according to Gallup [Poll]—*want* to live in cities, even small ones, whereas fully half prefer towns or rural areas."[4] The case was overstated. Americans do not hate their cities. Rather, they are ambivalent about them, and their ambivalence has ebbed and flowed with the prospects that cities have offered. Even when antiurbanism was ostensibly most pronounced, many people praised the city, moved there for fame and fortune, and remained in order to enjoy the good life. "Cities," an observer claimed, "express an ambivalence in the American soul."[5]

Antiurbanism and its more indulgent counterpart, ambivalence, are not unique to the United States. The country is unexceptional in this regard. "British animosity against urbanism," one commentator has remarked, began in Roman Britain and persisted through the twentieth century. In numerous countries, those living in the countryside have been, and continue to be, suspicious of city dwellers. Economic relations, not always favorable to rural areas, and contrasting ways of life fuel a tension with the urban upper classes and commercial elites. The latter are often viewed as parasitic, exploiting both the countryside and the urban laboring classes. Residents of capital cities, particularly those attending regal courts, working in government bureaucracies, or leading corporate dynasties, have also been singled out for special contempt by those who feel victimized by the power that they wield.[6]

Writings on American antiurbanism often make reference to John Winthrop's call in 1630 for a "Citty upon a Hill." When Winthrop wrote the famous sermon "A Modell of Christian Charity," which contains this phrase, the settlements of the then sparsely populated country, places like Jamestown, New Amsterdam, and the Plymouth Colony, were hardly the cities that postwar observers had in mind when they claimed that Americans were antiurban. Reading Winthrop's lines as a rare celebration of the city, later to be eroded by the industrialism and urbanization of the late nineteenth and early twentieth centuries, was and is a mistake. Winthrop spoke metaphorically. His "Citty" was an "experimental holy commonwealth" in which Christians would come together in brotherly affection and establish a covenant with God. It would be a spiritually united community "in which a genuinely ethical and spiritual life could be lived."[7]

The city on the hill did not address the functions, densities, and social diversities associated with contemporary urbanization. This was no model for the industrial city, much less for any real, inhabited place. Consequently, it is not the "ideal" that ostensibly was lost as the country grew. In fact, "the ideal of a great city never has occupied a comfortable place in the American imagination."[8]

The person most often mentioned as the country's first anti-urbanist is Thomas Jefferson. Writing in the late eighteenth and early nineteenth centuries, Jefferson was leery of large settlements. He believed that industrialization and capitalist competition would weaken agrarian society and, by severing the connection between people and their farms, would undermine freedom. One consequence would be the mob, a displaced workforce prone to authoritarianism and posing a threat to democracy. As president, he brought about the Louisiana Purchase in 1803 precisely to open up vast new territory for settlement and agriculture. At the same time, Jefferson appreciated the culture of the city—especially Paris—and recognized the inevitability of urban manufacturing in the face of possible foreign economic domination.[9]

Jefferson's worries were premature but prescient. When he wrote, manufactories were still of small scale and a minor element in the workings of the cities. The agrarian economy and its commercial cities were unchallenged. Jefferson's reasoning, though, was typical of what eventually became a cultural attitude wavering between dislike and an unstable mix of attraction and resignation. He based his aversion on the superior values of an agrarian society and on the way the city diminished close personal ties. Most importantly, he believed that the city weakened the psychological connection people had with the land.[10]

Within this argument sits an opposition between the countryside and the city and a nostalgic pastoralism that forms the core of urban ambivalence.[11] The countryside is aligned with nature and contrasted to society. Nature, in turn, is related to wilderness and the frontier, while the frontier is associated with freedom. By comparison, the city is artificial, contrived. There, people have to negotiate a public life together on unnatural grounds. Of course, this pastoral ideal is a product, not a precursor, of industrialization. It emerges, in Leo Marx's unforgettable image, when the machine enters the garden.

Coexisting with the opposition between the countryside and the city is a belief in a synthesis, a middle realm. Here is where the cultural resonance of the suburb was situated, particularly when suburbanization became a mass phenomenon in the postwar period. Its resonance was drawn not from the countryside but from the small town. The suburb—the garden city—is the synthesis. American urban ambivalence is thus doubly conflicted, contrasting the city with the countryside and conflating the suburb with the small town.[12]

From the 1860s to the 1920s, industrialization and urbanization were intense. During those years, cities pulled in rural migrants as well as immigrants from abroad and grew by leaps and bounds. Densities became greater and greater. The industrial cities were the centers of an increasingly national economy, and antiurbanism flourished for the first time outside intellectual circles. Its roots were in the more universal tension between rural and urban interests.[13]

This antiurbanism of the late nineteenth and early twentieth centuries had a great deal to do with the way urban elites were asserting control over the countryside and the rural-to-urban migrations that had been spawned. With the expansion of urban markets, rural agriculture and resource extraction became entangled with the city. Mechanization and later the rise of national corporations further established rural activities as part of an industrial economy. Consequently, the countryside became more and more dependent on the cities; the cities provided the markets, machinery, and financing that enabled rural industries to be profitable. By the late nineteenth century, with the frontier closed, there was no escape to a place untouched by the metropolis. Resentment followed.[14]

That resentment was exacerbated by the out-migration of rural youth in search of the opportunities and excitement. As machines displaced workers in rural activities and as farms were consolidated to reach the size needed to function in a mass-production economy, young people left to work in the factories and office buildings or to pursue careers as journalists, actors, or members of the many other occupations spun off by a prosperous and diverse economy. Parents lost their children to the city. Families were torn apart, and the solidarity and tradition of rural communities weakened.

Making the flight of youth to the cities even more appalling was the rural view of cities as threatening, sinful, and corrupting.[15] Cities shattered the familial and religious bonds of an agrarian society of small towns and created innumerable opportunities for sin and exploitation. In the cities, barrooms, brothels, and gambling parlors, along with other amusements of the flesh, tempted those with frail morals.

People bet their weekly earnings, smoked, and were lured into prostitution, kidnapped to become sailors, and mugged. Daughters and sons could be led into sin and left in destitution. To become citified was to lose one's values, to be corrupted. Rural migrants would be triply lost: to the countryside, to their families, and to rural values. The sins of the countryside, of course, were ignored.

One can only surmise that the epidemics and great fires that the cities experienced in the late nineteenth and early twentieth centuries also contributed to a sense of the city as dangerous. The pollution, grime, lack of sanitation, and sorry state of much worker housing probably only worsened popular opinions. Since most immigrants were concentrated in the industrial cities, neither can the nativist sentiments of the mid-to-late nineteenth and early twentieth centuries be discounted. During these times, native skilled workers and Irish and German immigrants frequently clashed over jobs.

The dislike that people of the countryside had for the city was further exacerbated by the wresting of control of state governments from rural legislators. The "one person—one vote" rule of the U.S. government meant that with the expansion of the cities relative to the countryside, cities gained seats in state legislatures and the U.S. Congress. Legislatures dominated by urban rather than rural interests were able to pass laws (for example, those regarding annexation) and mount public improvements (such as railroads) that favored cities. Politically, the countryside was less and less important and influential.[16] Along these paths, the patronage and corruption ostensibly endemic to city governments made its way to state capitals and even to Washington, D.C.

The antiurbanism of the postwar period was very differently constructed. It was not rooted in economic defensiveness, the loss of young people, or the condemnation of sin. Rather, it had more to do with fear of racial pollution, an aversion to physical decay, and a defense of property values and all that they symbolized. At the core of these concerns was the growing numbers of blacks who lived in the metropolitan centers. Urban ambivalence was no longer about the tensions between the countryside and the cities but about those between the suburbs and the central cities.[17]

During the late 1940s and early 1950s, one had to look wide and far for antiurbanism. People were beginning to leave the city for the nascent postwar suburbs, and the cities were rundown and shabby, yet city economies were still doing well. People and businesses left more because of the lure of open space than because of any particular dislike of cities. People could establish suburbs and not worry about being annexed by the central city. Commercial and industrial investment gave them the tax revenues they needed to provide their own public services; they had no need to consolidate. And as the suburbs grew, their representatives became more and more influential in state legislatures and in the U.S. Congress.[18]

Suburbanites could imagine themselves living in small towns, engaging in what one commentator called a "sentimental pastoralism: a bedroom community of detached, owner-occupied, single-family houses, located in a natural setting."[19] The world of the city—its workplace demands, its impersonality, its congestion and noise—could be temporarily forgotten. Security, with one's own kind, was available in the postwar suburbs.

Most important to this story is race. Postwar antiurbanism was racial animosity transferred to the cities. Its roots are in early conflicts between African Americans and whites over decreasing numbers of manufacturing jobs, increasingly scarce housing, and the integration of public schools.[20] Relations between these two groups have always been tense, and the simultaneous in-migration of blacks from the South and the collapse of manufacturing and the ports only worsened them. Whereas once the cities might have been symbolized by great factories and towering office buildings, these images were displaced by black faces, poverty, and African American slums. As conditions deteriorated in the cities, unemployment rose, slums spread, poverty intensified, and crime increased. Poverty was associated with black unwed mothers on welfare, while crime came to be associated with minorities and the cities. Viewed through the lens of television and newspaper coverage, city crime was black crime. Juvenile delinquency was mainly an activity of black teenagers. What white suburbanites feared was being mugged by a young black male.

The civil rights movement, the political militancy of such organizations as the Black Panthers, and the election of black mayors in the 1960s further exacerbated racial tensions nationwide and strengthened the symbolic link between the city and African Americans. This antiurbanism was brought to a peak with the riots of the mid-to-late 1960s. For a few years, urban violence and destruction became staples in national magazines and on national television. Images of the National Guard patrolling the streets of Newark, blocks of buildings burning in Detroit, black men stripped and handcuffed in Philadelphia, and looters running down the streets with television sets were unavoidable. By the mid-1970s, many of the declining cities were not only viewed as black and dangerous; they were also on the verge of bankruptcy. To violence, dependence, and criminality was added fiscal incompetence. One commentator observed in 1968 that "for generations we were taught to despise our cities until they became, indeed, despicable."[21]

Tempering this antiurbanism was the fact that office jobs and many manufacturing and service jobs were still concentrated in the central cities in the 1950s and 1960s, as were professional sports teams, movie theaters and nightclubs, and such cultural venues as concert halls and museums. The city enhanced as well as threatened suburbia. It was still central to the metropolitan economy, anchored cultural aspirations, and provided for the mass entertainment needs of metropolitan residents.[22] These suburban-city dependencies, however, were waning, and antiurbanism thrived during the years of racial unrest, fiscal crisis, and population loss. Yet people still moved into the cities, investors still built factories and office buildings there, and governments still funded urban infrastructure. (Relatively speaking, the numbers were small.) The cities even managed to lure young people, particularly those in the arts and in fields that had a strong urban presence (for example, health care, banking, and publishing).

When the throes of decline ended and the cities began to prosper in the 1980s and 1990s, antiurbanism ebbed and selected cities—San Francisco; Seattle, Washington; Chicago; or Boston, for example—came to be popularly viewed in a more positive light.[23] A noteworthy few rundown inner-city neighborhoods were rediscovered—gentrified—by developers and middle-income households. Retailers built shopping malls in a number of downtowns, such as White Plains, New York, and entertainment areas and festival marketplaces appeared in Baltimore, Cleveland, and Pittsburgh. New office buildings were constructed. In the 1990s, sports stadiums were being integrated into downtown neighborhoods, and trendy restaurants and clubs became ubiquitous. It became fashionable, rather than bohemian, to live in the city. Tourism, especially from the suburbs, boomed. It helped that crime had fallen and that race riots were no longer frequent occurrences.

The vacillation in ambivalence that Americans have for their cities became a cultural frame for postwar urban decline and suburbanization. In place well before the short American Century and the rupture in urbanization, this ambivalence was, nonetheless, slanted against the cities when they were most in need. It was part of the calculus of white households, investors, and government officials as they made their decisions about where to live, work, and invest. Not all of these decisions harmed the cities. Regardless, the bias was clearly in favor of the suburbs. "Zoning laws, developers, advertisers of home-related products, women's magazines, the Federal Housing Authority, and bank officials sought to make the sharpest possible contrast between the private, comfortable, safe, and protected environment of the suburbs and the open, competitive, dangerous, and seductive world of the central city."[24]

Government Complicity

In the postwar era, ambivalence toward the cities was reflected in and invigorated by the actions of government. Federal and state governments provided aid to the declining central cities in order to bolster investment, increase the number of jobs, retain middle-income residents, and improve the cities' image and attractiveness. At the same time, they promoted suburbanization. Overall, their policies and programs favored the suburbs.[25]

City governments have seldom been ambivalent about their core interests. Since the early nineteenth century, they have understood the imperatives of economic growth.[26] By the mid-1950s, however, growth was a lofty goal for most industrial cities; new residents and businesses were uncommon, tax revenues were stagnant or falling, the cities' reputations were tarnished, and their powers in the state legislature and region diminished. More pressing was survival. Nevertheless, "the pursuit of economic growth . . . [was] a central and defining feature of U.S. public policy in the half-century after the end of World War II."[27]

As the trauma of the cities unfolded, the ability of city governments to mitigate the problems besetting them was severely curtailed. Shrinking tax bases drove down revenues or forced cities to raise tax rates; numerous businesses and households fled to the suburbs where services were better and taxes less daunting. Furthermore, these cities were unable to annex growing peripheral areas in order to bolster their tax bases. To make matters worse, the flight of middle-income and college-educated households and corporate elites weakened urban leadership. "Our cities have lost the political ability and the political authority for large creative gestures," wrote one observer in 1967.[28]

City officials were turning to the federal and state governments for help. During the 1930s, the New Deal of President Roosevelt had launched programs that enabled the cities to weather unemployment and fiscal difficulties. The cities wanted to revive this partnership. They asked President Lyndon Johnson and federal legislators to do politically what was not available ideologically, that is, to recognize the importance of cities to the life of the country, to "federalize the problems of the big city," and thus to place cities on the top of the national agenda.[29]

Local leaders argued that they deserved assistance simply because the cities were in trouble. Once the proud centers of industrial dynamism, they were now struggling to generate jobs and retain industry. Property values were falling, especially in the downtowns. These cities were forced to take responsibility for the poor, more and more of whom were African American. They needed fiscal aid. If not, the burden that would have to be placed on city taxpayers to provide programs for addressing social ills and to mount economic development initiatives to reinvigorate the local economy would drive out investors and more-affluent households. Poverty, arguably, was a national, not a local, problem; its roots transcended municipal boundaries.

The primary issues were fiscal needs and social problems. The underlying premise was that state and federal governments were obligated to come to the aid of local governments in times of need. These governments had greater tax-generating capacities; the federal government could even operate with a deficit, something prohibited to local and state governments. In short, the federalist system under which cities functioned, a system that required them to generate most of their revenues from their own sources, hampered cities in crisis situations. The years just after World War II were such a time.

City leaders gave little attention in their arguments to the importance of the central city for metropolitan prosperity or to the city's cultural contributions. The first was not yet in doubt in the 1940s and 1950s.[30] Most observers still believed that the central cities would remain economically and demographically strong relative to the suburbs. To point to a need to assure this would be counterproductive. As for any cultural claim, it was likely to encounter significant and deep-rooted opposition. Not only has the national government traditionally been reluctant to become involved in local affairs, it has also avoided initiatives (such as a cultural policy) that smack of a coherent vision or centralized coordination.[31] The social diversity of the United States, the size and complexity of its economy, and the disjunctures in its peculiar form of federalism work against coherent and singular national visions.

All this said as background, one must further understand that the United States has never had a national policy focused on the distribution of the country's cities, towns, villages, suburbs, and rural areas.[32] Unlike such countries as Sweden, it has avoided explicit support of any one settlement pattern. Numerous policies and programs have aided specific types of settlement, but there has been no coherent policy that commits the country to one or another landscape. Population policies that control where people live, like cultural policies, are incompatible with the American embrace of personal freedom, consumer choice, and investor prerogatives. And while this understanding did not stop city officials and urban observers from calling for a national urban policy in the early 1960s and late 1970s, they did so in vain and mostly after the short American Century had ended.[33]

Still, state and federal governments have had land policies and have influenced settlement patterns. Probably the most coherent of these efforts were the land purchases and military excursions of the nineteenth century by which the federal government expanded the amount of land within the country's borders and then solidified their status as part of the nation with inducements to families to settle in these new territories. State governments were initially involved in canal construction that opened up areas to commerce, gave rise to new towns, and allowed existing towns (such as Buffalo) to become cities. They were also instrumental in financing and providing land for railroad expansion as well as in building roads. Not to be overlooked is the role that state legislatures played in the nineteenth century in authorizing city governments to expand their boundaries through annexations and consolidations.[34]

As part of the New Deal of the 1930s, the federal government did subsidize the construction of three new towns, communities built where none had been before. It was a short-lived experiment in settlement policy. In emulation of the new town policies of western European countries, an attempt was made to revive this program in the 1960s. Then, however, the idea was to clear slums and plant "new towns in town," as occurred on Roosevelt Island in New York City's East River.[35] For the most part, these efforts to define a settlement pattern for the country were isolated events and were unsustained. What urban policy existed in the country in the early postwar period focused on urban renewal and public housing, later augmented by support for local economic development and neighborhood upgrading. At the same time, federal and state governments also supported the decentralization of businesses and the suburbanization of stores and residences, with consequences detrimental to the older, industrial cities.

The two most important government programs addressing the ills of the declining cities were urban renewal and public housing.[36] The urban renewal program was approved in 1949 and engaged the federal and local governments in a joint effort to boost downtown property values by clearing blighted properties and creating large land parcels that would attract investors. These parcels were sold to developers at reduced costs. The subsequent investment in new office towers, apartment buildings, stores, and sports arenas, it was predicted, would reinvigorate the downtowns. The public housing program was also a joint federal-local effort. Its goal was to eliminate slums and replace them with subsidized housing for low-income families. Unlike the urban renewal program, its origins were in the 1930s, when federal financing of public housing was used to put men to work and reduce unemployment. After the war, the program was directed less at the temporarily poor than at minorities who were chronically disadvantaged. No longer living in slum neighborhoods and with their housing costs minimal, the poor would be better off and better able to take advantage of opportunities to move out of poverty.

Between 1949 and 1974, when the urban renewal program was at its peak, close to $10 billion was spent in approximately 1,250 cities. Over 2,000 specific renewal projects were undertaken, with most large cities having multiple projects.[37] Cities used urban renewal to eliminate obsolete buildings, create large-scale real estate projects with the critical mass to keep existing businesses from leaving, and attract new businesses into the downtown. These projects were long-term efforts that took years to complete. In many instances, the sites that were cleared remained empty because developers were simply not interested, even with the public subsidies. To support private investment, city governments constructed new office buildings for their employees and encouraged local investors to build sports arenas. They also built parks and plazas, probably the most famous being the arch and the park along the St. Louis waterfront. Through the 1970s, however, public investment had little success in attracting the massive amounts of private investment needed to reinvigorate the downtowns of declining cities. Building in the suburbs was less risky and more profitable. Consequently, capital was flowing disproportionately to the suburbs.

Urban renewal and public housing were linked. The slums targeted by the public housing program were often adjacent to the main commercial district, and their condemnation and demolition were central to the vision of a renewed downtown. Multiple and mid- to high-rise buildings set amid lawns and playgrounds replaced the slums. Between the late 1940s and the mid-1970s, approximately 500,000 housing units were demolished by urban renewal and over 900,000 public housing units were built. Most notably, and further racializing the image of the city, the percentage of minority tenants in public housing rose from approximately 25 percent to over 60 percent.[38]

In addition, the public housing program encouraged the segregation of land uses. Few stores and almost no businesses were included in these developments, and by style and overall layout they were distinct from the surrounding city and eventually isolated from it. In the worst of the declining cities, such as New Orleans, these projects eventually became the slums that they had ostensibly replaced. Public housing concentrated poor people, hindered community ties, and set minorities apart from the rest of the city's residents. Stigmatized and with a reputation for crime, these projects became another problem with which these local governments had to contend as well as being a blot on the cities' image.[39]

Neither urban renewal nor public housing nor the two together reversed the flight of white households, factories, department stores, and capital to the suburbs. Other policies were tried. Federal and state governments provided financing for various economic development initiatives—from industrial parks to loan guarantees—meant to retain businesses in the cities. They subsidized the construction of bridges and tunnels, water-treatment plants, sewers, schools, and playgrounds. In cooperation with state governments, the federal government financed and built limited-access highways that enabled intercity truck traffic to bypass downtowns and thus relieve traffic congestion there. Local governments offered tax abatements and other assistance.

In the 1970s, the federal government even had a program to share revenue with the cities, though its life was short. Had it been institutionalized, this would have been an important turn in U.S.-style fiscal federalism, one that might have freed city governments from the constraints of relying on own-source revenues. Revenue sharing was only one of numerous responses to the impact that the 1973–1975 recession had on big-city governments, though. A combination of shrinking tax bases, rising service and labor costs, and a tendency to balance budgets in creative and ill-advised ways set city governments on the edge of insolvency. With their debt limits nearly exceeded and their ability to borrow curtailed, the cities entered into a period of fiscal stress.[40]

What became clear was that cities would receive attention only if they were threatening the social order. The civil rights movement and the racial unrest of the 1960s garnered for the cities a host of federal programs from health clinics to welfare benefits, but as the riots of the late 1960s slipped into the political past, the cities lost their claim on the public's attention. Moreover, with the Republican Richard Nixon as president, the cities did not enjoy high priority in federal policy making. Associating the big, industrial cities with the Democrats, the New Deal, organized labor, and African Americans, Republicans and conservatives were disinclined toward them. As these cities stumbled through the 1970s, their political fortunes plummeted.[41]

During the 1970s, the Republicans developed their famous suburban strategy in which the Democrats would be ceded the cities and the minority and poor constituents who resided there. The Republicans would focus on the suburban vote.[42] It was not just the suburban vote that was coveted, though. Republicans also targeted the votes of whites who had fled the older, industrial cities for the burgeoning Sunbelt cities.

In fact, many urban commentators blamed the federal government for the decline of the older, industrial cities: "Throughout the decades of the 1950s and 1960s, the government articulated a national interest in central city revitalization, while at the same time promoting massive redistribution of population and capital investment from central cities to suburbs."[43] By subsidizing home ownership, building highways to connect suburbs to downtowns, underwriting the cost of operating an automobile, underfunding mass transit, and subsidizing the building of infrastructure, the federal government drew households and investors away from the urban cores. Consequently, the suburbs became relatively less costly and much more attractive than the central cities.[44]

At the center of this suburban policy bias was the Federal Housing Administration (FHA) mortgage program that was originally conceived in the 1930s. This program was designed to encourage home ownership and thus expand demand for home building and related activities. It restructured the home-buying process to allow for lower down payments and longer terms for mortgages, thereby reducing monthly costs. Moreover, it made it possible to amortize loans, that is, to pay down the principle as the interest was being paid. In addition, the FHA established guidelines for subdivisions (and thus suburban home building) and for the selling of residential mortgages. FHA-insured mortgage debt in structures housing from one to four families went from just over $5 billion in 1945 to nearly $45 billion in 1970.[45]

Central to the FHA program were the underwriting guidelines that discouraged lenders from using the program in most city neighborhoods. Residential areas with mixed land uses (for example, businesses near housing) or with minorities were considered undesirable. This bias was known as redlining, a reference to the use of a colored line to designate such areas on maps. Suburban development on open land did not face these obstacles. Thus, the great majority of the loans went to home buyers in the suburbs and not to home buyers in the cities.[46]

From 1934 to 1972, home ownership increased from 44 percent to 63 percent. Home construction boomed, with 24 million new private housing units started between 1945 and 1960.[47] New residential construction was disproportionately concentrated outside the central cities. In Philadelphia, nearly 400,000 new housing units were built in the suburban communities of the metropolitan area between 1954 and 1973; just over 115,000 were built in the city.[48] And Philadelphia is an anomaly among the declining central cities. Just after World War II, it still contained a large area of farmland. Combined with a local law that mandated that fire and police personnel live within the city, this meant that it could undertake suburban-like development within its borders. Once that area was built-up, it lost this advantage.

With developers mass-producing tract housing, returning veterans looking to start families, and the government subsidizing home purchases, the suburbs were very enticing, particularly when compared with shabby and congested central cities. Middle-income households could escape the city and also avoid the growing African American population.

The emerging suburbs were not open to racial minorities. Discriminatory real estate practices joined with discriminatory lending practices to discourage minority households from living in these new communities. That the federal and state governments did little to eliminate these practices, at least until the mid-1960s, was additional evidence that governments were more interested in protecting the suburbs than in reviving the cities. State laws regarding zoning, annexation, and control over school funding also enabled suburban governments to resist encroachment from what they might consider undesirable elements. State and federal laws enhanced the ability of suburban municipalities to protect themselves. At the same time, they weakened the city government's ability to exploit its advantages.[49] Add to these factors a federal tax law that allowed home owners to deduct local real estate taxes and the interest paid on home mortgages, and the lure of the suburbs was even more irresistible.

In the decades immediately after World War II, middle-income, white-collar jobs were still disproportionately in the downtowns of the central cities.[50] This is where the interstate highway program did its damage. Developed by the federal government in the 1950s, its goal was to link all of the major cities of the United States via limited-access highways, both to facilitate commerce and to enable the movement of military equipment around the country in the case of an enemy attack. (This was the height of Cold War paranoia.) The highways would be jointly funded by the federal government (90 percent) and state governments (10 percent) and would be maintained by the state governments. This funding principle would apply also to access roads built from one interstate highway to another and from downtowns to interstate highways. Over 40,000 total miles were initially authorized, of which more than 2,000 urban miles had been built by 1979.[51]

Culture and Institutions

The interstate highways harmed the central cities. First, they gave impetus to the trucking industry and improved its competitiveness relative to railroads and intercoastal shipping. This led to the shrinkage of urban rail yards and ports. Interstate highway extensions also enabled businesses (such as wholesale distributors) that relied on trucking to relocate outside the city, where they would have better access to the metropolitan market via the new regional highway network.

Second, these highways made it possible for suburban workers to commute to their jobs in the central cities. With commuter rail capacity low, and nonexistent in many cities, and with suburban housing spread across the landscape, the automobile was a logical choice of transport. Local governments made it even easier to commute by having urban renewal authorities build parking garages to accommodate commuters and suburban shoppers. And with the federal government maintaining relatively low gasoline prices and building toll-free highways, the commute was relatively inexpensive. As an economist would say, the social costs were hidden. The major private costs were gasoline and parking. Government subsidies plus low-density suburban development, the shrinkage of mass transit (especially buses), and the growth in the overall population and number of households resulted in a sixfold increase from 1945 to 1973 in urban travel by automobiles and a threefold increase in annual automobile sales between 1940 and 1973.[52]

Third, limited-access highways created high-value intersections throughout the suburban periphery, and these locations became ideal sites for regional shopping malls. These malls diverted retail expenditures from central business districts. This was not the only way that the government aided suburban retailing, though. Federal tax policy, specifically the accelerated depreciation allowance, enhanced the profitability of investment in shopping centers.[53]

Fourth, interstate highway extensions sliced through urban neighborhoods, thereby eliminating housing and disrupting communities. They generated noise and pollution that discouraged adjacent development, and their physical bulk was an aesthetic affront to the fabric of the city. Moreover, these highways, perversely, did not relieve downtown congestion but, rather, encouraged more automobile usage.

The federal and state governments also made suburban development attractive by subsidizing a range of infrastructures, particularly water and sewer systems. (See Figure 8.) This lowered the expense of building at low densities. Without water and sewer systems, suburbanization would have been slowed. With them, suburban developers could continue to buy more and more open land and build farther and farther away from

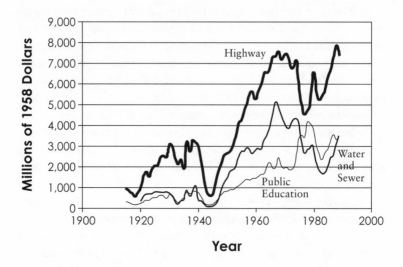

Figure 8. Selected public expenditures, 1915–1989. The data for this figure are from U.S. Department of Commerce, Value of New Construction Put in Place *(Washington, D.C.: Government Printing Office, various years).*

the metropolitan cores, thus requiring more and more roads and highways. Government expenditures that provided new, campuslike schools also served as an incentive for families to move into these communities. The sprawl that resulted eventually made the suburbs congested, difficult to traverse, and too far removed from the central cities.[54]

As the suburbs grew, they had to provide services and build schools, parks, and sports fields. Tax revenues had to be collected. Thus, many suburbs began to compete with the central cities for business. First there were suburban industrial parks and then suburban office parks. Research parks in particular benefited from military expenditures and public monies flowing to the universities for research.[55] It was one thing to lose residents to the suburbs, another to see manufacturing firms and wholesalers flee, but to lose one's office functions constituted an affront to the centrality of these older cities. When professional sports teams began to build stadiums in the suburbs, all seemed lost. Here were the seeds of the edge cities of the 1980s.

On balance, the central cities were harmed more than helped by federal and state policies during the early postwar decades. *Newsweek* in 1967 put it bluntly: "The [federal] government spends less a year rebuilding cities than it does a month on Vietnam, more federal money is spent on soybean research than on urban studies."[56] Urban policies were stopgap measures meant to slow the rate of disinvestment and

| Culture and Institutions

encourage new investment but not to reverse the overwhelming loss of manufacturing jobs, the decline of port activities, and the decreasing competitiveness of downtown retailing. Nor did they address the racial tensions that were central to the suburbanization of white households. Combined with the overall flow of people and private capital, the result was unfavorable for the older, industrial cities.

Still, we need to keep government policy in perspective. It favored the suburbs, but the forces driving the decline of the industrial cities and the suburbanization that engulfed them were not confined to state and federal policy. They included more than white flight and the decentralization of manufacturing, wholesaling, and retailing businesses.

First of all, government policy failed to ameliorate the racial fears and animosities that led whites to flee the cities when blacks entered them. In fact, the civil rights laws of the 1960s could be said to have exacerbated racial anxieties, particularly on the part of an always-vulnerable white working class. Antidiscrimination laws were passed, and many efforts were made to address the consequences of discrimination at the workplace and in housing and schools, but these actions inflamed racial tensions. Many black families eventually moved into the middle class and to the suburbs, even into predominately white suburbs, but any more than minor racial mixing met white resistance. During the short American Century, blacks carried the burden of urban ills and whites kept their distance.

Second, federal and state policy only took passing heed of the collapse of heavy manufacturing and the ports. The United States has never had, and has been reluctant to even consider, a national industrial policy along the lines that other countries, notably Japan, developed in the late twentieth century. The federal government is "weak" in the realm of economic and industrial policy and willing to let competition and "the market" (or economic elites) determine the direction and nature of the economy.[57] The collapse of heavy industry and the ports—deindustrialization—was pivotal for the declining cities. In the United States, not only state and federal governments but financiers, investors, and developers were disinclined toward the cities. The economy itself was biased against them.

Frontier Capitalism

During the height of parasitic urbanization, investors and real estate developers favored peripheral expansion over development in the central cities. Postwar capitalism had a suburban bias that drained the older, industrial cities while also producing new, low-density, and automobile-dependent metropolitan areas in the West and Southwest. Returns on investment, ease of development, and levels of risk were more attractive in the open spaces surrounding the cities and in areas of the country ripe to be urbanized. Renewal and intensification, required for development to have followed a more pro-urban path, were generally, but not wholly, avoided. A "wasteful and divisive [pattern] of American urbanization" took root.[58]

Of course, this bias was of its time. In the period of distributive urbanization, American capitalism had favored high-density, concentrated development. And it would—ever so slightly—shift its emphasis back to the cities in the 1980s and 1990s. A balanced perspective must also recognize that these cities had experienced over fifteen years of neglect, resulting in deterioration and a general shabbiness. This, too, discouraged new investment. Nor can we overlook the pent-up demand for new housing that erupted after World War II, a demand that the dense, industrial cities could not easily or profitably accommodate. All of this contributed to the greater attractiveness of the suburban periphery. The postwar cities grew "by 'sheer chance' and by the whims of developers," a claim that aptly captures the suburban bias, even as it distorts the motives of investors and the degree to which their decisions coalesced in time and space.[59]

The people of the United States have had an enduring affinity for open spaces, even when building the great industrial cities. The idea that a frontier exists to be relentlessly challenged has persisted since colonists first arrived on the country's shores. "It is part of the American character to be stingy with time but spendthrift about space."[60] Throughout the period of distributive urbanization, the national government was continually adding land and encouraging people into unsettled areas. The country was expandable, able to accommodate immigrants, and hospitable to growth. The proliferation of new settlements, moreover, became an inducement to further expansion. In the early postwar era, though, open spaces were less a matter of going westward than a matter of filling the spaces around and between the major cities.[61]

New development will always draw households and investors from existing places. During distributive urbanization, as households left the cities to start new ones, they were replaced by immigrants and rural migrants. This replacement function collapsed after World War II. Investment capital had a similar spatial dynamic. The capital available for suburban development expanded, in part, because of disinvestment in the central cities.

|

This general argument requires elaboration. Begin with a simple fact: The U.S. economy is "an inherently expansionist force."[62] It is an economy in which private investors pursue profits by pursuing growth. Office buildings, factories and their machinery, trucking and airline companies, and investment capital are privately owned, and the benefits associated with this control are privately appropriated. To increase profits or even hold them steady, though, businesses must grow. The existence of competitors, assured by laws prohibiting monopolies, means that market positions are always vulnerable. To stay still, to remain comfortable or complacent, is to risk extinction. In a capitalist economy, businesses grow by expanding markets, introducing new products, procuring favorable government regulations and subsidies, and becoming more competitive (that is, by increasing productivity and lowering both costs and prices). Through growth, they are able to boost profits and gain more control over the markets in which they operate. Investment decisions are based on the opportunities for growth and profits and the risks such opportunities pose.

In theory, risk and profitability move together. Large profits are related to high risk, but high risk also raises the likelihood that an investment will turn sour and the investor suffer a loss. Because actual risk is inherently unknowable, except probabilistically, investors have a tendency to do what other investors have found rewarding. Certainly, there are mavericks and risk takers, but overall most investors follow "success." As more investors enter a market to provide goods or services, however, market shares are eroded, production is routinized, and profits begin to fall. When this happens, some investors move to other opportunities. This imitative behavior and the relation of risk to profitability have much to do with the postwar suburban bias.[63]

Despite the potential gains from competition, most capitalists would prefer to limit it, that is, to have fewer rather than more competitors. Oligopoly sounds fine, especially if monopoly is illegal. Limited competition reduces the possibility that competitors will institute sudden price reductions or introduce innovations that take away market share. Oligopolistic arrangements create leeway for setting prices, controlling supply, and better managing profits. And they allow for growth, even if it falls below the levels of more speculative investments.

All of these factors, particularly the drives to control markets and to pursue high profits, make the economy inherently unstable. In search of profits, concerned about risk, fearful of competition, and avoiding saturated markets, investors move their investments from one sector of the economy and from one place to another. When profits fall, they disinvest and place their capital elsewhere. Where investors are crowded, as in cities, competition also creates a frontier dynamic that encourages investors to seek less developed areas. The result is an economy seesawing across the landscape.[64]

Economies, however, operate on more than economic calculations, or, to say it differently, there is no economic decision that is not infused with social, cultural, and political considerations. Despite this, the usual, neoclassical description of "free markets" cordons off the economic realm from noneconomic realities. It views neither cultural predispositions and social institutions nor government as essential to the functioning of the economy. Markets, it is assumed, "control the fate of communities." In reality, without an acquisitive spirit, concerns about social status and consumption, and the trust that enables transactions of all types to occur, capitalism could not function. Moreover, without laws that circumscribe markets and legitimize technologies and products, along with government investments in public goods such as highways, private investments would be less profitable and would be very different in type and location.[65]

Investors in the United States pursue profit, avoid risk, mimic each other, and try to dominate markets, but they also exist in a capitalism specific to the country's institutions and culture and of its time. Enduring across the decades are two tendencies of U.S. capitalism, at peak strength in the postwar era, that had a profound impact on cities and suburbs. One was a strong commitment to growth that translated into territorial expansion. The other was a dominance over the government that allowed capitalists to dictate the type and timing of urbanization.[66]

After World War II, a contract of sorts was signed between capital and the government. In return for constant and rapid growth in the economy, the government would minimize the encroachment of the welfare state and its planning apparatus. Private investors believed that growth would be threatened by the expansion of government involvement in social provision (for example, income supports, full employment, health care) and by increased government control over development, particularly through land-use planning. The examples of the Scandinavian and western European states were particularly noteworthy in this regard. Not only were they establishing welfare states, but they were also extending their planning controls and building new towns.[67] Private-sector interests were being subordinated to public interests.

Internally, the lingering remnants of wartime planning and the experience of the New Deal were equally foreboding to business. Before

| *Culture and Institutions*

the war had ended, national legislators were proposing full-employment policies that would involve the government in managing the labor market. The federal government subsequently adopted Keynesian macroeconomic principles as a way to regulate investment and disinvestment. In addition, unions were gaining strength as a result of the heightened demand for such durable goods as automobiles, kitchen appliances, and trucks. At least for a few years, it seemed that the United States might move to a corporatist model of national economic policy in which business would have to accept parity with government and labor.[68]

This did not happen, in part because of the traditional freedom from government interference that investors, financiers, and corporate leaders enjoyed and in part because the U.S. government has always been fundamentally averse to infringing on the prerogatives of the private sector. "Unrestrained growth" historically has dominated the creation of wealth in the United States.[69] The private sector controls the capital and investment decisions that generate growth and, via taxes, fund welfare activities. Any government interference might dampen its enthusiasm. So the national government acquiesced. It realized that its political goals required making peace with capital. National planning was not placed on the agenda. As one critic suggested, postwar "growth allowed policies that substituted economic performance for political ideology." Labor also struck a bargain. In return for high-wage jobs and job security, unions agreed to routinize labor-management relations.[70]

Of course, this had local consequences. The reluctance of the federal government to mount efforts toward a national settlement policy or to establish a planning body for dealing with national development kept planning and land use regulations confined to the local level, where they had been placed during the Progressive Era. And with state governments similarly averse to growth policies, the ability of local planning bodies to coordinate across jurisdictions was further weakened. This prevented the central cities from influencing metropolitan growth and enabled suburban municipalities to resist encroachment.[71]

In addition, local governments were then, as now, dependent on own-source revenues, particularly real estate taxes. If suburban communities wished to grow and provide the public services that would support new residents and businesses and attract future growth, their tax bases had to expand. They needed either wealthy families willing to pay relatively high property taxes or commercial and industrial development to share the tax burden. Local governments and their planning bodies, though, were powerless in institutional terms to negotiate with investors and developers. Consequently, they readily acquiesced to the latter's interests in return for investments that increased their tax bases. These institutional relations formed the backdrop for the development peripheral to the central cities.[72]

There was also a cultural side to postwar urbanization that included not just an urban ambivalence shaded against the older cities but also attitudes toward private property and land. Private property, the capacity to possess and control it, is a cherished value in the United States; "Euro-Americans have long held to the acquisition of property as a fundamental cultural injunction."[73] Traditionally, the private ownership of real property has been seen as essential to freedom. This was the issue being debated around the closing of the frontier in the late nineteenth century, and its roots extend as far back as the colonial period. Control over property is a way to avoid the intrusions of government.

The twinned notions of private property and of a country whose frontiers are always expanding have anchored deep-rooted attitudes to the land. Freedom in the United States has meant the ability to move away from that which brings displeasure. From the country's initial colonization, and no more dramatically than in the postwar period, Americans have accepted the fact that open space was perpetually available for escape and development. "From the 1790s on, an indifference to place has been a hallmark of American life," and this indifference has fueled a constant restlessness.[74] The vast land area of the United States, still with broad reaches of unsettled and sparsely settled spaces, and the joining of freedom to mobility established a cultural attitude that underpinned postwar expansion. Americans seemed to harbor a "contempt for natural limits."[75]

Not to be overlooked in this equation was the postwar portrayal of home ownership as a reflection of one's freedom. A family might be unable to amass vast land holdings, but it could have a quarter-acre lot in a low-density suburb. In this way, it would have the symbol if not the reality of being released from the bonds of urban society. As one commentator noted: "The American idea that [communities] could be made almost entirely of free-standing private houses with their own garden was . . . a powerful cultural ideal."[76] Urban land area more than doubled between 1950 and 1974 as low-density development increased the amount of land used to support each inhabitant. (See Figure 9.) In 1960, the average amount of urban land occupied by a resident was 0.20 acres. Driven by metropolitan sprawl, it increased to 0.23 in 1970 and 0.28 in 1980.

The open spaces around cities, however, were not empty and

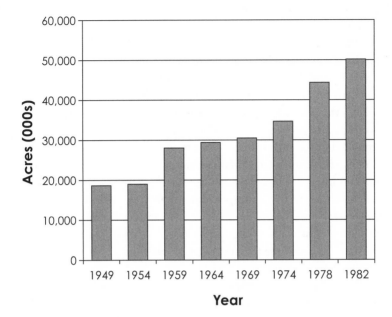

Figure 9. Urban land use in the United States, 1949–1982. The data used here are from U.S. Department of Agriculture, as collated by the Urban Land Institute (www.uli.org). Urban land is land within an urban area (that is, a place with 2,500 or more inhabitants) that contains an improvement such as a house, sewage plant, or cemetery.

simply awaiting new development. In many instances, they contained small towns and villages and rural industries such as farms, quarries, and lumber operations. Relatively undisturbed woodlands, lakes, wetlands, and rivers were also part of the landscape. The peripheral expansion of development was not expansion into a vacuum. It disturbed existing settlement patterns and ways of life. Moreover, it threatened the natural environment: "The loss of prime farmland to urban development accelerated in the postwar years."[77]

These were the concerns neither of developers nor of suburban governments, both of which favored growth. Small towns were of little value when it came to "progress," and rural industries had little moment in an economy increasingly reliant on business services. Nostalgia for small towns was not pervasive enough to resist the attractions of brand-new suburbs. And with the turn to large-scale farming and the consolidation of food distribution in supermarket chains, the smaller truck farms that had thrived in the hinterlands of older central cities became less important. Other rural activities suffered similar fates. In the late twentieth century, the country imagined itself not as a rural society but, to the contrary, as an urban and, thereafter, a suburban one.

Equally salient was the near absence of an environmental ethic. Americans, on the whole, were not environmentally aware in those early postwar years. Little legislation existed to protect the environment, particularly open space. If environmental damage was even recognized, the general attitude seemed to be that such damage was the price one paid for development. Hence, suburban expansion proceeded unmindful of the impacts that new development had on existing communities, rural industries, and the natural environment. Developers "built without regard for the environmental consequences."[78] It mattered hardly at all that suburban development might despoil the environment and be more damaging than investment in the cities. Such a perspective existed only on the fringe of contemporary understandings and was wholly outside the mind-sets of investors, developers, governments, and suburbanizing households.

No wonder that low-density development and sprawl came to characterize postwar suburbanization.[79] Developers built subdivision after subdivision of single-family detached homes, limited-access highways spurred a search for land further and further from the central cities, the reliance on the automobile encouraged the scattering of retail stores and other facilities (with regional shopping malls the exception), and suburban governments gave their imprimatur to decentered development. Streets were wider, lot sizes were bigger, and lawns were more common. *U.S. News & World Report* noted in 1950 that "the average family . . . wants space in which to live, room for the children to play."[80] Many commentators, though, attacked the suburbs as an inefficient form of development when compared to the cities—"the unplanned, unpredictable, to-hell-with-tomorrow haphazardness of sprawling growth."[81]

One result of low-density development was a rapid rise in land values as speculators drove up prices. On Long Island, "the price [sic] of land has gone from 10% of a house's cost to 25% in five years," *Time* magazine reported in 1964. Developers were undaunted. One large developer in the Washington, D.C., area was quoted as saying that "it's been my practice to pay [for land] what is asked, within reason. It may seem high at the time, but five to 10 years later it will look like a steal." Plus, developers knew they could pass along land costs to the home buyer.[82]

The institutional freedom enjoyed by investors, especially those involved in real estate development, and the cultural attitudes of postwar Americans as regards private property, the environment, and rural life set the parameters of postwar urban decline and suburbanization. Investors were attracted to the suburbs, and they avoided the intensification and renewal that would have been required if the cities were to grow. In effect, a classic avoidance-attraction situation emerged. On the one side was a generalized indifference to the cities. On the other side was the allure of the undeveloped metropolitan periphery. Although investors and households did not shun the cities altogether, most gravitated to the suburban frontier.[83]

What was it about urban development in the early postwar period that discouraged investors? First, real estate development in cities is always more difficult than in less developed and less dense places. Property is usually arranged in relatively small parcels owned by numerous people and businesses, thus making it difficult to acquire and consolidate sites. Once land has been purchased, existing buildings often need to be demolished. Demolition and the subsequent construction pose numerous logistical problems in the tight confines of cities and thereby raise construction costs. Because cities are densely developed, their governments have established a multitude of regulations to protect the health and welfare of the residents and to assure that any new development is compatible with current planning guidelines. Such regulations also increase costs.

Second, during the early postwar period, urban development had to contend with general decay and blight in the city. Any new construction in the downtown or adjacent neighborhoods was thwarted by the possibility that development would be risky and might stall and that the project might then fail. Disinvestment had been underway for a number of years, and businesses and households were leaving for the suburbs. A single developer could not hope to build a project so large that it would reverse this trend. This is why local governments undertook urban renewal projects, provided development subsidies, and financed new low-income housing; it was precisely to lower this risk. The large size of an urban renewal project would provide a critical mass of new development that would, at least in theory, entice additional new investment. Many of these projects, though, simply became enclaves within a less prosperous city.

Third, development in the cities would have to be at a higher density than in the suburbs in order to be profitable. The relatively higher land values were the culprit. To justify land costs, apartment buildings, office towers, and stores had to occupy more of the land and rise multiple stories from the ground. Intensification, however, increased the risk of a project. Much more capital was involved, and the project took a relatively longer time between conception and realization. There was more to lose and, because one could not be sure that the cities would once again become prosperous, a stronger likelihood that the investment would falter.[84]

Nevertheless, a number of investors did develop projects in the older cities and build housing, office buildings, and stores. Large-scale development, though, required government subsidies, and even then many never came to fruition or, if built, were not very profitable. Real estate investment—shopping centers, housing subdivisions—was more likely to be successful if it occurred on undeveloped land near the city's boundaries. Few cities offered such opportunities. Although Philadelphia had open space, many of the older, industrial cities, such as Pittsburgh and Boston, were fully built up and could not offer developers the kind of land that was available in the suburbs.

Fourth, it was less risky and easier to build on the city's fringe. The flow of businesses, households, and investment was in that direction, and any investment in shopping malls, tract housing, or industrial parks was likely to attract tenants and buyers. New developments would be quickly surrounded by other new developments, thereby enhancing the value of the initial investment. The cities could not match these conditions.

Fifth, suburban governments placed fewer restrictions on developers.[85] Environmental regulations hardly existed, and municipal bureaucracies were small and inexperienced at planning and overseeing development. Subsidized by state governments, local governments were also more than willing to extend the infrastructure further into the countryside, in the same way as the state and federal governments were connecting cities and suburbs with limited-access highways. Developers did not receive the same kinds of direct subsidies they could obtain in the cities, but neither did they have to navigate city regulations or worry about the decrepit state of roads and sewer systems.

Last, property acquisition, property development, and financing were less onerous in the suburbs. Land was often configured in large parcels, and there were fewer owners with whom to negotiate. Planning regulations were lax, and actual construction was unconstrained by adjacent buildings and infrastructure or by burdensome regulations. Financing was also readily available. Banks were more than willing to provide capital for such low-risk ventures, particularly when the government was underwriting home mortgages. Additionally, developers were becoming larger and thus better able to manage big projects.[86]

The whole institutional apparatus of real estate development was predisposed to the suburbs.

Of course, conditions favorable to the suburbs and unfavorable to the cities did not always exist. They are intrinsic neither to urbanization nor to capitalism. The suburbs were less attractive prior to World War II. The cities were not shunned in the 1920s. Risk is always a matter of perception, and for some developers, the greater risk of urban development was precisely its allure—the potential profits were also greater. American capitalism is a frontier economy. The development frontier, however, is less the edge between highly developed and sparsely developed areas than the line between acceptable profits and higher profits. Consequently, the frontier can be redefined, as it was in the 1980s when the city once again attracted significant numbers of investors.[87]

Parasitic Urbanization

The suburbs and the Sunbelt cities were parasitic on the cities in three ways: by siphoning households out of the older, industrial cities of the Northeast and Midwest; by attracting urban retailers and manufacturing firms; and by absorbing capital that might have been used for urban redevelopment.

Suburban development, of course, was bound to draw families and individuals from the cities. During the early postwar years, however, the older cities could least afford to give up households; replacements were scarce. Black migrants from the South were entering these cities at a rate insufficient to cover the loss of white households, and immigration had so ebbed that compensation from this source was highly unlikely. Finally, the high rate of formation of new households that occurred in the early postwar years was an impetus for relocating to the suburbs rather than an incentive to stay in the central cities. Young married couples were enticed by new housing and easy financing to move out and were discouraged by overcrowded conditions from staying.

Although the population of the country was growing and people were marrying and having children in increasing numbers, neither trend favored the existing cities. Demographic conditions restricted the growth of the older cities, and they subsequently lagged behind the suburbs and the new cities of the Sunbelt. The African American households that entered the cities and the babies they had mitigated a portion of the population loss but also contributed to it, both through the perception that the cities were becoming predominately black and because African Americans were disproportionately mired in poverty and living in slums. With the country's population growing more slowly than it had at a time of distributive urbanization and with immigration merely a trickle, the suburbs could grow at the rate that they did only by drawing on residents from existing cities.

Regarding business flight, suburbanites initially continued to rely on urban retailers for high-priced goods and services. Once people relocated in significant numbers, though, the major retailers followed. Between 1940 and 1954, "almost half of the 28 million national population increase [took] place in residential suburban areas, anywhere from ten to 40 miles away from traditional big-city shopping centers." Many large urban retailers moved, and department stores opened suburban branches. These losses tarnished the image of downtowns and further discouraged shoppers from going there. And even though many department stores maintained their flagship locations in the central cities, by the 1980s many had been closed or downsized.[88]

As for manufacturing firms, they had been moving to the periphery since the early part of the twentieth century.[89] Industrial suburbs, in fact, became one of the first peripheral attractions for working-class households. After World War II, the exodus accelerated. An official for IBM noted in 1966 that "it has been [our] policy to locate manufacturing and engineering installations away from big cities."[90] Eventually, these firms occupied industrial parks or corporate campuses and contributed to the tax base that suburban governments used for funding sports fields, sewage disposal, and public education. Lured by lower land costs and access to the new interstate-highway system and displaced by urban renewal in the city cores, wholesaling followed. Together, these firms provided jobs for local residents as well as for residents of nearby municipalities.

Investment capital also played a central and necessary role in parasitic urbanization. Without the capital to finance tract housing developments, shopping malls, new industrial buildings, industrial parks, new roads, water and sewer systems, electricity networks, stores, and schools, postwar suburbanization would have been merely a secondary phenomenon to the redevelopment of the older cities. One flow of this capital stream passed through the consumers who purchased the housing, shopped at the malls, and paid taxes to suburban governments.[91] An expanding economy, with higher levels of productivity, boosted workers' wages and salaries. With prosperity entrenched, credit was more readily available. Buying on an installment plan, and later with credit cards, became common. Of course, this expanded the amount of money in circulation. With the government underwriting mortgage lending and thereby freeing up capital for suburban (but not urban) home buyers, the forces were in place for new suburban households to spend on their homes, automobiles, and children's education.

Another part of this stream involved public capital expenditures, that is, the monies used to fund the building of schools, roads, bridges, playing fields, and water and sewer lines. Once again, the expanding economy was essential; it increased tax revenues and enabled the federal and state governments to support the capital outlays of local governments. Local governments also benefited from a prosperous economy. With expanding tax bases, they could borrow from financial markets more easily and at lower interest rates than could governments in the older cities. The latter faced shrinking tax bases. Because lenders believed that the suburbs would continue to grow and thus generate the revenues needed to pay for the loans, they were willing to provide the necessary capital.

The private sector provided most of the money for postwar development. With the trade balance favorable and with the economy growing in real terms, investment capital was abundant. Industries were expanding, and this absorbed between 50 and 80 percent of private fixed investment in the 1960s.[92] Another large portion went into the bond market for use by governments, and a third to commercial and residential real estate development.

These flows of public and private capital were connected to the decline of cities in two ways. First, their suburban bias contributed to the inability of cities to attract capital for large-scale developments that would stabilize downtowns and city neighborhoods. Second, and more important for the claim of parasitic urbanization, the disinvestment in the city freed up capital for suburban growth. Suburbanization would not have proceeded at the scale and the pace it did if those who invested in the cities had not withdrawn capital from manufacturing firms, office buildings, stores, and housing. The deferral of maintenance and the decision not to renew properties or expand existing operations made capital available for use elsewhere. Conversely, any significant reinvestment in the cities after World War II would have detracted from suburban investment, even with a growing economy.

Still, the suburbs were not built wholly on the backs of the older, industrial cities. Parasitic development was a general tendency and not the sole mode of investment or the only quality of postwar urbanization. Nevertheless, one cannot wholly dismiss the bias that American capitalism then had for low-density suburban development. Renewal and intensification in the older cities was of secondary importance.

In sum, postwar urbanization took place against a backdrop of cultural attitudes and institutional inclinations that worked against the older cities. An enduring ambivalence to cities turned any urban flaw into a debilitating condition. The industrial cities entered the postwar era shabby and overcrowded, and this set the stage for disinvestment, while white flight created a climate in which cities enjoyed little popular or political support for significant reinvestment. Government policy reflected this ambivalence. Assistance was available, but it was hardly sufficient. As always, private capital took advantage of conditions that promised low risk and substantial profits. Consequently, the cities were disadvantaged in multiple ways. As one commentator observed in 1963, "There are powerful economic forces spoiling plans for curing urban ills."[93]

Industrialists, department-store executives, government officials, and bankers made decisions in this cultural and institutional setting. Many made decisions that helped the cities and that went against the prevailing trend. A number did both—for example, building new production operations in the suburbs while locating management functions in office buildings in the central city. Overall, the bias could have been less. Although postwar urban population loss and decline were not inevitable, it takes quite an optimist to imagine how it might have been otherwise.

The emerging suburbs and Sunbelt cities were parasitic, drawing residents, businesses, and investment capital from the older, central cities. That this occurred during a period of national demographic and economic growth attests to the rupture in the country's underlying processes of urbanization. At the same time, suburbs and Sunbelt cities fueled the very economy that made their rapid growth possible. Like parasitic urbanization, the domestic prosperity of the short American Century was of its time.

5

Domestic Prosperity

No one factor brought about the parasitic urbanization of the post-war period. Cultural attitudes were biased against big cities, while the institutional tendencies of government and business favored nearly unfettered growth and ceaseless expansion into adjacent farmlands and open spaces. Without the great burst of prosperity that followed World War II and the corresponding expansion of the middle class, however, the forces of deconcentration and the seemingly inexorable decentralization stemming from demographic growth would not have reached such an unprecedented scale. An "affluent society" encased within the world's first trillion-dollar national economy made possible a great wave of consumption that carried forward the era's low-density development.[1]

Yet the postwar suburbs and the Sunbelt cities were not solely consequences of economic growth. They were also antecedents, simultaneously reaping its benefits and spurring the economy's expansion. Parasitic urbanization was consequence and cause. Domestic prosperity owed its existence, in part, to the widespread adoption of a consumption-focused suburban lifestyle and the communities that supported this way of life. The construction of single-family homes, the automobiles that they necessitated, and the public infrastructure that served them fueled the economy. The modest reinvestment occurring in declining cities also contributed to economic growth, but as a factor it paled in comparison to suburbanization and to the more encompassing disinvestment these cities experienced. The fact that the older, industrial cities were not re-developed when the country was at its most prosperous is indicative of the profound rupture in urbanization processes. Essential to parasitic urbanization was decline in the midst of prosperity.

Much like the urbanization story, the story of postwar domestic prosperity benefits from a global perspective.[2] The affluence that the United States enjoyed after World War II was due largely to the country's dominance of the world economy. For many of these postwar years, the nation ran a trade surplus, and the dollar occupied a privileged position in international currency markets. The restructuring of the international division of labor, with developing economies taking on manufacturing functions and developed economies specializing in business, educational, and financial services, buttressed what was happening domestically. The Cold War conflict that pitted the United States against the Soviet Union—capitalist markets against central planning, democracy against communism—further energized domestic production, of which military consumption was a leading component.

Parasitic urbanization and domestic prosperity are two of the three pillars of the postwar transformation of the national identity. They enabled the country's shift from an urban to a suburban society. The third pillar is the peculiar global dominance that the nation enjoyed during these decades. Because of the ideological challenge posed by the Soviet Union, suburbanization became ensnared in the international projection of American interests. The second pillar of this transformation involves the domestic prosperity that reigned from the late 1940s to the early 1970s and the role that suburbanization played in giving it visibility. "Postwar affluence took hold of the American imagination," and Americans imagined themselves to be suburban.[3]

Postwar Economic Growth

From just after World War II to the recession of the mid-1970s, the period of the short American Century, the country experienced unprecedented domestic affluence. One historian wrote that "never in the long annals of mankind had so many people in any nation enjoyed so high a level of prosperity." The United States had become the world's largest economy, and its place in the international web of trade and finance, diplomacy, and Cold War militarism "helped produce the most sustained and profitable period of economic growth in the history of world capitalism."[4]

During this quarter century, the gross national product (GNP) expanded threefold. From 1948 to 1973, the economy grew at an annual rate that was over one and one-half times as large as that for 1929 to 1948 and over twice as large as that which held sway after the recession of 1973–1975. Most importantly, this growth occurred while inflation and unemployment were at all-time lows. And since the country's population increased at a lower pace, a broad swath of residents were financially rewarded; median family income more than doubled. The proportion of households that could be considered middle-class was twice as big at the end of this period as at the beginning. Poverty declined, and income disparities shrank. The nation had recovered quickly from the war; the perils of the Depression and wartime sacrifices were replaced by the advantages of affluence.[5]

As the Depression receded in the late 1930s, the U.S. economy began to expand. The initial impetus was aid to Britain and France in support of their resistance of the German juggernaut. The economy surged when the attack on Pearl Harbor in December 1941 triggered America's war with Japan. Soon thereafter, war was declared against Germany. Military-related spending produced a nearly 60 percent growth in the GNP in the 1940s. Even after the war had ended, the economy continued to become even bigger, growing by 47 percent in the 1950s, 37 percent in the 1960s, and 44 percent in the 1970s. Across the short American Century, investment in the construction of industrial buildings and structures doubled; new commercial construction investment expanded fivefold.[6]

The growth in the national economy was less than that which was occurring in France, Italy, the United Kingdom, or Germany. These economies had been wholly disrupted by the war. Consequently, their growth rates were higher. In 1950, though, none of them had an economy more than one-fifth as large as that of the United States. The proportion of the gross world product going to the United States then was 42 percent. Even though this figure had declined by 1970, it still exceeded that going to any other nation. In that year, no western European countries exceeded one-third of the U.S. GNP. The country's healthy economic growth maintained its dominant world status.[7]

During these years, and especially in the early decades after World War II, the United States benefited from the fact that the war had taken place elsewhere. Its industry was intact and its cities undamaged by aerial bombardment. Japan, England, France, and Germany were not so lucky. The United States had dropped atomic bombs on Hiroshima and Nagasaki. Dresden had been firebombed. Much of London had been set upon by German rockets. Rotterdam had to be nearly wholly rebuilt.

The Bretton Woods Agreement of 1944 made the U.S. dollar the benchmark for world currencies and established Washington, D.C., as the center of international finance and home to the World Bank and the International Monetary Fund. Consequently, the country was well positioned to engage in foreign trade and investment. It had the industrial infrastructure—having quickly retooled to produce nonmilitary goods—to meet demand in world markets. Politically, protectionism was being ceded to free trade.

During the 1950s, U.S. exports constituted between 15 and 20 percent of world commerce. In every year from 1956 to 1973, with the exception of 1972, the country enjoyed a trade surplus, particularly in machinery, transportation equipment, chemicals, agricultural products, and military equipment. Much of what the United States was exporting went to rebuild the economies and infrastructures of western Europe, a consequence of the Foreign Assistance Act of 1948, known as the Marshall Plan. This plan's purpose was to sustain European reconstruction, and it did so with $11.5 billion of aid. By 1973, total exports reached $110.2 billion. Exports, in turn, helped expand the domestic economy while imports satisfied a rising consumer demand.[8]

While the United States was producing for the world economy, U.S. corporations were investing overseas. Spurred by a strong dollar, a Keynesian expansionary fiscal policy, low inflation, and privileged access to capital secured by the trade surplus, production moved to foreign markets. "Total overseas investments increased from $36.9 billion in 1945 to $166.9 billion by 1970."[9] U.S. foreign investment in manufacturing increased ninefold. Making foreign investments even more attractive were Federal Reserve Bank ceilings on interest rates in the United States that kept rates of return higher in Europe. U.S. transnational corporations expanded into world markets.

The domestic economy also availed itself of military expenditures. The Cold War was the excuse. As the leader of the "free world," the country maintained the world's largest military-industrial complex while engaging in a dangerous nuclear arms race with the Soviet Union. Even though wartime defense spending fell precipitously when World War II ended, peacetime defense spending ballooned in the early 1950s in response to the Korean conflict (1950–1953) and, later, to finance the war in Vietnam. During this time, overall defense spending hovered around $200 billion annually in real dollars, and through the 1950s and 1960s military expenditures approximated 6 percent of GNP. During the latter decade, military aid as a proportion of foreign aid was nearly twice what it had been in the late 1940s.[10]

Defense spending by the federal government funded research and development in the airplane, electronics, military hardware, and computer industries. These expenditures, in turn, supported key employment sectors and leveraged vast amounts of private investment, particularly in southern California, where they established a significant aerospace industrial complex. One team of researchers estimated that in 1966, military expenditures directly supported 2.4 million jobs, 3 percent of the country's total. The federal government became responsible for more and more of the national economy, although defense spending as a percentage of GNP fell from the mid-1950s through the late 1970s.[11]

Postwar domestic prosperity was also a consequence of technological advances, investments in new fixed capital, and a peace between the labor unions and the large corporations that created favorable labor-management relations. The result was a boost in productivity. Productivity rose through 1973; it more than doubled between 1946 and 1969. On average, workers were producing more and more goods per hour of work, and wages and salaries increased accordingly. Combined with the savings that had been amassed during the war years, this spurred a rise in consumption that was sustained until the recession of the mid-1970s. Mass consumption supported mass production, and the wages paid to unionized labor amplified the process. America became a consumer society.[12]

Yet productivity growth lagged behind that of Japan, the United Kingdom, France, Italy, and Germany. Nonetheless, the United States remained the dominant world economy. Its large internal market relative to these other countries and the corresponding scale of its economy were distinct and powerful advantages. Moreover, it had entered a period of relatively friendly relations between organized labor and big capital. In the years from 1947 to 1955, work stoppages involved 5 percent of the labor force on average. From 1956 to 1973, by contrast, that yearly average fell to 3 percent. This also contributed to high levels of productivity and, when combined with the country's trade advantages, compensated for lower levels of productivity growth relative to the other advanced economies.[13] (See Figure 10.)

Employment grew. Total nonagricultural jobs more than doubled in the thirty years from 1945 to 1975 while unemployment rates remained comparatively low, hovering below 7 percent throughout the 1950s and 1960s. (By contrast, in the 1970s, these rates would reach double-digit proportions.) Once again, though, by comparison to Japan and the western European countries, the United States was not doing so well. In these economies, unemployment rates were even lower.[14]

A number of significant changes occurred in the U.S. economy during these years. Manufacturing moved away from the steel and

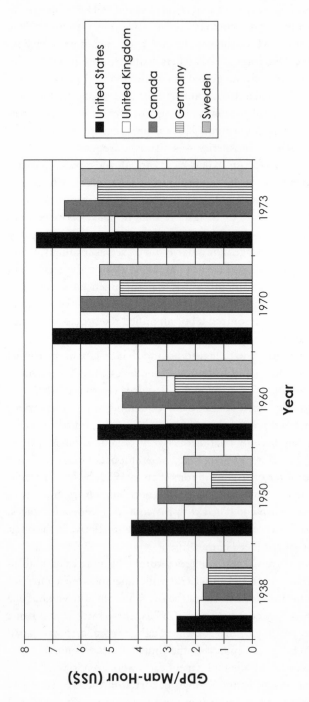

Figure 10. Annual productivity for selected countries, 1938–1973. Gross domestic product (GDP) per man-hour is in 1970 U.S. relative prices. The data used here are from Angus Maddison, Phases of Capitalist Development (Oxford: Oxford University Press, 1982), 212, table C10.

shipbuilding industries to the chemical, electronic, and automobile industries. Heavy manufacturing declined in importance to be replaced by light manufacturing and a wide array of services: business, financial, educational, retail, and health, to name just the major ones. From 1945 to 1975, employment in goods production fell from 32 million to 25 million while employment in services rose from 8 million to 57 million. As the country became more affluent, consumption became more important. Indicative of this shift, personal expenditures on services as a proportion of GNP rose by more than 60 percent.[15]

Productivity gains and changes in the mix of industries engendered a decline in blue-collar jobs and a rise in white-collar employment.[16] Correspondingly, the proportion of salaried workers was also on the rise. The expansion of higher education produced a better-trained workforce and one less suitable for manual labor. Economic prosperity and the government's GI Bill enabled many veterans to attend college who would not have otherwise done so. Consequently, more and more people began to work in offices. White-collar employment doubled between 1940 and 1982 as a percentage of all jobs. Movement into the managerial ranks meant higher salaries and middle-class status. By 1973, an estimated 63 percent of all families fell into the middle class. A new managerial stratum had come into existence.

Suburbanization played a role in creating a middle-class, consumer society. The percentage of households owning homes increased from about 44 percent in the early 1940s to 62 percent in the early 1970s. With property ownership came wealth and financial stability. One historian, looking back on these years, has commented that "as suburbanization gave a majority of Americans for the first time ever the opportunity to become people of 'property,' it also seemed to promise a surefire way of incorporating a wide range of Americans into a mass consumption–based middle class."[17]

Relatively speaking, the big job growth was in producer services and social services; the big declines were in the extractive industries of mining and agriculture. And although manual workers fell as a proportion of all workers, their actual numbers increased. The value-added portion in manufacturing also went up because of rising productivity and the changeover to more specialized goods.[18] Further contributing to the transformation of manufacturing was the rise of U.S. transnational corporations, American investment in overseas manufacturing, and a corresponding shift in the international division of labor. Worldwide, total manufacturing production increased more than twofold during the time that the U.S. manufacturing sector became smaller.[19] European and Japanese goods production rebounded from the devastation of the war, and countries like Brazil and South Korea became competitive with U.S. industries. None of this boded well for the economy.

The transition to a service economy, with its reliance on highly educated workers, and economic growth produced a much more affluent society. Disposable personal income in 1958 dollars rose from $210 billion in 1946 to $577 billion in 1973. Married couples saw their incomes more than double. At the same time, poverty rates declined. By 1973, they were one-half what they had been in 1960. Public policies, most importantly those that addressed poverty among the elderly, also contributed to the decline in poverty rates.[20]

Postwar domestic prosperity led to mass suburbanization. By increasing disposable incomes, expanding home ownership, enabling widespread automobile purchases, and providing the capital to build acre after acre of single-family homes and mile after mile of highways, an affluent society established the necessary conditions to draw people and investment from the central cities and settle them in the surrounding suburbs. In the absence of such prosperity, the forces of parasitic urbanization would have been substantially diminished. At the same time, the quest for global profits, the recovery of the European and Japanese economies, the spread of manufacturing to developing countries, and the subsequent challenges to the U.S. dollar in world currency markets were setting in motion forces that would bring an end to this burst of economic growth. Parasitic urbanization would subsequently be dampened.

Low-density peripheral development and central-city decline were not just consequences of economic growth. They also precipitated it. One commentator put it bluntly: "People in suburbs were buying more than their share of what America was producing."[21] A mobile population opened up new areas for development, and suburbanites (whether on the fringes of Pittsburgh or San Diego) increased their demand for a variety of goods and services. Some of these consumer products, such as televisions and lawn-care products, were relatively novel, while others, such as washing machines and home mortgages, were relatively familiar. Even what was familiar was transformed to fit the mass consumption of the era. This consumption, in turn, led to mass production. The economy soared.

The Suburban Contribution

The geographer David Harvey wrote in 1973 that "much of the expansion of GNP in capitalist societies is in fact bound up in the whole suburbanization process."[22] While the geographical scope of his claim was premature and the influence of suburbanization probably overstated, his core point cannot be ignored. Domestic affluence and suburbanization were mutually supportive during the early postwar decades.

Rising disposable personal incomes provided the money that made a suburban lifestyle possible. In turn, the services and goods, from homes to patio furniture, that suburban living required fueled the economy. Lawn-mower manufacturers and kitchen-appliance companies expanded, and new businesses emerged to provide food-waste disposers and backyard swing sets, all designed to serve the suburban way of life. A single-family, detached house was like a car: "a crucial element in the new economy of mass consumption."[23] Simultaneously, suburbanization required massive public expenditures on highways, water-filtration plants, and schools. Suburbanization was one of the prime engines of postwar economic growth.

The biggest purchase most people made was a house, and housing was one of the largest boosts to the postwar economy. During the Depression and the war, fewer than 500,000 housing units had been built each year. This was not nearly enough to meet the demand. One result was housing shortages; another was overcrowding in the cities. The rapid increase in marriages, babies, and new households, coupled with the rise of large, suburban home builders, brought about a surge in home construction. Over a million new units were added to the housing stock in 1946, and by the early 1970s over 2 million dwellings were being built each year. In constant dollars, investment in private residential construction increased 120 percent. Moreover, of every ten housing units built, eight were single-family homes. Not until the late 1960s, as garden apartments began to appear in the suburbs, did this ratio fall to below six of ten.[24]

With single-family homes making up the great majority of new dwellings in the 1950s, the physical landscape was transformed. These homes were usually constructed in subdivisions on individual lots ranging from one-seventh to one-quarter of an acre. Uniformity was the key to their low price and to the developers' profits. Each house was similar to the one next door and was often small—750 square feet was the size built initially by Levitt and Sons—and each house was surrounded by a lawn.[25] Densities were much lower than in the nearby central cities. Consequently, infrastructure (such as water mains) was utilized less intensively. In addition, land was developed at a faster pace than it would have been if another housing type had been adopted. The effect on the economy was significant; "new suburban home building was a pump primer for the postwar economy."[26] New homes have what economists call a large multiplier effect. Their construction involves a multitude of prior purchases—land, lumber, the labor of plumbers and electricians, built-in appliances, concrete—and their purchase and subsequent occupancy trigger a corresponding cascade of expenditures: mortgage fees, lawyer's services, dining-room sets, lawn sprinklers, curtains, an automobile or two. Annual total construction costs alone rose from around $10 billion in constant dollars in the late 1940s to around $15 billion in the early 1970s, while average sale prices went from $7,000 to almost $10,000. From the late 1940s to the mid-1960s, real estate capital made up one-fifth of the nation's GNP on an annual basis.[27]

Suburban homes were purchased "on time." New mortgage arrangements developed in the 1930s by the FHA made it possible for families to buy homes with small down payments and to amortize the loans over twenty to thirty years. By standardizing the basic elements of mortgage lending, the FHA made it easier for families to buy. It also enabled them to move more freely around the metropolitan area and the country, selling one home and purchasing another. These guidelines, though, were not only designed to benefit the consumer. They were also meant to boost the economy by invigorating the home-building and banking industries. The result was an eightfold expansion in residential mortgage debt, tripling to nearly 40 percent of GNP by 1973. Most of this debt was incurred by suburbanites.[28]

While suburban homebuyers were acquiring debt, they were also amassing wealth. In an expansive economy, home values appreciated and equity grew. In the aggregate, and in real terms, residential wealth increased by 75 percent between 1952 and 1968.[29] What made this possible was a growing real estate industry of mortgage lenders and real estate agents who advertised homes and worked with potential buyers to match their needs with the appropriate property. Of course, the wealth one had in a house could only be realized upon its sale. A whole industry thus emerged to encourage renters to buy and home owners to move up when their families changed or when they ascended another rung on the ladder of social mobility. Property had to circulate so that money could be made and the economy could expand.[30]

These market pressures spawned a fixation with property values. Rising property values meant appreciation and greater wealth that could be tapped during retirement or used to send the children to college. One result of this fixation was the defensiveness of suburban municipalities. These new middle-class enclaves resisted the encroachments of the

Domestic Prosperity

city, whether via annexation initiatives, minorities, or poor families. To maintain property values was another reason to establish a distance between the suburbs and the central cities.[31]

The other major consumption item in the postwar expansion was the automobile. Automobile ownership increased dramatically. From 1950 to the mid-1970s, 60 million cars were added to the roadways. Annual sales went up astronomically. Whereas 70,000 cars were bought in 1945, by 1973 sales had reached nearly 10 million. Automobile-related expenditures increased by a factor of six. And as the years passed, households came to own more than one automobile. This was a trend peculiar to the suburbs, where the low-density dispersal of activities created a need that was not equally present in the cities. Cities also lacked the parking space to support multiple automobiles per household; even one automobile posed parking and storage problems.[32]

Suburban families lived in wholly residential neighborhoods and had to drive to drugstores, doctors' offices, and the public library. They had children who had to be taken to school and to birthday parties. These destinations were spread out in low-density patterns. The single wage earner, usually the husband, often needed a car to commute to work. If not, and if the family owned only one automobile, the wife would have to drive him to and from the train station each workday. With mass transit mainly designed to carry commuters between the suburbs and the central cities, suburban families were dependent on the automobile.

The costs of automobile ownership were not only its initial purchase but also its operation and maintenance. Gas and oil had to be bought, and repairs were frequent. Storage was also a big expense: A garage or carport added to the cost of a home, and a car entailed parking fees at work. The automobile spawned networks of assemblers, suppliers, dealerships, parts stores, insurance companies, gas stations, and repair shops. Each of these functions, in turn, left a mark on the landscape. Gas stations became ubiquitous and could be found at almost every major highway intersection. Car dealerships clustered along suburban roads so as to better compete with each other. Stores selling automotive parts became a common tenant in commercial strips. And assembly plants occupied vast tracts of suburban land outside cities like Atlanta; Kansas City; Los Angeles; Arlington, Texas; and, of course, Detroit. Highway construction and maintenance, and the policing of the roads, further expanded the automobile's impact on the metropolis and daily life.

Then there was obsolescence. Manufacturers brought out new models each year and encouraged owners to trade in their old ones for the latest designs, colors, and gadgets. If the advertising was to be believed, a driver needed to purchase a new car with each style change. A car became a status symbol. Having a new car was a sign of upward mobility. Consequently, Americans were never free from car loans. This dynamic created a subindustry of used-car dealerships, which joined gas stations and new-car showrooms in giving character to suburban and city landscapes.

The automotive industry grew to be a pivotal component of the national economy by "ushering in a new era of profitability and capital accumulation in many related sectors."[33] The automobile was the dominant transportation innovation of the era. Public expenditures for highway construction and maintenance as well as for regulating automobile and truck use joined with the private expenditures for purchase and operation to create a dominant economic sector. Annual personal consumer expenditures on motor vehicles and the gasoline and oil to run and maintain them more than doubled in real terms between 1948 and the early 1970s to nearly $60 billion. As a proportion of GNP, these expenditures hovered between 9 and 10 percent. Moreover, it was estimated that one of every six jobs was directly or indirectly tied to the automobile industry.[34]

This economic impact was not only a function of rapidly expanding automobile use; it was also tied to the tremendous growth of trucking for shipping goods around the country. The volume of freight handled by the trucking industry went from 67 million tons in 1945 to 760 million tons in 1975, while the number of trucks in use quadrupled to 27 million.[35] Truckers also bought gasoline, paid for maintenance and repairs, and purchased new tires. Moreover, the demand for their services expanded as low-density development spread.

The automobile was increasingly a necessity. Yet purchasing an automobile has a significant discretionary component as well, particularly when it comes to replacing a working but out-of-style car or purchasing a second car. Such decisions are sensitive to economic cycles; new purchases fall precipitously as unemployment rises and the economy recedes. As the automobile industry grew, then, it came to play a larger role in national business cycles. Expenditures on cars and trucks spurred expansions but, when the economy slackened, amplified contractions.

Automobiles and homes, the two most costly items in a suburban household's budget, were bought on credit. Savings and loan associations provided short-term loans for buying automobiles—as did credit unions—and long-term loans (twenty to thirty years) for home purchases. In real terms, consumer debt for automobile loans was twice as large at the end of the postwar era as at the beginning. Fueled by suburbanization, residential mortgage debt as a percentage of total personal disposable income went from 10 percent in 1946 to 54 percent in 1975. Overall, private debt as a percentage of GNP doubled. Savings and loan associations did eight times the volume of loans in the mid-1960s as they had when World War II ended. Total mortgage debt outstanding expanded by a similar proportion during the short American Century. In brief, and "more than anything else, the explosion of consumer credit and borrowing kept the postwar mass consumption economy afloat."[36]

The rise in consumerism involved more than homes and automobiles. New homes, particularly for young and growing families, required new furniture, carpets, drapes, washing machines, lawn mowers, picnic tables and benches, and swing sets, among a multitude of other items. Growing families needed baby clothes, diapers, toys, and pediatricians. The rise in disposable income not only made these purchases possible but also expanded leisure opportunities for this new middle class. Recreation became a defining element of the suburban lifestyle. Golf clubs, tennis outfits, sailboats, croquet sets, and vacations at the shore or in the mountains became items in the household budget. Suburbanization also spawned fast-food restaurants for harried parents; households began to spend an increasing proportion of their food budgets on "eating out."[37]

Retailers made these and other purchases easier by expanding the use of charge cards and installment loans. This also boosted sales. The Diners Club introduced the first credit card in 1950 and made it even easier to buy now and pay later. The use and pleasure of the purchase could be immediately experienced while full payment could be deferred for months and even years. Consumer credit in 1958 dollars rose dramatically, from approximately $11 billion in 1946 to $120 billion in 1975, when it constituted 12 percent of GNP.[38]

A few examples illustrate this great burst in consumer purchases. Although the television industry existed prior to World War II, it was very small. By the 1970s, it had become a multibillion dollar industry. After the war, only about 60,000 households—less than 0.2 percent of all households—owned televisions. By 1960, 90 percent did. From the years just after the war to the 1970s, yearly sales of dishwashers went from 200,000 to 2.1 million; of food waste disposals, from 300,000 to 2.0 million; and of power lawn mowers, from 1.1 million to almost 5 million. Reflecting the move from tenements and apartment buildings to single-family homes, the cost of operating a household went up 15 percent.[39] (See Figure 11.)

With the consumer society came growth in businesses that produced consumer goods and provided consumer services. The home-building and automobile industries were two of the more obvious beneficiaries of postwar domestic prosperity, but producers of consumer electronics (radios and televisions), makers of home appliances, and plumbing-fixture manufacturers among many others also did well. Retail demand went up, giving rise to the suburban shopping mall and boosting the sales of mail-order retailers such as Sears, Roebuck. One consequence of all this was that unemployment reached record lows in the 1960s.

New forms of retailing came to distinguish the suburbs from the central cities. Large regional shopping malls are the most often mentioned example. Just after World War II, few of these malls existed. Even in 1958, regional shopping centers captured less than 5 percent of shoppers' purchases. By 1967, though, that share had more than doubled, and by 1979 it was 31 percent. The number of shopping centers tripled from 1958 to 1963 and tripled again from then until 1980.[40] In addition, strip retailing—with stores arranged linearly along a highway—became ubiquitous. Commercial strips provided the veterinarians, convenience stores, automobile parts dealers, bakeries, and supermarkets that were rare in regional malls. Access to all of these places required an automobile.

As retailing grew in the suburbs, it stagnated in the central cities. During the 1950s, metropolitan retail sales grew by more than 50 percent while central-city retail sales hovered in the low single digits. In the 1960s, "one major retailing chain report[ed] that it expect[ed] to close 10 to 20 downtown stores per year as leases expire. At the same time, of the 348 new stores it [had] opened in the past five years, 308 [were] located in suburban shopping centers."[41]

Business expansion boosted the revenues of local, state, and federal governments and also brought pressure on governments to spend public funds on roads, police and fire services, and water and sewer infrastructure. More and more households, the great majority of which took up residence in small towns on the suburban fringe where public goods and services were few, also increased the demand for state and local government spending. Federal budget receipts went up from $52 billion in 1946 to $149 billion in 1973 in 1958 dollars; state and local

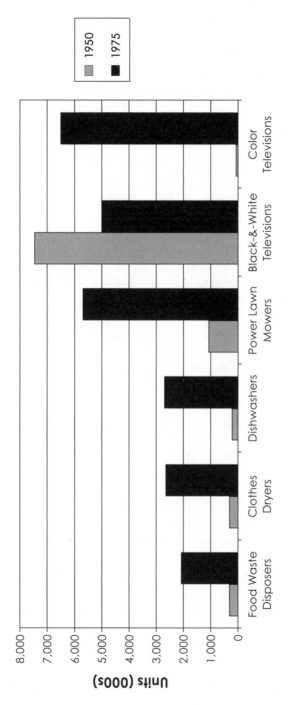

Figure 11. Selected consumer purchases, 1950 and 1975. Based on manufacturers' sales data from U.S. Bureau of the Census, Statistical Abstract of the United States (Washington, D.C.: Government Printing Office, various years). Color television sales began in the late 1950s, so the first year for this item is 1960, not 1950.

government expenditures expanded eightfold. As a percentage of GNP, federal expenditures climbed to 22 percent in 1980 from 10 percent in 1940. The state and local government shares, however, remained constant at 10 percent.[42]

Suburbanization and Sunbelt-city growth required not only new road networks but also water and sewer lines, filtration plants, waste treatment facilities, new schools, parks and playgrounds, landfills for trash, and police and fire stations. All of these public services had to be staffed and maintained. Together, federal and state government outlays on the interstate highway system averaged $1.3 billion for each year in the 1960s and early 1970s. By 1973, state and local governments were spending $181 billion annually.[43] These expenditures provided an additional spur to the economy.

The costs facing suburban and Sunbelt-city governments were exacerbated by low-density development and by the fact that many of these suburban communities had few public services prior to suburbanization. Water and sewer lines had to be built in the suburbs, and, compared to those in high-density cities, they extended further and were used less intensively. Schools had to be constructed and children bused to them. More roads were needed, as were more fire stations. Of course, sidewalks could be dispensed with, as few people had reason to walk in their neighborhoods except to cross the lawn to visit neighbors. These costs were also contributions to the economy. Building more roads and extending water mains meant more public jobs and more government purchases that, in turn, fed an expanding private sector. The inefficiencies of parasitic urbanization made the economy even more prosperous than it would otherwise have been.

The Economics of Parasitic Urbanization

To what extent did postwar affluence depend on parasitic urbanization? How much of the domestic prosperity can be attributed to suburbanization and the growth of the Sunbelt cities? How much to central-city decline? That suburbanization and Sunbelt growth dominated national growth in these years, with the older, industrial cities and rural areas lagging behind, is irrefutable. The more challenging claim is that urban decline also enabled domestic prosperity.

The connection between parasitic urbanization and postwar prosperity is built on two premises. One is that growing areas of a country contribute more to national economic growth and prosperity than do stagnant and declining areas. The other premise is that decline also enhances overall economic growth by freeing up capital to be invested more productively elsewhere and by casting off households and thus taxpayers and consumers. Declining areas are more than simply a burden imposed on the national economy. In the United States, as has been often said, even the demolition of a historic building is a contribution to the gross national product.

In growing areas, as compared to declining ones, more private capital is being invested in homes and businesses, more public capital is put in infrastructure and public services, and more money is being spent by households with rising incomes. New housing is more common, and this means larger expenditures on plumbing services, new furniture, and many other consumption items. Under parasitic urbanization, the growing areas were also low-density areas, lacking in mass transit, and thus requiring greater reliance on automobiles, thereby boosting spending at gas stations, car washes, and auto repair shops.[44]

Rapid and significant growth made the suburbs and the Sunbelt cities major factors in postwar prosperity. In the 1940s, residential expansion in the suburbs accounted for nearly one-half of national population growth. The suburban share of this growth rose to just over 70 percent in the 1950s and over 85 percent in the 1960s; by the 1970s, population loss from the central cities was so severe that suburban growth compensated by exceeding 100 percent. To give an example of the dominance of suburban growth, in the first seven months of 1947, 6,983 new homes were started in the Philadelphia-Camden metropolitan area, but only 2,542 were within the municipal boundaries of these two cities.[45]

New and young households in the suburbs also meant babies. Together—new homes, growing families—they contributed to a spurt in the consumption of homes, automobiles, and highways as well as of elementary schools, life insurance, and medical facilities. Housing was being built in the cities, and newly married couples were having children there, but on a scale much less than on the urban periphery. Because public expenditures in the cities did not involve building new school systems and extensive highways and water and sewage systems, the multiplier was much less. Domestic spending in general had a suburban bias; the postwar suburbs, one commentator has claimed, were "deliberately planned to maximize consumption of mass-produced goods."[46]

Exports during this period were high, but they never contributed more than 7 percent of the gross national product.[47] Domestic private investment in durable goods (for example, machinery) increased throughout this period in real terms and as a percentage of all fixed investment. Investment in nonresidential structures such as factories, office buildings, and farm milking sheds exhibited a similar trend. Domestic private investment in nonfarm buildings and structures, however, went up over 600 percent in real terms on an annual basis.[48] To a great extent, postwar prosperity was a domestic phenomenon. And, I would argue, the main forces of economic growth were constituted out of suburban development.

Admittedly, the expansion in restaurant patronage, clothing expenditures, the purchase of televisions, and the construction of new homes also took place in declining cities. The incomes of city residents were falling relative to those of the suburbs, however. Home building was concentrated in the metropolitan periphery, and mass transit still functioned sufficiently to deter many central-city residents from buying an automobile. Consequently, consumption expenditures on a per capita basis were probably lower in the cities than in the suburbs. As one historian has commented, the postwar economy was "built in large part on the consumption of new housing and automobiles," and these were very much attributes of a suburban lifestyle.[49]

Central-city decline, though, was not solely an economic burden. Decline attracted government investment and subsidies, particularly for urban renewal and public housing, that otherwise might not have been made. Additionally, not all private investment fled the central cities. New housing, new office buildings, and new factories were built; many existing properties were renovated and redeveloped. In Philadelphia, for instance, $152 million was invested in industrial buildings from the mid-1950s to the mid-1970s, and over $415 million, in real terms, was put into commercial buildings. Over 117,000 housing units were built.[50] Public investment also increased after the war with the building of new schools, bridges, and water-filtration plants. Nationwide, the public housing program alone added nearly 1 million new dwelling units, and the urban renewal program spent billions of dollars.

Of course, the cities still contained a significant amount of economic activity. In the early postwar years, almost all of the metropolitan office function was concentrated there. Many factories had yet to move out or close down, while banking, business legal services, and accounting remained primarily in the central city. Almost all of the suburban commuters worked in the city's central business districts, particularly if they were in management or other white-collar occupations.

My point is that the suburbs supplanted the central cities during the short American Century and that their contribution to the economy, an economy increasingly driven by consumption, was proportional to their contribution to growth. Higher rates of new development rather than redevelopment, higher incomes, and a more consumption-based lifestyle were the keys to the suburbs' economic impact.

At the same time, disinvestment was a positive force in the national economy even if not for the cities where it originated.[51] The abandonment and demolition of tenements and factories, the shrinkage of retail space, and the dismantling of piers and railroad viaducts all contributed to economic prosperity. Over 500,000 dwelling units nationwide were demolished to clear slums. The urban renewal program was responsible for the closing of 100,000 businesses in the cities to make way for new commercial development. Interstate highway construction also demolished scores of buildings and uprooted numerous industrial, wholesale, and retail businesses. In Newark, New Jersey, in the 1960s, 9,000 homes were demolished, and in Philadelphia yearly demolitions reached a peak of nearly 4,000 in 1968.[52] To accomplish this, machines had to be bought, laborers hired, supervisors trained, and consultants paid. Redevelopment expanded the economy. It also created opportunities and freed up capital.

In short, destruction and disinvestment—undermaintenance, abandonment, demolition—are good for the economy. They are one side of the creative destruction that is at the core of capitalism's vitality. Destruction, whether it takes the form of product obsolescence (which can destroy a thriving industry), war damage, or natural disaster, has benefits. The demolition of slums, for example, required city governments to expand their planning departments, which, in turn, gave the government greater capacity to improve its zoning, develop plans for future development, and track building activity. Development also released the capital that had been committed to these buildings by owners and investors. It allowed investors to escape from prior sunk costs. No longer attached to that specific investment, the capital could be redeployed to more profitable uses.

When landlords held back on maintenance in the inner cities and subsequently abandoned or sold their properties to urban renewal authorities for demolition, they were then able to reinvest their capital elsewhere. Banks no longer held mortgages on these properties and thus had additional funds to lend for suburban home buying. A similar logic holds for store owners, factory operators, and others who left the declining central cities. Value was lost, but it was also gained and redirected. A portion of this capital was probably reinvested in the cities, but, given the decline these cities suffered, it was probably small.

Central-city decline also cast off households so they could relocate to the emerging suburbs, liberated retailers from existing markets, and provided factory owners with compelling reasons to build new plants in suburban industrial parks. All of these shifts involved costs (for example, moving one's family or business), and these costs expanded economic activity and served as the prelude to new investments.

During the roughly twenty-five years from the late 1940s to the early 1970s, then, parasitic urbanization was crucial for economic growth. Suburbanization and Sunbelt growth—low-density development—were the biggest contributors. Central-city decline was also a factor, one that is too often ignored. The latter provided people and businesses to occupy new suburbs and burgeoning Sunbelt cities, liberated private capital, and justified extensive public-sector investments. "Cities are economical; suburbs are costly"—precisely the condition that made suburbanization and low-density development central to postwar domestic prosperity.[53] And while we cannot definitively quantify these impacts, neither can we summarily dismiss them.

Prosperity's Limits

The domestic prosperity of the short American Century eventually came to an end. A deep recession in the early 1970s marked its closure. Rising energy prices, unemployment rates rarely seen since the 1930s Depression, rampant inflation, and stagnant wages all contributed to the shrinkage in consumption and the deceleration of growth. European countries no longer welcomed U.S. investment or offered the favorable trade relationships that had been available in previous decades. Japan began to compete in U.S. automobile, steel, and electronics markets.

In retrospect, the cessation of this long expansion could have been predicted. Long waves and business cycles have been an integral part of capitalist economies for centuries. Moreover, the economies of western Europe and Japan were bound to regain their international competitiveness. The emergence of the Eurodollar in the 1970s kept capital in Europe rather than allowing it to flow back to the United States. As a result, trade deficits became more common. For a variety of reasons, inflation rose worldwide. U.S. overseas investment in manufacturing was spreading technology and spawning industrial growth elsewhere, and interest rates began to climb as the economy slowed. With immigration minimal, birthrates falling after the baby boom, and the spurt of new households having passed, consumption-driven growth dampened.

A number of commentators looked back at this historic juncture and claimed it was the beginning of the decline of America itself, not just of its industrial cities.[54] The edge of U.S. global competitiveness had become dull, and militarily, the nation was no longer able to assert its will. The stalemated Korean conflict, the debacle of Vietnam, and, later, the Iranian hostage crisis (1979) took a toll. Diplomatically, Germany and Japan were less pliable in the face of U.S. policy. Internally, the antiwar protests, the women's liberation movement, and the lingering civil rights movement combined with the "culture wars" of the 1980s to suggest a country in disarray. Of course, there was truth in the evidence. The dominant position of the United States in the world—economically, militarily, diplomatically, culturally—had been eroded, but then only slightly and certainly not erased. The domestic economy was still strong.

While these events seemed to bring an end to parasitic urbanization, *diminished* is a more accurate characterization than *deceased*. Suburbanization continued, and Sunbelt cities still outpaced Rustbelt cities in population growth and economic prosperity, though New York and Chicago maintained their positions in the country's urban hierarchy.

The large industrial cities, though, began a subtle deviation from their earlier path and showed signs of renewal. Population loss slackened. Industrial decline, after the recession of the early 1980s, virtually ceased—little was left to close or relocate. Racial tensions eased. Elements of revival appeared in the form of gentrification of inner-city neighborhoods and of downtown commercial investment in office buildings, shopping malls, and festival marketplaces. Immigrants once again began flowing to the cities, although white out-migration continued.[55]

Suburbanization encountered obstacles: the environmental movement, antigrowth and antisprawl initiatives, higher gasoline prices, crowded highways, and the increasing physical distances from the center city. Overall, urbanization was less parasitic. Another wave of development had peaked. Notwithstanding, the country did not fully return to an earlier era of distributive urbanization.

In effect, the United States had become a suburban society. Large cities still existed, and highly dense ones—New York, Boston, Chicago—at that, but the dominant mode of growth was low density and automobile-centric, even in the cities of the Sunbelt. Anchoring this shift was the eruption and spread of a way of life associated primarily with suburban living. This shift in the core identity of the country was inseparable from the short American Century and from the parasitic urbanization that shaped the movement of people and capital across the American landscape.

6

Ways of Life

The consumption that drove the postwar economy was, in style and content, distinctly suburban. Its novelties included greater individual mobility, increased leisure, higher rates of product obsolescence, and a tighter bond between status and consumption. As the famous housing developer William J. Levitt noted about postwar suburbanization, the suburban homebuyer is "not just buying a house, he's buying a way of life."[1] Much as it had in the mid- to late-nineteenth century, the United States was undergoing a profound transformation, not from a rural to an urban society, as then, but from an urban to a suburban one. The country's dominant identity was in flux.

Of course, no distinct boundary divides that which is urban from that which is suburban.[2] Correspondingly, no unequivocal distinction can be made between a city-based and a suburb-based way of life. Yet a new way of living was spreading throughout the country. Its roots were in the suburbs, and its qualities shaped by the people who lived there. Cities were also included. Their residents adopted similar buying habits and even a few "suburban" daily activities.

The transition from an urban to a suburban way of life is the element that connects parasitic urbanization to national identity and to claims about American exceptionalism. No longer shaped by its industrial past, America would now draw its identity from the suburbs. The claim that the dominant way of life in the United States changed from urban to suburban, however, might well seem disingenuous. The famed ambivalence toward cities, at times becoming dislike, would seem to undermine any such assertion. If an urban way of life was never embraced, how could it subsequently have been cast aside?

Americans never so loved their cities that they celebrated city life with fervor. Neither was there a specific and unique urban way of life to be defended as the suburbs rolled across the landscape. What changed were tastes and habits, consumer preferences, social norms, political ideas, forms of business organization, and varieties of popular culture. In the late nineteenth and early twentieth centuries, these were all centered in and associated with the large industrial cities. How people lived, at least how the largest grouping of people lived, was anchored there. Prior to World War II, cities dominated national life. They were the sites of popular and elite culture and the sources of news and ideas, and they had a major influence on politics. These cities were also the engines of growth and prosperity for the countryside. If one wanted fame and fortune, if one wanted to be successful, one went to the city.[3]

How this way of life was interpreted in any particular place varied widely. People far removed from the city—living relatively isolated in the hills of North Dakota or in the marshlands of Florida—crafted an existence whose connection to a city was tenuous at best. Those living in the streetcar suburbs of Boston could hardly avoid it, while residents of inner-city neighborhoods were urban to the core. The nation was inseparable from its cities. It was in this sense that the postwar era transformed the country's identity by establishing a "suburban ethos." The transition was neither sudden nor complete, neither sharply defined nor indiscernible, neither immutable nor endlessly malleable. Yet it would be wrong to assert without any doubt, as one observer did, that "there are no grounds for believing that suburbia has created a distinctive style of life or a new social character for Americans."[4]

Suburban Life

In the early twentieth century, small-town life challenged rural life for the position of preferred alternative to living in the big cities. The countryside held fewer and fewer opportunities. Notwithstanding, Americans retained a strong attachment to rural-agrarian ideals and a sense of themselves as free, unhampered by legal constraints, and independent. For such people, the city represented closure and restraint. Rural life, by contrast, allowed Americans to own land and to insulate themselves from the institutions of society. By the early twentieth century, however, rural life was simply untenable for most people. A half century later, Americans began another struggle to reconcile the places available to them with the pursuit of the good life. In the postwar period, one observer commented, Americans wanted "the economic benefits of urbanization while resisting the way of life usually associated with living in cities."[5]

Rural life could be stifling. Small towns were restrictive: Demanding conformity, they made it difficult to escape the scrutiny of one's neighbors. Both offered limited opportunities for social expression, economic advancement, or professional accomplishment. For those with wider aspirations or inclined to pursue lifestyles or dreams not sanctioned in their hometowns, the city was necessary and irresistible. Fame, fortune, and anonymity were its draws.

Yet while Americans were drawn to the city for its opportunities, they kept alive and nurtured the ideal of small-town life.[6] In the twentieth century, the search began for an alternative to both the small town and the dense and hectic industrial cities. The expansion of the economy in the 1920s gave impetus to this search. Rising incomes and an emerging emphasis on mass consumption made home ownership and leisure time accessible to larger numbers of people. The federal government, newly interested in bolstering the economy, joined this endeavor in the 1930s. To stimulate the economy, and by using a variety of government programs and initiatives, it encouraged home buying.[7] Home buying, government officials knew, would also stimulate other purchases, expand production, and boost the economy.

Not until after World War II did construction techniques, financing arrangements, and business practices make it possible to realize the dream of greatly expanding home ownership and thus to replicate small-town America on a mass scale. Into existence came the automobile-centered, mass-produced suburb with its landscape of single-family tract houses, highway shopping, and single-story school buildings. Symbolically fused to it were images of family life, domesticity, safety, and the innocence of childhood. Here people could live with others like themselves and bring up their children free from the threats and temptations of the city. Still, it was a compromise: "In suburbia people [had] the advantage of electing a place where they prefer[ed] to live," even if it was not the "ultimate rural residence."[8]

Central to all of this was the association of middle-class values with a specific understanding of what family life meant in the suburbs. To be middle-class meant more than aspiring to a college education and a white-collar job. It also meant having a family—the point of view is decidedly male—with a homemaker wife and three to four children all living together comfortably in their own home. The family was to be the center of social life. One consequence was an emphasis on family vacations and the active involvement of parents in the lives of their children through organized sports and the local parent-teacher association. Bringing together families in this way offered a "retreat from the utilitarian world of work and into an expressive world of friendly community."[9]

Despite its humble aesthetic qualities and relatively low cost, the suburban home took on a high symbolic value as mass suburbanization "brought the dream of small-town life within everyone's reach."[10] Of course, it was not quite a small town. These newly built communities lacked shopping areas within walking distance, town squares, local employment, and history. Generations of families did not live within blocks of each other. The newcomers lacked roots. Yet many people considered them better than the cities. People voted with their feet and rejected the older, central cores. Housing shortages and rising prices for good apartments and homes drove out urban dwellers. In addition, the high densities and limited land that was available in the industrial cities made building there costly and particularly difficult at a scale that would accommodate the large numbers of people in search of new homes and neighborhoods. Home builders, supported by financial institutions and government programs, offered mainly one choice: the suburbs. It was easier to purchase there than in the city, and many families were happy to take advantage of this opportunity. "People liked [suburban life], anyhow, were grateful for it, got used to it, grew fond of it."[11]

Migration from the countryside to the city still occurred. The "magnet's pull," though, was to the suburban rings, and more and more people—white, upwardly mobile, young—were leaving the cities for these new communities. Federal programs and suburban developers "transformed a country of urban renters into a nation of suburban property owners."[12] *Business Week* asserted in 1960 that a fundamental demographic change had taken place: "Once a rural country, [the United States] turned urban in the 1910s; now it has turned suburban," though it would not be until the 1990s that more than one-half of the country's population would live in the suburbs. Ten years later, another mass-market publication echoed those observations: "The pull of the suburbs has been so strong that suburbanites are becoming the most numerous element in the U.S. population" and suburbanization the "dominant growth pattern of the United States."[13]

Suburbanization became the reigning pattern of development and defined a style of consumption and way of life for suburban and nonsuburban residents alike. People lived differently, not because moving to a suburban community changed their values and made them different in some fundamental way but because suburbanization was linked to a new mode of consumption. That mode required that people do normal activities (for example, clothes washing or churchgoing) in unusual ways as well as perform new tasks such as mowing the lawn and driving to work. One observer in the late 1950s presciently commented that the alterations that suburbanites experienced in their lives came from the aspirations and pressures afloat in the larger society. These changes were not essentially suburban, but they had "led [people] to the suburban builders."[14]

The novelties were many. Take work: As the economy shifted away from manufacturing, more and more people were employed in white-collar positions. Many of them were commuting by bus or subway within the city, but an increasing number were traveling by automobile from the suburbs. The suburban commute to the central business district became a defining activity for an increasingly mobile population. The typical commuter was highly educated and wore a suit and tie rather than coveralls. Moreover, he—seldom she—was likely to be employed by a large corporation. The latter was also true of blue-collar suburbanites, who often found themselves working in automobile assembly plants or steel mills. For both groups of workers, commuting by automobile was common.

These workers were primarily men. Women were underrepresented in the ranks of unionized blue-collar and educated white-collar workers, though not among secretaries and service workers such as department-store clerks. The labor that women performed in the suburbs was associated with the home; it was domestic work. (This was, however, more true for middle-class than for lower-middle-class women; the latter were more likely to be employed.) Men, as well as many women, expected women to care for the children, maintain a home, and make the purchases that allowed her to be successful at both. Women were housewives and the managers of and impetus behind the household's purchases—"Mrs. Consumer." Even with a college education, her obligations were to the family, first, and to the home.[15] This meant grocery shopping, trips to the drugstore for cough medicine, taking the children to the dentist, and driving to the shopping mall to buy clothes and lunchboxes for the children's new school year. Almost all of these trips were taken in the family car; there were no other alternatives.

The suburban housewife was also responsible for the care and personal development of the children. Children were at the core of family life. New theories of child rearing emphasized their social and intellectual development and placed the woman in a pivotal role. The mother watched over her children at the playground, read to them at night, attended parent-teacher association meetings at the local elementary school, and monitored the foods they ate. Despite their absence during the week and lesser household responsibilities, men participated in these obligations as well. Still, the husbands were often served by wives who cooked and cleaned for them and managed the house. Although the husband brought home the weekly paycheck that made this lifestyle possible, absent the housewife and the "cult of domesticity" that justified her efforts, the suburban lifestyle would have been considerably altered.

The design of the typical tract house reinforced these values. Whether Cape Cod or ranch style, the suburban house contained, if not a family room, a kitchen-dining area (perhaps with a breakfast nook), a den where the family could gather each night to watch television, and, just off the kitchen, a backyard for play. Though small, tract houses were expandable and grew along with the family as rooms were added. Mass society, U.S.-style, had found its "dream life."[16]

Men made repairs to the house, tended the yard, and organized construction of additions to accommodate a growing family. In fact, the postwar years turned the normal chores of home ownership into hobbies and do-it-yourself activities. In order to afford their homes, and as part of leisure-time activities, many men mowed and raked the lawn, built bookshelves for the den, replaced light fixtures, and changed the oil in their automobiles. The economy was moving toward greater self-service even as the suburbs spawned a whole array of house-oriented service workers from television repairmen to house painters. Leisure was redefined. For men, it included work on the house, yard, and car; for women, their work-leisure counterpart was shopping.

As women took up shopping as a source of social engagement outside the home, shopping was simultaneously depersonalized. Suburbanization was one of the driving forces. Except for department stores and specialty shops in central business districts, most retailing in the cities and in small towns prior to World War II was community based. The stores were locally owned and staffed, customers and clerks knew each other, if not personally, at least familiarly, and a purchase was more than a monetary transaction. Stores were the "focal point[s] for the community."[17]

Mass consumption and the expansion of highway-oriented retailing on the city's fringe changed this. Shopping became more physically and socially remote, and shopping increasingly meant traveling by automobile—even in the cities. In the suburbs, most shopping was done in national chain stores and outside the neighborhoods or small towns where people lived.[18] One could still find "local" stores and "personal" service, but it was less and less available. From the perspective of suburban developers and planners, retail activities and services such as doctor's offices were incompatible with the family-centeredness of residential subdivisions. Lingering to chat with the pharmacist or greeting the children's pediatrician on the sidewalk were less and less likely to happen. Shopping was disengaged from sociability.

Not only were people traveling more to shop, but they were also eating out on a more regular basis and finding more and more entertainment outside the home, even as home entertainment became more common. Suburbanization and its related mass consumption brought changes in how people consumed food. Supermarkets replaced corner grocery stores. In addition, the food that was cooked at home was more likely to be prepackaged. TV dinners exemplified this trend; they combined a labor-saving benefit for the housewife with an opportunity for the family to watch television together. Even as developers and advertisers touted the modern appliances of electric kitchens and as advice books encouraged women to have their families "eat right," more and more of what the household consumed at home came from cans and packages.

At the same time, people were eating outside the home more often. Whereas once restaurant choices divided about equally between a few fancy restaurants and roadside or downtown diners, many more different types of opportunities became available in the postwar years. Investors were responding to an increasingly car-oriented culture and the need for food services along the highways, not to mention places to stop—motels—for overnight stays on long car trips.[19] They were tapping into the larger amounts of disposable income brought about by postwar prosperity. And they benefited from a combination of greater leisure time and pressure to engage in family-oriented activities. The suburban landscape became dotted by fast-food restaurants, many of them national chains. These suburban restaurants, by contrast to their city counterparts, were like the new retail stores—disengaged from the local community.

Entertainment options were changing in similar ways, becoming both more home centered and more available outside the home. Even mass entertainment, as epitomized by Disneyland, was family centered and reminiscent of suburban values.[20] These changes were driven by

Figure 12. Kaffeeklatsch in Park Forest, Illinois, 1954. Courtesy of Library of Congress, Prints and Photographs Division [LC-USZ62.132141].

the peculiar qualities of suburbanization and its emphasis on consumption. The encouragement of family-centered leisure supported the watching of television, backyard play sets for the children, family or "rec" rooms in the house, and outside decks and patios for socializing with friends and neighbors. Entertaining people in one's home became more prevalent, part of an inward-oriented privatizing of social life generally but also related to the pride that families had in their homes and in the skills of the housewife and husband-handyman.

Suburban housewives brought friends and neighbors into the home for coffee or "get-togethers." Being at home during the day, and specifically when the children were in school, created opportunities to socialize. Moreover, social life in the suburbs was different from what it would have been back in a city neighborhood.[21] Often people moved to the suburbs "away" from their extended families and the older generation. Family gatherings thus involved traveling some distance. Neighbors and friends were nearby, though, and "couple visiting" became more common.

The age and class homogeneity of the suburbs further narrowed a family's range of friends. Men, of course, had friends and acquaintances from work. Advancement at the office might be enhanced by playing golf with colleagues on the weekends, dining at a downtown restaurant with them and their wives, or inviting coworkers for a backyard barbecue in the summer. Some of these were formal occasions, but much of the socializing associated with the suburbs was casual. This was in line with "the new ideal of the relaxed, informal family lifestyle, with its emphasis on outdoor activities and its stress on enjoyment and personal satisfaction, [that] was incorporated into the personal ideals of middle-class suburbanites."[22]

Yet this generation was also deeply engaged in the civic life of the community, more so than the generation before and the ones that followed. Church attendance was high, and union membership was at a twentieth-century peak. Participation in league bowling was common and neighboring was prevalent. The rootedness of home owners was one reason. "Americans, it seemed, were rediscovering the civic virtues of small towns."[23] As suburbanization continued, though, and sprawl intensified in the 1970s, civic engagement ebbed.

Family socializing was, in part, child dependent. Children made friends in the neighborhood, the parents became acquainted, and neighborly relationships followed. Unlike city children, children in the suburbs had yards in which to play; younger children also roamed through the neighborhood or to the local playground much as older children do. In addition, child's play became more routine. Suburban communities spawned all kinds of scheduled recreational activities, from swimming pool parties to Little League baseball and ballet classes. All of this added another task—driving the children to their many social activities—to the many responsibilities borne by suburban mothers.

Adults had numerous entertainment options outside the home as well. Movies, sports events, concerts, and nightclubs had been around for decades. In the very early years after World War II, the suburbs had few of these attractions. As the population in the suburbs grew, investors began to build movie theaters there. The number of drive-in theaters, where one never had to leave the confines of the automobile, multiplied from 100 in 1946 to more than 3,000 in 1956.[24] Sports arenas, concert halls, and nightclubs remained mainly in the central cities. Strongly influencing these many activities was a general optimism:

"the flush of military victory, the staggering prosperity, the renewed faith in the future," as one observer described it.[25] Personal affluence, the opening up of higher education, and a growing society with expanding opportunities encouraged a belief in the inevitability of advancement. Middle-class suburbanites were upwardly mobile. At the office, the husband expected to be regularly promoted and granted the perquisites of a bigger office, a personal secretary, and a higher salary. The collective embrace of success translated into a fixation on and anxiety about social status and its accoutrements.[26] One's home, one's automobile, the landscaping of the lawn, the way one entertained, the vacations one took—all spoke to the status one had in the community. The level of one's consumption was a function of necessity and affluence and a prod to anxiety about status and the desire to signal that status to others. Not new, these pressures were amplified in the postwar period.[27]

None of this is meant to imply either that these daily activities and concerns were novel to the short American Century or that they were confined to the residents of suburban municipalities. Neither of these implications is defensible. The suburbs "set the tone of American living" in these early postwar decades; they did not dictate how people had to live.[28]

That the suburbs did not reflect the diversity of the American population is also important. Most new suburbanites were young, white families. In addition, there was economic homogeneity. The poor were excluded, and the rich had other options than a tract house in a suburban subdivision. Elderly households remained in the cities. Single women and black households were blocked from obtaining home mortgages. On the other hand, a variety of Christian religions were present, as were a broad array of ethnicities. The suburban lifestyle in its full glory was the province of young, white, educated, married couples with children. All others participated to a lesser extent.[29]

By the mid-1970s, the suburbs had come to signify a new lifestyle, one rooted in the metropolitan periphery and the emerging Sunbelt cities. This way of life, at least elements of it, was also available to those still living in the older, industrial cities. In the early postwar period, "it was an article of faith that the style of America was being set in the suburbs."[30] The new postwar lifestyle was shaped by the low density of development, the reliance on the automobile, the stark separation of land uses, the social similarity of residents, the magnetic attraction of the malls, and the scarcity of employment centers. By far the most important factor, though, was the consumption-centered economy.

The United States became a suburban nation not in terms of mass culture, elite culture, or commerce and finance, but in terms of lifestyle. The suburban way of life rose to a position of dominance by the choices people made—and the choices people were offered—of where to live and how to live. They practiced this lifestyle in suburban communities and Sunbelt cities. "The suburban single-family home became the American home and suburbia the American way of life."[31] Living in the cities and living an urban way of life became a demographic and, more importantly, a social abnormality.

Life in the City

Life in Levittown or Phoenix was different from life in Chicago or Boston. Whom one encountered in public, how one traveled from place to place, the kinds of homes one lived in, and the types of public spaces where people congregated were hardly comparable. Thus, when a majority of the populace took up residence in suburbs and low-density Sunbelt cities, a condition that occurred at the end of the short American Century, the urban way of life became the norm for a minority of the country's residents. Dense, diverse, and transit-dependent cities no longer shaped how most Americans lived.

In popular and elite culture, the central cities were still important. Metropolitan newspapers remained, as did most metropolitan television stations. Sports teams, even if their venues were increasingly in and their fans increasingly from the suburbs, mostly kept the names of their cities. Institutions of higher education, particularly the large research universities, stayed in the cities even as a number of them considered relocation and others flirted with establishing research parks in outlying, low-density communities.[32] Museums, symphonic orchestras, opera houses, and legitimate theater companies also resisted the lure of the suburbs. Fashion, in a variety of fields, was dictated from an urban base, even as it catered to the desires of suburban consumers. Midway through the postwar period, in 1960, one anonymous observer could write that "although many people are deserting the cities proper, they are not severing their ties with them or their reliance on them."[33]

Cities also retained their preeminence as the centers of corporate control and finance. A few corporations moved their headquarters to suburban locations; the major banks, law firms, and accounting firms, though, stayed in the cities.[34] The rise of edge cities in the 1980s threatened this dominance but, except in the most devastated of older cities, did not seriously erode it.

As residents of the cities were swept along by the wave of mass consumption, their lives also began to change. No law prevented urban households from buying TV dinners and spending each evening in front of the television set. Neither were they ostracized for buying a car and using it to shop at suburban malls. Nonetheless, how one lived in the city was popularly viewed as quite unlike how one lived in the suburbs. Of course, as in the suburbs, the residents of the cities lived differently from each other as well.[35] One could imagine a modal way of life—a norm—but what was most common did not exhaust the actual possibilities. Neither did the distinction between city and suburb constitute a boundary impervious to the migration of lifestyles. Despite this complexity, observers from academics to television producers to newspaper editors fixed on a small number of dominant images—urbanity, slums, and ethnicity—to depict life in the cities.

Mass suburbanization did not suddenly arrive full throttle after the end of World War II. Its acceleration was gradual. Between the early years and when it reached top speed, the cities could still be portrayed as vibrant and urbane. For some observers, decades later, the cities were most desirable in the 1950s, when urbanity was ostensibly at its peak.[36]

During the early years of this decade, the central business districts were bustling with shoppers, their corporate offices were filled with local employees and commuters from the suburbs, movie theaters and nightclubs were attracting patrons, and the sidewalks were safe. Residents from the city's neighborhoods went downtown to work or shop and on the weekends took the bus, subway, or trolley to find entertainment there. Traffic congestion was on the rise, but the city itself was still relatively untouched by the automobile. Although few new office buildings or department stores had been built in recent decades, buildings were being renovated, and the decay and deterioration that would soon settle into these business districts had yet to accelerate.[37] Postwar prosperity boosted the city's economy and energized public life.

Surrounding these commercial centers were the city's docks, warehouses, and industrial areas. They too were bustling with activity. The domestic freight business was keeping the rail yards busy, foreign freight filled ships and warehouses in the harbors, and burgeoning airports generated another cluster of businesses. These activities provided jobs for blue-collar workers as machinists, crane operators, stevedores, truck drivers, and deliverymen. Many of these jobs were taken by city residents who walked to work or took public transit.

Although shabby and overcrowded, urban neighborhoods were

nonetheless viewed as viable. They contained a range of retail stores that provided personal service and were mostly locally owned and operated. Churches were still neighborhood based. People were outside on the sidewalks or in front of their houses socializing throughout the day and into the evening.

No one captured this view of the urban neighborhood more brilliantly than Jane Jacobs, a community activist and reporter who lived in Greenwich Village in New York City. *The Death and Life of Great American Cities,* her book on how diverse activities and peoples were essential to urban life, became a classic among urban planners and even drew popular attention.[38] Jacobs's portrayal of her neighborhood focused on the myriad activities—barbershops, meat markets, bookshops—that were jumbled together in odd patterns, the vibrancy of street life, and the sociability of people as they traveled to and from work or wandered out for groceries.

Being forced to coexist, people grew tolerant of each other. The combination of diversity and tolerance, in turn, created a level of civility that made this and other urban neighborhoods places of "community." People knew each other or, at least, could distinguish between local residents and perfect strangers. They also helped one another. And they shared an identity as residents of Adams-Morgan or Beacon Hill or Pilsen. These were tightly knit neighborhoods, and they were relatively stable compared to the suburbs. They were also more or less racially and ethnically segregated, a factor that contributed to their strong sense of community.[39]

Segregation had not yet become a daunting public problem. On the race side, three dynamics operated. One was the general indifference of a predominately white society to the plight of African Americans. A second was the small scale of most minority neighborhoods, at least in the early postwar years. The third was the presence of a range of social classes in black neighborhoods. In short, the ghetto had yet to be crafted out of public housing and black migration from the South.[40] Educated and professional African American households still lived with their working- and lower-class counterparts. By choice and by necessity, their neighborhoods had a range of retail and personal services, and jobs were still plentiful both there and in the larger city. Consequently, racial segregation had less of a negative impact than it would after civil rights laws and integration enabled the black middle class to move away.[41]

In a similar vein, predominately ethnic—Italian, Irish, German, Chinese—working-class neighborhoods were also celebrated.[42] Ethnicity was the glue holding them together. Family connections and roots in the "old country" filtered people's local relationships, while ethnic-based socializing, foods, religious practices, and entertainment defined the local culture. Such neighborhoods functioned as the small towns that immigrants had left. After the postwar urban crisis had passed, they too, like small-town and rural America, became places that suburbanites romanticized.

What is important about this perspective on life in the cities is the emphasis on community, that is, the concern with the way people knew each other, provided support, constructed family networks in close proximity, and shared a common identity. The suburbs did not offer this, at least initially, and although friendships were formed, neighbors were invited for dinner on Saturday evening, and car pools and babysitting were arranged, none of this substituted for the ethnic homogeneity and generational ties that existed in the urban neighborhoods that had once repelled these suburbanites. The sharp distinctions of ethnic diversity were blurred in the suburbs by the relatively narrow range of incomes.

The city in the early postwar years also represented other ways of life, lifestyles at odds with the family-centered world of the suburbs.[43] One was bohemia. Mainly in big cities like San Francisco, New York, and Chicago, these areas were occupied by artists, musicians, novelists, poets, gays and lesbians, and numerous other escapees from the mainstream. Stereotypically, the bohemian lifestyle consisted of intermittent work, long hours spent talking in coffeehouses, and often a disdain for conformity and upward mobility, qualities that were incongruous with the suburbs. Such people were living against the grain of postwar prosperity and the mass consumption that it encouraged. Personal relations were more fluid, and life was less acquisitive. Accomplishment was valued, but never unequivocally celebrated.

Even more dominant as an image of the postwar city, supplanting the cohesive and relatively prosperous black and numerous white working-class neighborhoods, was the slum.[44] For many suburbanites, this was the city they had fled. Here were overcrowded tenements, noisy streets, and poor-quality goods and services. Slums offered too few opportunities to rise in status and income. For whites, they also symbolized the "old country" and an unhealthy inability to sever ties to the past.

The ghetto was an even more intimidating image of the city. As blacks migrated from the South, they found that many neighborhoods were closed to them. Manufacturing jobs were shrinking, and they

Figure 13. Shopping in downtown Providence, Rhode Island, 1967. Photograph by the author.

were exploited by corrupt landlords and real estate agents. The earlier stable black neighborhoods began to disintegrate. With public housing driving the forces of segregation, the "second" ghettos emerged. Here, lower-class and working-class blacks were segregated in neighborhoods without decent private or public services. Unemployment was high, poverty entrenched, and drugs and street crime common.[45]

As the 1960s unfolded, the civil rights movement spread and racial tensions (and even violence) became prevalent in the cities. The way people lived in ghettos became merged in the public imagination with the way people lived in cities generally.[46] Race filtered popular perceptions. In the city, one was either poor and dangerous or living a defensive life. (The many affluent households that remained in the cities, mostly in segregated enclaves, became imperceptible to the majority of observers.) At the peak of the urban crisis, the city elicited few regrets from those who had fled.

Just as this perception of the city is both historically specific and a distortion, the earlier image of communal, vibrant, and culturally cohesive central cities is also problematic. The city of the late 1940s and early 1950s existed on the cusp of postwar urban decline and the massive flight of white households. Downtowns were attracting investment, though not enough to overcome the spreading shabbiness or their inability to accommodate the automobile. Neighborhoods were overcrowded, struggling to break free from years of disinvestment. Racial tensions were on the rise, and city governments were unprepared to address the consequences of job loss, white flight, and racial transition. Some new housing was being built and some new stores were being opened, but they were too little and too late. These neighborhoods were no longer competitive with the newly built suburbs.

The view of the city as robust and viable during these early postwar years owes a good deal to nostalgia. Looking back after suburbanization had become the dominant way of life in the country, critics of the suburbs searched for an earlier time when consumption, individualism, and self-advancement were not as pronounced. Their search led them to the city of the 1950s and the lives people ostensibly led then. Rose-colored glasses were a necessity, especially when it came to looking at issues of racial harmony. What was found was less a fact of city life than an imagined community portrayed as a lost ideal.[47]

Later in this period of mass suburbanization and central-city decline, as parasitic urbanization receded and the city developed a new allure, the view of city life from the suburbs took another turn.[48] Having for years distanced themselves from the cities, many suburbanites began to write the city back into their history. As the early suburbanites aged, they developed an appreciation for the city's heritage and for the history of their parents. The community that once felt stifling now seemed vivid and supportive. The violence of the 1960s and the fiscal crisis of the mid-1970s had passed. Many of the older neighborhoods were experiencing gentrification, and the downtowns were beginning to be revived. A visit to the city seemed possible and even potentially pleasurable, though it would still be a few more years before actually living there became attractive to more than a few middle-class risk takers. This resurgence of the city, occurring after the short American Century had ended, was a further dilution of the urban way of life of the early twentieth century. In some respects, it was the suburbanization of the city.

Criticizing Suburbia

Although suburbanization was the choice of most upwardly mobile households, pundits and other intellectuals came to view the suburbs with a combination of alarm and distaste.[49] Their critiques took two forms: one aimed at the sterility, conformity, and isolation of suburban life, and the other (less critical than concerned), at the problems generated by rapid growth. Negative public commentary dominated the media; unmitigated praise was rare. People were moving to and living well in the suburbs, but most public commentators could not accept this. Such was the view from the metropolitan core.

Critics characterized the suburbs as a social and aesthetic wasteland.[50] They accused suburbanites of being conformists, "organization men" at the office and, at home, driven by a need to "keep up with the Jones's." Suburbanites were joiners and not mavericks. They lived in identical houses on identical streets, bought identical cars, and were surrounded by people of the same age, race, and income. This conformity had its roots in an emerging mass society in which people allowed their personalities to be homogenized, their individuality to be erased, and their actions to be dictated by advertisers or political demagogues (a concern whose origins were a still-vivid fascism and totalitarianism in the Soviet Union). In mass society, most virulent in the suburbs, people were atomized, alienated, depersonalized. Consequently, whatever sense of community people had was false. The suburbs were seen as weakening the real community that one had found, and still could be found, in the ethnic enclaves of the city. The kind of community produced by "the mass movement into suburban [areas]" after World War II "caricatured both the historic city and the archetypal suburban refuge" of the 1920s and late nineteenth century.[51]

The suburbs were bereft of cultural venues and activities of the mind and were molded by the leveling influence of television. Housewives and children were bored. "Quiet despair" quickly set in, particularly for women, along with incipient alcoholism and adultery. One of suburbia's most flamboyant critics described it as "a jail of the soul" and a "national failure." "Here is a place," he offered, "that lacks the advantages of both city and country, but retains the disadvantages of each."[52] Yet that same critic was nagged by the possibility that suburban life was not so bad and that, maybe, people were actually happy there. At the end of his article, he allowed a fictional suburbanite to retort: "What are you crabbing about? We never had it so good." But instead of taking this response seriously, he accused the speaker of being shallow and a moral failure.[53] While such a negative view was extreme even for these years, this and similar comments were much more common than public acclaim.

Eventually the critique of suburbia became more specialized and more influential. It turned to the life that women led as housewives. Socially isolated, bearing the bulk of the responsibility for the children and the home, blocked from using their college educations, and viewed as subordinate to their husbands, many women began to rebel.[54] Whether in the suburbs or in the cities, women were prevented from realizing their potential. A male-dominated society was holding them hostage to gender stereotypes and a single model of the "ideal" woman: the suburban housewife. Many women, of course, did find fulfillment as housewives and mothers, and many women engaged in a rich civic life or found employment. The feminist critique was not necessarily dismissive of or incompatible with their choices.

Conformity had its roots in mass consumption, which, in turn, drew its strength from widespread affluence and the numerous opportunities for upward mobility. Together, they bred anxiety. Critics noted the extent to which social striving and the "fear of falling" created personal neuroses as well as a political inwardness that kept suburbanites from compassion and empathy for the poor.[55] The suburbs created both a social and spiritual homelessness. Life, for example, could no longer be lived in one place, either socially or geographically. Families had to be on the move, acquiring and nurturing their status and scaling the corporate ladder. At the same time, affluence bred alienation and estrangement that, at least in popular novels, turned into self-pity. Beneath the surface, discontent was the prevailing mood.[56] Suburbia crystallized these social and psychological pressures and focused postwar critiques of American society.

Aesthetically, the suburbs were considered monotonous and banal.[57] In order to mass-produce affordable homes and make a profit doing so, developers made each lot identical and built only a few styles of houses for sale. Standardization was the key to lowering costs, and "cookie-cutter" design was a common term of derision. Moreover, so as to maximize the returns on investments, the goal for developers of most subdivisions was uniformity of design and saturation of the land. Only the most enlightened of developers interspersed public open space with home lots or built recreational facilities. The advantage for young families was affordability.

Even commentators who took a more balanced view could not resist pointing out that the suburbs had problems.[58] Most were related to growth. Municipalities had to be incorporated, governments elected, taxes collected, public services funded, and schools and infrastructure built. Developers were putting up homes faster than local governments could respond. Consequently, there were too few classrooms, the roads were congested, parks and playgrounds lagged behind need, and taxes were on the rise. Suburbanites would eventually manage, but in the early years the mass-produced character of the suburbs and the pangs of growth provided ample ammunition for critics.

Very few commentators came to the defense of the suburbs. Noting the "national endorsement" of suburbanization, a writer in a 1959 issue of *Commonweal* praised the fact that people could now avoid the cities. He rejected a short-term perspective that focused on the suburb's problems and called instead for a longer view of them as a "healthy corrective" to urban life. We should not expect the suburbs to be perfect or to redeem us from urban and technological influences, he argued. Rather, we should recognize that a new American landscape and national character were in the process of "becoming."[59]

Phyllis McGinley, a resident of a commuter town just east of New York City, offered a less resigned defense. She bemoaned the fact that suburbia had become a symbol of all that was wrong with the middle class—the consumerism, smugness, and mediocrity. McGinley declared: "I like it." She praised her yard and home, the freedom from the city's noise, and the lack of soot on the windowsills. Her neighbors were involved in numerous social and civic activities and were interesting to her. The schools were excellent, as were trash collection and the water supply, even though taxes were a bit high. Better designed than the city, her commuter town was also "planned for the happiness of children." Some day, she mused, people might well look back on these suburbs with nostalgia and respect. "In a world of terrible outcomes, it will stand out as the safe, important medium."[60]

Where the suburbs were treated uncritically was in advertising and on television. Advertisers celebrated mass consumption and used family life and status anxieties to sell automobiles, dishwashers, and life insurance. More generally, the goal was to sell suburban living in order to maintain the never-ending cycle of consumption. One contemporary commentator remarked that "never before had the power of the media been used so significantly in the creation of a new definition of family life."[61] Television was another friendly arena. Family-oriented situation comedies such as *Ozzie and Harriet* and *Leave It to Beaver* portrayed suburban living in a positive light while emphasizing what later came to be called family values. *The Life of Riley* was a blue-collar rather than a middle-class offering that, like its competitors, presented suburban living without the dark side uncovered by intellectuals and novelists. And in the early postwar years, television still offered analogous shows about city living. *The Honeymooners*—a comedy about working-class and childless couples living in Brooklyn—became a classic of the genre.[62]

Large numbers of people moved to suburbia. Yet it was unacceptable in intellectual circles to find these places attractive. Anything so associated with consumerism, the expanding (and leveling) middle class, and mass production could not be anything but inherently suspect. A small minority of the population resisted and derided what a large majority enthusiastically embraced. Was this simply disappointment that the American ideal, once again, had failed to materialize? Or was it the snobbishness of city-based intellectuals?

The romanticism and nostalgia of the criticism was hard to ignore. Commentators had waited nearly two decades for the country to return to prosperity and to bring back the vibrancy and excitement of the 1920s. In that decade, urbanism had thrived as a way of life. Construction and hedonism soared. People had fun. By the late 1950s, it was clear that all that would be dashed against the hard surface of reality. Industrial cities were in decline, men and women were intent on careers and families, and suburbs mushroomed across the landscape. At a time when the national government had embraced Keynesian prescriptions for managing the economy and the social sciences were overflowing with ideas and methods for shaping society's destiny, here was a society hell-bent on being average.

Elitism was essential to these critiques. American individualism, it seemed, was dissolving in mass consumerism and tract housing projects of endless banality. This being the height of the Cold War, the political Left was under scrutiny by the government and under attack from the anticommunists. Intellectuals were suspect, particularly in light of a heightened appreciation of American technical know-how and innate common sense. The beatniks rebelled but pulled few of the "drones" into their camp (not that they proselytized heavily). No self-respecting intellectual, artist, or iconoclast would live in the suburbs.

So public commentators resisted. Their resistance was not so much an attempt to return the country to an urban way of life as to keep alive their image of what cities could have been. In an important sense, their disdain for the suburban lifestyle was a profound disappointment that America had once again fallen short in its quest for urbanity. The American Dream was too broadly American and too concrete for city-nurtured intellectuals. Where were the country's ideals?

Toward a Dominant Lifestyle

Critics could bemoan the sterility and conformity of suburbia; they could not roll back its advance. More and more people were revealing their preferences by moving to a single-family house on the urban fringe. Fewer and fewer people were opting for the older, industrial cities. And while an argument could be made that such preferences were hardly innate, distorted as they were by advertising and by the limited choices made available to consumers, nevertheless, the claim that "people moved to the suburbs because it was their best financial option" is too narrow a characterization.[63] The suburbs had much to offer as well. Nor is it accurate to proclaim the "suburbanization of everything."[64] The era of the large, industrial city of high densities, vibrant street life, and mass transit seemed to have passed. Yet these cities did not disappear. As one of the celebrants of the early postwar city wrote, "If America reached its peak as an urban civilization in the 1950s, it has since become a quintessential suburban one—*even in its cities.*"[65]

Suburbanization was both a shift in where people lived and a change in the country's dominant way of life. Energized by the prosperity of the times and carried along by new patterns of consumption, the suburban lifestyle spread throughout the country. "Americans in the postwar years saw the prospect of affluence and respectability, the opportunity embodied in the suburban ideal, as a birthright."[66] By the late 1970s, most people resided in suburban communities. There, they lived the American Dream and enjoyed the good life unhampered by the chaos and frictions on which cities thrive. "First the city made the middle class possible," one commentator has noted, "and then it made them want to move away."[67] The dense, industrial cities no longer served as the destination for the upwardly mobile. A suburb would do.

The dominant American way of life came to be rooted in and crafted around the suburbs. "Whereas once work and family had dictated residence, now increasingly consumption—of homes, goods, services, and leisure—did."[68] Neither the style of consumption nor the ways of suburban life were confined there, however. And by the end of the short American Century many people still lived in an "urban" fashion, though now much diluted. Most people, though, did not.

This profound change in the dominant American lifestyle and identity was not only a matter of the physical configuration of the places of work, home, and leisure. It was more deeply embedded in and emergent from the social relations spawned by these changes. It was widely believed that "the postwar suburb was producing a new kind of American." Suburban ideals, "nearly two hundred years in the making," became widespread.[69] Ironically, one could be suburban without living in the suburbs.

Of course, while the suburbs were physically open—spaces between houses, backyards open to view, the boundaries between lawns indistinct, the streets ungated—they were not socially open. The identity being formed was a white identity. It was also one that dissolved ethnic differences. In the metropolitan periphery, distinctions of class and status took their place. Consequently, the suburbs were both democratic and racially exclusive. The leveling that mass consumption and mass suburbanization promised had its limits. Many—black, poor, unmarried—were left outside.

This confluence of domestic prosperity, economic growth, and suburbanization eventually became a powerful weapon in fighting the Cold War. Like parasitic urbanization and the country's postwar domestic prosperity, the suburban way of life was globally dimensioned. It drew strength from the growth generated by exports and a strong U.S. dollar and served as a sign of American accomplishment, values, and economic prowess. To this extent, the suburbs and the cities were politicized; they entered into a Cold War ideology that championed the country's international dominance.

7

America's Global Project

Not only was the suburban way of life essential to America's post-war prosperity, it also contributed to the crafting of America's global dominance. Suburbia's consumer-based lifestyle epitomized the freedom and prosperity that figured prominently in the ideological construction of the United States as an international power. The urban way of life held much less appeal. Cities were vulnerable to atomic-bomb attack, conjured up images of socialistic public housing, and harbored cells of communist subversion. The spreading slums and growing numbers of poor African American families combined with the seediness of industrial and commercial districts to lower cities' propaganda value even further. By contrast, the suburbs figured prominently in U.S. global projections that were designed to create a "better world abroad and a happier society at home."[1] One consequence was to further entrench the parasitic urbanization that was undermining the industrial cities.

The global dominance of the United States after World War II, a dominance that remained intact until the mid-1970s, was not about subjugation or territory. Neither colonialism nor expansion was the goal. Rather, the United States hoped to establish itself at the center of an international economy based on free trade. It would occupy the position of world political leader with distinction, and it would spread democracy and publicize the American way of life. "More than ever before—or since—Americans came to believe that they could shape the international scene in their own image."[2] The key was the casting of the country as a model to be emulated. Desire rather than fear would drive global dominance, with the United States portrayed as a place of freedom, democracy, and economic opportunity. To achieve legitimate status in the eyes of the world, the nation needed to ground its values in a distinctively American way of life. The suburbs were the solution. They stood for achievement at home—the realization of the American Dream—and American exceptionalism in the world.

Manufacturing had elevated the United States to the commanding heights it enjoyed in the postwar era. Industrial prowess enabled the country to triumph in foreign wars while reaping the benefits of economic growth at home. Yet when the postwar era began, the industrial cities were in poor shape, rundown and increasingly abandoned by factory owners and well-to-do, mostly white households. Heavy manufacturing eventually collapsed, and light manufacturing moved to the suburbs along with even more white families, retail stores, and, later, office activities. With African Americans flowing to the inner cities and with slums more and more the dominant image of urban life, the industrial cities were unworthy of foreign envy. How could the country's industrial cities—polluted, shabby, and chaotic—ever compare with such capitals of Europe as Paris, Madrid, and Amsterdam or compete with the history and civilization they embodied?[3]

The industrial cities were additionally tainted by America's racial dilemma. African American ghettos and entrenched poverty anchored the stigma of urban decline and eliminated the older cities as candidates for international publicity. In addition, contemporary African Americans brought forth memories of slavery, the Civil War, and the decades of institutionalized discrimination that had followed emancipation. During the Cold War, Soviet propaganda "delighted in publicizing news of American racial discrimination and persecution."[4] Racial inequity was the country's shame, and it was not easily dissociated from the large, industrial cities.

In 1954, the editors of a national magazine commented on the spreading slums of Washington, D.C. Their ruminations led them to the intersection of urban decay, race, and Cold War ideology. After noting the lack of heat, lights, and toilets in the homes and the overabundance of rats, the editors noted that "a favorite Communist propaganda picture shows some dirty Negro kids playing in a yard of garbage against a backdrop of the sharply focused Capitol dome."[5] Such irony, visual or otherwise, made Americans uncomfortable. Their vision of the nation was one of prosperity, freedom, and tolerance, and it was this vision that they hoped to project to the rest of the world.

Another commentator, trading on the prevailing Cold War vocabulary of the 1950s, asked whether cities were not, in fact, un-American.[6]

His question was more rhetorical than substantive, and his article turned away from the implied ideological point to the flight of people from the cities and the cities' deepening extremes of wealth and poverty. The Jeffersonian concern with cities and democracy was left unaddressed. Still, the allusion should not be summarily dismissed. Here was the power of the Cold War rhetoric on display, along with a hint of its potential use against the cities.

Seen in this light, the designation of "All-American" cities by *Look* magazine during these years takes on new meaning.[7] These cities were selected for their efforts at civic improvement "in the public interest." The awards were not meant to be political; they were simply meant to recognize places where people (Americans) had created prosperous, pleasant, and stable communities. Nevertheless, inherent to the awards was an ideological message. Implicitly, they counteracted the ascendance of mass-produced suburbs and the decline associated with the industrial cities. These "All American" cities were often small towns such as Clarksburg, West Virginia, and Neosho, Missouri. The label itself linked cities with patriotism. In this period, to be American was to be fervently nationalistic and staunchly anticommunist.

With the racial disturbances of the 1960s, race, cities, and communism were once again joined in a symbolic triumvirate. South Carolina's U.S. senator Strom Thurmond, an archconservative and anticommunist, coupled the riots with "Communism, false compassion, civil disobedience, court decisions and criminal instinct."[8] With the exception of the communist accusation, this was the conservative critique of the city that was standard during these early postwar years.

Only a minority of observers of the city, though, blamed communists for Negro unrest. U.S. attorney general Nicholas Katzenback, for example, pointedly noted in 1966 that the riots "were indeed fomented by agitators, agitators named disease and despair, joblessness and hopelessness, rat-infested housing and long-impacted cynicism." The National Commission on Civil Disorders, set up to explain the causes of the riots, found no evidence of any organized or international influence. Still, the symbolic combination of urban decay and the oppression of African Americans was enough to eliminate city living as a candidate for the American Dream.[9]

The suburban way of life was ideologically and substantively "clean" and uniquely American. No other country engaged in mass suburbanization. Some—for example, Sweden and England—had "new towns" that were basically suburbs, but none had Levittowns. In turn, the suburbs represented freedom of choice in the market, including the freedom to live wherever one wanted. Suburbs were all about consumption and prosperity. Consequently, other countries—having to rebuild after the war, facing shortages of goods (including housing), and having experienced, often firsthand, totalitarian or fascist regimes—were enticed by the affluence and democracy that the United States and its suburbs represented. "The transformation of American society [became] an integral part of the continuing transformation of the global economy."[10]

That Japan and the countries of western and eastern Europe rebuilt their cities after the war in ways the United States failed to do in no way implies that their citizens were immune to the allure of the American suburbs or to American-style consumerism. Many of these countries established significant welfare states—exceeding social provisions in the United States—to protect their citizens from the uncertainties and insecurities of markets. This did not preclude a desire for individual homes and automobiles, supermarkets, televisions, and the other accoutrements that were associated with American suburban living. Convincing them of the legitimacy of their desires and helping them to act accordingly was a central objective of American's postwar global dominance.

This linking of cities and suburbs with the short American Century was hardly an ideological imperative. Neither did it appear as an explicit and monolithic argument. Rather, the touting of the suburban way of life and the symbolic abandonment of the cities was woven into a variety of debates about how the United States should position itself in the world. From fear of the atomic bomb, which gave rise to a call for the decentralization of cities, to U.S. Cold War propaganda, cultural exchanges, foreign aid, and congressional debates concerning the provision of low-income housing, the project of global dominance embodied a need to hide, if not to abandon, the industrial cities.

The Cities and the Cold War

In August 1945, the United States destroyed two enemy cities. Hiroshima and Nagasaki were reduced to rubble not by saturation bombing, as had been the fate of German cities, but with atomic bombs. Suddenly, the destructive power of these weapons, and the ostensibly peaceful use of the atom for energy and health care, became part of the American psyche. Although the Soviet Union, the former World War II ally turned Cold War foe, did not develop the atomic bomb until 1949, from 1945 until the early 1960s, Americans fretted about the possibility that an enemy, especially the Soviets, would launch an atomic attack on American cities. The purported consequence was daunting: near-total destruction. "The reality of the bomb, and the stark images of devastated American cities that it evoked, did for many Americans what two grinding wars had done for [the Europeans and the Japanese]." Consequently, at the top of the public policy agenda was the need to address the vulnerability of urban areas and the questionable likelihood of "urban survival in the nuclear age."[11]

If such an attack were to occur, cities, particularly industrial cities, would be prime targets. Military strategists noted the importance to an enemy of undermining the ability of the United States to produce war materiel, mobilize defensive forces, communicate, and keep the economy functioning. Such key industries as steel, motor vehicles, and airplane assembly were high-priority targets, and the cities in which they were concentrated—Pittsburgh, Detroit, Seattle, Los Angeles—were correspondingly at risk. San Francisco, Chicago, New York, and Boston, with their corporate headquarters and their banking and communication functions, were also high on the agenda of likely first targets. Military installations and ports (for example, the submarine base in Groton, Connecticut) could count on being struck during the first wave of bombs. Washington, D.C., was especially vulnerable. The federal government estimated that at least 140 cities could be potential targets. In a statement typical of the paranoia of the times, one popular magazine noted that "cities are pretty much defenseless and their populations are naked under the enemy."[12]

Dropping an atomic bomb on these cities would result in massive casualties and near-total destruction of vast areas, particularly at ground zero, the location one-half mile below the point at which a bomb would be detonated. Scientists and reporters described this destruction to the American public in graphic detail and frequently. For a distance of up to three-quarters of a mile from ground zero, buildings, bridges, and roadways would be reduced to rubble, and everyone there would either be instantly killed or would soon die from lethal radiation. For another two miles, heavy damage and high levels of casualties would be the norm. From there and for the next few miles, the destruction would be only serious, though people would still receive heavy doses of radiation and most of them would die within a short time. Fires would rage throughout the city. Water and power supplies would be heavily damaged and probably made inoperative. Mass transit systems would be disabled and most major highways destroyed.

Those still alive, the scenarios went on, would flee in panic. With roadways destroyed or clogged and mass transit shut down, people would be unable to escape in any organized way. Emergency medical, police, and fire services would be mobilized, but the loss of life among these personnel and the breakdown of communication systems would severely hamper any assistance that they might be able to provide. The injured, untreated for the most part, would die painful deaths. One scenario, with ground zero over Union Square in Manhattan, predicted 150,000 dead and dying just after the bomb exploded and offered the opinion that "in Central Park, ditches would be bulldozed for mass burial of the dead."[13]

The United States had never been so exposed to a foreign enemy. Geography alone had provided security. Oceans separated it from Asia and Europe while Canada to the north and Mexico to the south were friendly neighbors with insignificant militaries and small economies dependent on the United States. Now, however, long-range bombers, intercontinental ballistic missiles, and atomic bombs made the country's physical barriers much easier to breach.

The federal government responded with a variety of initiatives. Just after the war, the United States had managed to isolate the Soviet Union from Allied sharing of the knowledge needed to build an atomic bomb. The policy was to contain the proliferation of production capabilities, institute international controls over production and testing, and maintain aircraft and missile superiority. Missiles would intercept enemy bombers as they approached, and large bombers would be used to retaliate after an attack. Later, missiles became the delivery vehicle of choice for nuclear weapons. In fact, the U.S. government continued to make atomic bombs and went on to develop the hydrogen bomb. Stockpiling, moreover, was essential to a strategic posture of massive retaliation. It was meant to be a deterrent. Many believed that the presence of large numbers of bombs alone would discourage aggressors.

The defense against atomic attack also included the establishment of a complex early-warning radar system that would facilitate interception of incoming bombers. It would provide time for people to evacuate the cities or seek shelter there. To this end, the federal government set the Federal Civil Defense Administration the task of planning for an enemy assault. Its job was to identify emergency resources, develop plans for coordinating personnel, and provide for civil-defense shelters in public buildings and spaces. Individuals were encouraged to build personal fallout shelters to house their families. Protected from the initial blast and subsequent fallout of radiation, they would stay in the shelters until emergency personnel had brought the situation under control. After that, however, they would probably "wander helplessly through a useless city."[14]

Fear and anxiety were widespread and were exacerbated by civil-defense preparations, which included having schoolchildren participate in air-raid drills that required them to hide under their desks for protection. At the height of the Cold War in the early 1960s, requests for the U.S. Department of Defense's thirty-two-page pamphlet *The Family Fallout Shelter* went from 260,000 copies per month to 600,000 copies, and the Bendix Corporation experienced a jump in sales of its "Family Radiation Kit" to be used to detect nuclear radiation. The home became a "bulwark against the dangers of the atomic age."[15]

Home fallout shelters posed an interesting moral issue.[16] Individual households were expected to build shelters where possible. This occurred, as might be expected, mainly outside the cities. The government would provide public shelters in the cities. One common ethical scenario involved the dilemma posed to the shelter-rich when confronted with the shelter-poor on their doorstep. Would space, purified air, and food supplies last if the shelter-poor were accommodated? More specifically, would suburban households with shelters be willing to admit to safety the hordes fleeing a bombed city?

One solution was obvious: encourage individuals to live outside the cities and businesses to invest away from the enemy's primary targets. Not everyone, however, could move far from where jobs were located or could purchase the fifteen-acre estate just outside Saratoga, New York, that was advertised in the *Wall Street Journal* as having "good bomb immunity." And businesses still needed to draw their workforces from relatively nearby.[17]

The more encompassing solution, one that would provide affordable housing and place workers near jobs, would be for the government to disperse the cities. This solution resonated with incipient suburbanization, the trend to lower densities, and the emergence of smaller cities embedded in multicentered metropolitan areas. Moreover, it built upon a policy of decentralization that had been managed during World War II by the federal government's War Production Board. "Space is our ally," claimed one observer, who further pointed out that cities like New York and Chicago were too vulnerable to be allowed to persist: "In an Atomic Age, no nation can afford to present such a perfect target to an enemy."[18]

A number of city planners proposed that "successful protection" could be achieved by gradually dispersing population and industry to new satellite communities in the periphery of the large central cities.

The satellites would be located twenty to twenty-five miles from the urban core and would be spaced equidistant from each other, thereby making a single bomb less effective in destroying industrial, corporate, and commercial functions and in killing a large percent of the population. In order to further diminish the damage, these peripheral cities would be located upwind from radioactive fallout. Back in the central city, neighborhoods would be ringed by parklike strips containing highways and railroad lines. These buffer zones would block the spread of fires, isolate transportation links from other potential targets, and serve as safe areas after the attack.[19]

In addition to lowering densities and creating buffer zones, planners also called for zoning by function (for example, secluding factories and separating industrial from residential areas) and for building housing in parklike settings on lots no smaller than two acres. No more skyscrapers would be built. Rather, office functions would be placed in low-rise, two-story buildings. Retail shops and stores would be encouraged to move to drive-in locations in commercial strips along highways.[20]

Many with an interest in urban development pointed out that the atomic bomb would provide another reason for doing what needed to be done, that is, improving the lives of people by releasing them from congested cities. One commentator wrote that "the decentralization of our cities on the spots on which they stand, plus the release of our whole communication system from the threat of a disastrous tie-up, are reforms which are long overdue, war or no war."[21] This attitude was pervasive; it was not just the atomic bomb that compelled dispersal of the large, industrial cities but also the failure of these cities to continue to prosper. For those who considered the atomic bomb a threat, the bomb was an excuse to decentralize the cities and lower densities.[22]

A report by the Population Research Bureau in 1953 noted that people were still migrating to the cities "at a time when atomic-hydrogen warfare could blow our cities to bits."[23] Urban growth was seen as increasingly unhealthy, and the threat of nuclear attack was viewed as an opportunity to place more people in "semi-rural life on the urban periphery." The result would be a much better balance between the city and the country and better living conditions for all.[24] With people living in semi-independent communities of 30,000 to 50,000 residents clustered around an urban center and with each of those satellite communities surrounded by open space, they would be less vulnerable to attack. And they would live in a healthier environment.

Easing this way of thinking was the discovery that the optimum size of a city could be calculated from the destructive capacity and strategic intent of the enemy. It was estimated that an atomic bomb would cause instant death to 90 percent of the people within a half mile of ground zero, 50 percent of those between one-half and one mile away, 15 percent of the people from one to one and one-half miles away, and 3 percent of those from there to two miles distant. If the enemy's goal was to kill 5,000 people instantly, then a city with a density of 1,893 people per square mile would be safe. Within a two-mile radius, the requisite population would not exist and, therefore, an attack would not yield the deaths that were strategically required. The city would not become a target.[25] A city with this density and whose population was spread evenly up to two miles around the central business district thus could have a total population of 24,000 people and remain immune to attack. At three miles in radius, it could grow to 53,000 people. That these calculations depended on a rapidly changing and often-secret technology, on a deliberately obscured (but nonetheless assumed) strategic intent, and on the belief in the inherent rationality of one's enemy makes them highly suspect.[26]

Proposing to respond to the threat of atomic bomb attack by dispersing the industrial cities is nothing if not an endorsement of suburbanization and a foreshadowing of the rise of edge cities in the 1980s. The atomic bomb extended an antiurban ideology whose roots stretch back to well before nuclear physics embarked on the "taming" of the atom and the creation of fission. In short, "civil defense plans . . . suggested a particular atomic age rationale for the American retreat to the suburbs."[27] Providing reinforcement for this perspective were the debates around the establishment of a national highway system and public housing. They too drew on anxiety about foreign attacks and national defense.

The federal policy that created the interstate highway system was titled the National Interstate and Defense Highway Act of 1956. It had been preceded by the Defense Highway Act of 1941.[28] The latter had designated certain highways for the movement of troops, war materiel, and supplies and had emphasized constructing roads to military installations. The former had as one of its goals, albeit a minor one, the creation of a road system that would enable military personnel and equipment to be moved quickly to points of attack on the continent's coastal borders. Whereas the large size of the United States made it possible to disperse population to thwart nuclear attack and mute its consequences, that same size made it awkward for the military to provide protection against an enemy invasion.

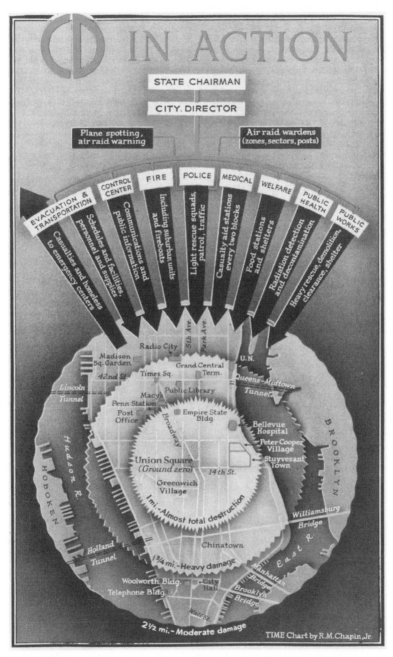

Figure 14. Preparing for an atomic-bomb attack, New York City, 1950. From
"The City under the Bomb," Time, October 2, 1950, 13.

In an era of long-range aircraft and, later, intercontinental ballistic missiles, moving troops and equipment along highways was not the most efficient way to counter the initial attack, even though it was important for repelling a subsequent invasion. Military leadership and in particular President Dwight D. Eisenhower, a former army commander, were concerned about the difficulties the current road system posed to troop movements. In fact, President Eisenhower named General Lucius D. Clay, former American military governor of occupying forces in Berlin during the onset of the Cold War, to head his Advisory Committee on a National Highway Program.

The dearth of limited-access highways linking cities to each other, the quality of the interurban and interstate roads that did exist, and the ability of these highways to accommodate large military equipment—in terms of both the width of the roads and the height of bridges and tunnels—were all at issue. Consequently, the 1956 interstate highway act contained guidelines that standardized the quality of road construction and designated the width of lanes and the clearances underneath crossover bridges. Although the military did not always adhere to these standards by controlling the size of its equipment, the intent was there. More importantly, the national defense goal was crucial for changing the funding formula from 50:50, with the federal government and state governments sharing the costs equally, to a 75:25 federal-to-state ratio.[29] This made the program even more enticing to the states and helped to assure construction of interstate highways across the land.

Congress liked the idea that high-speed, limited-access, divided highways could be used to evacuate the cities in case of an atomic-bomb attack. The highways would enhance civil-defense preparedness. With prior warning, people would be able, quickly and safely, to drive their automobiles or take buses away from the central cities. After the attack, emergency fire and medical personnel would be moved efficiently into the cities from the surrounding suburbs.

In effect, the highway system that contributed to mass suburbanization after World War II was made possible, in no small part, by a rationale that linked highways to the possibility of foreign invasion and the need for national defense. Further strengthening the rationale was the specific threat of an atomic-bomb attack and the commonsensical notion that dispersing people, business, and industry would not just make a concerted attack harder but also diminish the destruction that an attack might cause. Of course, the decline of the industrial cities and the spread of low-density development hardly needed these arguments to come to fruition. As one commentator wrote, a "new world order" might well save the country's cities from atomic bombing, but it would not save them from decay.[30]

Simultaneously, the federal government was working with local governments to address the problems of the cities, even as it was funding civil-defense activities, highway construction, and mortgage-insurance programs that shrank them. One of the programs aimed at reversing urban decline was public housing.

Unlike urban renewal, which subsidized private-sector real estate investment, public housing was enveloped in both Republican distaste for the New Deal programs of the Democrats and the real estate industry's interest in protecting its prerogatives. Consequently, both Republicans and real estate people opposed public housing. To press their case, public housing's critics took up the banner of anticommunism. For some, public housing was the first step along the path to socialism and would bring about the demise of free enterprise. For others, public housing projects were a threat because subversives supposedly thrived in them. "Suspiciousness about Communist evil had been internalized and [it] generated widespread" anxiety, not the least of which was fear about the erosion of property rights.[31]

At the end of World War II, the United States faced "the worst housing crisis in [its] history."[32] Demand was projected at 1.5 million new units each year from the late 1940s to 1960, but the private sector had produced only half that in 1947. Moreover, private developers and investors invariably targeted the top of the market, whereas the need was for housing for low-income households. While middle-income households could purchase new homes in the suburbs, low-income households (including many African American migrants from the South) were confined to the city—and were desperate.

The real estate and home-building industry was embarrassed. Frequent mention of the housing shortage and the possibility of government intervention lessened its prestige and posed the threat of interference by the public sector. Developers and their bankers responded with tract housing in the suburbs and apartment buildings in the cities; however, neither was sufficient to meet demand. Overcrowding persisted in the metropolitan cores. Despite this, the real estate industry attempted to defeat the bill proposed in 1947 to expand the Housing Act of 1937.[33]

The main line of attack was a defense of the free-enterprise system that emphasized freedom of choice. One official of the National Association of Real Estate Boards claimed that one could "trace back the history of every country that's gone Communistic or Socialistic, and it all started with public housing."[34] The enemy of capitalism was socialism. Socialism involved public ownership rather than private property, and it meant not just government control over business but also government takeover of the housing industry. Private businesses were eager to accept government subsidies (for example, the assistance provided by FHA mortgage insurance); they were opposed to the government as a producer of housing. Public housing was seen to be insidious and the "cutting edge of the Communist front."[35]

Home ownership was considered a bulwark against socialism. As the suburban developer Levitt put it: "No man who owns his own house and lot can be a communist. He has too much to do."[36] Being committed to a home and to private property rights would make people responsible and less likely to work against the system that provided these opportunities. Ostensibly, home ownership brought people into the political mainstream.

The real estate industry found a champion in U.S. senator from Wisconsin Joseph McCarthy, a relatively new senator whose name would later become an "ism"—McCarthyism—and synonymous with anticommunism, intimidation, and demagoguery. McCarthy saw an opportunity to use public housing as a tool to attack the Democrats, weaken the legacy of the New Deal, and establish a reputation as a foe of communism. In 1947, he engineered the creation of a joint congressional committee designed to hold hearings on the proposed public housing legislation; he maneuvered to place himself in charge. Hearings were held in thirty-three cities, and nearly 1,300 carefully chosen witnesses testified, most of them unsurprisingly opposed to public housing.

McCarthy's attack was two-pronged: first, to convince people that public housing did not really help the poor but instead was allocated to friends of the Democrats who governed the cities, and second, to link it with communism. (Private housing, on the other hand, was essential to democracy.) McCarthy believed that public housing projects "menaced the republic" and were deliberately created slums that became "breeding ground(s) for communists." Throughout the hearings, McCarthy labeled public housing a "socialist danger."[37] Nevertheless, he was unable to derail the legislation, and the bill eventually became the famed Housing Act of 1949 that promised a decent home and living environment to all Americans.[38]

Ironically, the supporters of public housing also drew on the fears associated with communism. President Harry Truman argued that "there is nothing more un-American than a slum. How can we expect to sell democracy to Europe until we prove that within the democratic system we can provide decent homes for our people?" The housing expert Nathan Strauss agreed. When the government provides healthful, livable, low-rent homes and eliminates slums, he wrote, it "cuts the ground from under the Communists."[39] For both opponents and proponents, the threat of communism, whether external or internal, was pertinent to the debate. At the same time, proponents of public housing and urban renewal were also motivated by the desire to project a positive global image, one that presented the United States as accomplished and compassionate.

In the end, accusations of communist conspiracy and claims that public housing would open the door to socialism delayed but did not defeat the legislation. The real estate industry subsequently turned its attention to convincing state and local governments to reject public housing. Earlier legislation had limited the number of new public housing units in any city to the number of dwellings demolished as part of slum clearance. This one-to-one rule meant that the supply of homes would not increase and the government would not compete with the private sector. Providing public housing only to those with the lowest of incomes further protected the prerogatives of the home-building industry, since it was generally not interested in building homes in a price range that low-income households could afford. Needless to say, anxiety about a nascent socialism and fears of a communist menace were unfounded. Except for small minorities, the citizens of the United States found neither socialism nor communism to their liking. As for the national government, it was equally, perhaps more, obsessed with disseminating the American way of life across the globe.

Exporting the Suburban Dream

The suburbs were not immune to anxieties about nuclear attack and communist infiltration. "Civil defense plans . . . suggested a particular atomic age rationale for the American retreat to the suburbs, and such plans helped to taint the otherwise innocent and safe quality of life" there.[40] Planners and others framed the dispersal of the cities as a way to minimize the risk of and damages from an atomic-bomb attack and as inherently desirable because of the low-density living it offered. These rhetorical moves still left intact the possibility of widespread and unpredictable death and destruction. Given the tendency of radioactive fallout to drift with the winds across city boundaries and given the hordes of city dwellers fleeing the city after an attack, the suburbs were still vulnerable.

Elaine Tyler May, a cultural historian, positioned suburban growth within this postwar anxiety.[41] During the first half of the short American Century, marriage rates and birthrates were higher and divorce rates were lower than they had been in the previous generation and would be in the subsequent one. Moreover, the women of this era embraced traditional gender roles, with many of them staying home to raise children. The parents of the baby boomers were unlike their parents and unlike their children. The children married later, had fewer offspring, divorced more frequently, and joined the ranks of postwar feminist and gay social movements. They also fueled the first round of gentrification in the cities in the late 1970s and 1980s.

What explains the anomaly—the commitment to family and domestic tranquility—of this postwar generation of suburbanites? These households were more prosperous than their predecessors, but prosperity has always been associated with marrying later and having fewer children and commonly makes the breakup of families easier. None of this occurred. The answer, May offered, lies with the larger political culture—the domestic ideology—in which the postwar suburban family was situated. Forming a buffer between the family and the anxieties of the atomic bomb, McCarthyism, and communist subversion was a family-centered culture that was relatively isolated in the suburbs. This domestic ideology was a haven from these disturbing eventualities. With the parents protecting the children, defending the hearth, and providing for all needs, suburbanites were safe in the nuclear family.

Adding to their sense of security was the suburban home. It was surrounded by its moat of grass and set in a residential area in which all other families were racially and economically alike; foreign influences were absent. Suburban families were also far from the cities on which postwar anxieties were focused. In addition, their homes were self-contained. The mother could do the washing, prepare meals, and entertain without having to leave the nest. Her children could amuse themselves watching television or, when the outside beckoned, play on the backyard swing set or swim in the family pool. Near at hand, ever ready, was the family automobile, in case a flight from danger became necessary.

When the father returned from a day at work, he would be greeted by his wife and children and reassured that even if he had to go into the world and be exposed to its threats, a place existed where being safe and cared for was assured. His family was even protected from the world of corporate growth and organizational loyalties where promotions often meant relocations. With a suburb on the fringe of Atlanta hardly different from one outside Boston, and with his family and home life stable, the rootlessness of social mobility was diminished. There were costs, but in the suburbs the postwar family's "deepest wish to build a warm hearth against the cold war" was realized.[42]

One group denied this option was homosexuals.[43] In the 1950s, gays and lesbians were just beginning to develop collective identities and view themselves as oppressed minorities. As they crafted communities in the cities, they came under attack by anticommunists for the corrosive impact their sexual practices had on others and for the security risk they posed. (Homosexuals were deemed more susceptible to blackmail than heterosexuals, an implicit comment on their double-victimization.) Homosexuality was also perceived as a threat to marriage and motherhood, and the "feminization" of gay men was seen as eroding the masculine vigor that might be used to resist communism. Gays and lesbians, though, were not present in the suburbs, at least in any numbers—or visibly. Rather, they resided mainly in the cities. Homosexuals amplified the city's subversive reputation, and this further extended the symbolic distance between suburbs and the declining urban cores. Here was another issue to add to the woes of the industrial cities.

It was not just homosexuals who threatened peace and security. Many family professionals were concerned that the anxieties of the age would lead to promiscuity by heterosexuals. Premarital sex was particularly feared. Sexual chaos would hinder reproduction and deprive the country of the children needed to keep the country strong. Those holding this view encouraged early marriage and traditional gender roles. They also offered courtship advice that warned against sexual intercourse prior to marriage. At a time of national insecurity, sexual freedom was unacceptable.[44]

The family and suburbs, though, were not simply retreats from an ominous world; they were also points of pride and celebration. They were at the center of the postwar American Dream. By contrast, the postwar discussion of America's global aspirations excluded the industrial cities from this rosy view of American life. They were liabilities: They were vulnerable to attack, they hid communist sympathizers, and they were the origin of arguments meant to transform the country from a capitalist democracy to a democratic (possibly, even, undemocratic) socialism. To put it bluntly: "Cosmopolitan urban culture represented a threat to national security."[45] By contrast, the suburbs were essential to the postwar American Dream, and that dream was a significant element in the country's global aspirations. The suburban way of life crystallized Americans' sense of themselves as capable, prosperous, and free. The "perfectionist impulse . . . [that] swept through postwar American society" had to be shared with the world.[46]

Since the rumors of the New World first spread amongst the courts of the European powers in the fifteenth century, the Americas have been a coveted place. Early explorers came for fame and fortunes, early colonists for religious and political freedom. With its vast geography and ever-expanding economy, the United States came to be perceived as a land of possibilities, elevating hopes and attracting waves of immigrants. The roots of the American Dream extend to other lands, its imagery fueled as much by alien aspirations as by homebred accomplishments.

These hopes represent a host of revered values: independence, freedom of choice and mobility, tolerance, democratic institutions, and free enterprise.[47] Consumption and social mobility, moreover, vie for equal status with political and cultural freedom. People once migrated to America because they thought that the streets were paved with gold; they came because economic opportunities were greater here than there. Once here, they wanted to experience that dream: start families, earn a fair wage, and live well. Through the years, the dream took on different colorations. In the early postwar period, it involved a college education, home ownership, a secure job with a large corporation, and a comfortable life that combined work and leisure with the nuclear family. With productivity on the rise, the economy growing, and incomes increasing, realizing that dream, at least for white Americans, was relatively easy. And it was realized in the suburbs.[48]

Postwar planners believed that "expansion, domestic prosperity, and the world's well-being were complementary goods."[49] World War II brought the United States out of the isolationism it had embraced as far back as the early decades of the century. More and more, elected officials, federal bureaucrats, military advisers, and corporate leaders began to believe in the importance of free trade and overseas investment as keys to domestic prosperity. In a world of nuclear weapons, jet aircraft, and missiles that could carry payloads across national borders, isolationism simply was less and less an option. This internationalism included trade and cultural exchange as well as a flow of ideas that carried the American way of life to the world. "Science, technology, and even the arts became strategic resources to be mobilized in the nation's quest for world dominance."[50]

At the end of World War II, "America stood in a position of material and moral supremacy."[51] Unlike those of the world's other industrial powers—England, Japan, Germany, the Soviet Union—its factories had not been destroyed, its railroads and highways were intact, its financial markets were functioning, and its population had escaped decimation. U.S. cities did not have to be rebuilt because of enemy bombing, nor did the country have to rely on international agencies for financial assistance to restart its economy. The United States could retool its factories with relative ease and begin the shift to an economy focused on consumer goods and services. Moreover, the mass production and organizational techniques that had enabled it to be victorious could also be used to meet the demands of a growing and mobile population and to restructure its urban areas.

That the United States had successfully turned back fascism and saved the world from the imperial designs of Japan and Germany conferred a moral superiority on the nation. Coupled with its vaunted and international reputation as the land of freedom and democracy, this moral position compelled the country to meet its international obligations and take on the leadership of the Western world, as Henry Luce and others encouraged it to do. The United States was primed for this task, believing that a world free of dictators and of barriers to trade and investment would bring peace and prosperity to all peoples. A nation so capable and accomplished could easily, and would gladly, bear the weight of world leadership.[52]

Most Americans agreed with the assertion that the United States—its economy, government, and social customs—was a model for the rest of the world. Despite an avowed commitment to a marketplace of "alternative visions of human possibilities," as one historian noted, Americans still "believed that America's own formula for advancement would inevitably triumph in the global marketplace."[53] The components of this formula included democratic institutions, civil rights, economic opportunity, and religious and ethnic tolerance. The freedom of choice and the social mobility they enabled were central to the economic prosperity enjoyed by its citizens. In the postwar era, that prosperity was inseparable from the massive growth of middle-income suburbs and the suburban way of life associated with them.

Consequently, in projecting its image across the globe, the United States also projected its commitment to suburban living as the quintessential American way of life and a way of life that might be copied by others. Through Cold War propaganda, cultural exhibitions, and trade relations, the country exported its values and social practices. None could be easily distanced or imagined independently from the suburbs.[54]

Trade was a primary conduit for transferring American values to other countries, particularly to those of the United Kingdom and western Europe. The story begins with the Marshall Plan, known officially as the European Recovery Program (ERP), the country's post–World War II effort to help European nations reconstruct their economies and, by doing so, resist the postwar blandishments of communism. Passed by the U.S. Congress in 1948, the Marshall Plan was based on the belief that domestic prosperity would be achieved only in a world of free trade among prosperous nations. It was preceded by the Lend Lease Agreement of 1942 and the Truman Doctrine in 1947. The first provided assistance to the United Kingdom and the Soviet Union prior to America's entry into the war against Germany. The second served as Truman's commitment that the United States would support all free people in their resistance to internal subjugation or external pressure. The former established a policy of trade assistance, and the latter a rationale for standing in the way of the communist advance.

Against this earlier background, Secretary of State George C. Marshall in June 1947 proposed that the United States help Europe cope with postwar recovery. In a famous speech at Harvard University, he called on western European governments to propose a plan to work together to rejuvenate their economies. The U.S. government was dissatisfied with the pace of recovery in Europe and the limitations of international aid agencies. He noted in reference to the U.S. embrace of world leadership that "[we are] deeply conscious of our responsibilities." The Marshall Plan gave substance to America's new internationalism.[55]

The European nations subsequently engaged in a complex set of multilateral negotiations in order to produce a reconstruction scheme. In the end, sixteen countries proposed a multibillion-dollar approach to bolstering their economies, an approach that relied heavily on trade with the United States and improvements in production capacity. Using loans and grants, the United States would make financial assistance available to these countries, and they would apply the funds to the purchase of American goods. The Marshall Plan would raise European living standards, make European economies more congenial to U.S. investment, provide the means for the Europeans to pay their share of the costs of rearmament, and remove the destitution in Europe that might make people susceptible to communism. Coincidentally, it would boost the U.S. domestic economy. The act itself stated that "Congress finds that the existing situation in Europe endangers the establishment of a lasting peace, the general welfare and national interest of the United States, and the attainment of the objectives of the United Nations." Despite its complex humanitarian, economic, and political motives, and most importantly for our concerns, it "allowed the United States to remake the European economy in the image of the American economy."[56]

Under the auspices of the Marshall Plan, the United States exported two types of commodities—goods and American business know-how—and the government engaged in a great deal of propaganda. High on the list of commodities were raw materials such as wheat, tobacco, cotton, oil, sulfur, and borax; intermediate producer goods such as aircraft parts and drilling equipment; and capital equipment such as tractors. American business experts, in turn, consulted with European firms about technology, human relations policy, and manufacturing techniques. The transfer of technology and knowledge also occurred through direct foreign investment by American firms and the sending of American managers, with their families, to live in Europe for extended periods of time.

Many European firms embraced American business practices. They introduced automated production and new marketing schemes and adopted U.S.-style advertising and management philosophies. The Marshall Plan "aimed to get as close as possible to the people it was benefiting in order to channel attitudes, mentalities and expectations in the direction America understood, the direction of mass-production for mass-consumption." An expert on the Marshall Plan characterized it as one of the "greatest international propaganda operations ever seen in peacetime."[57]

The Marshall Plan provided just over $13 billion to European recovery between 1948 and 1952, when the effort ended. More than $5 billion was used to purchase industrial goods, and an almost equivalent amount went to buy food and other agricultural products, mostly from the United States. About $800 million was spent just on freight charges to the U.S. shipping industry. To state the obvious, these expenditures boosted foreign trade. As a portion of the country's overall economic activity, trade increased by two-thirds between 1945 and 1955.[58]

In fact, throughout the short American Century, from the business cycle peak in 1948 to the valley in 1973, exports expanded as a portion of GNP, though since foreign trade was less than 10 percent of the domestic economy, the country was never dependent on it. During that time, total exports in 1958 dollars more than tripled, to just over $70 billion. Even more striking was the growth in direct foreign investment. U.S. investors were aggressive in purchasing businesses in Europe and in establishing overseas plants and offices there. Across this period, U.S. direct foreign investment increased more than fourfold, to $66 billion.[59] Exports and direct foreign investment carried the American way of life to Europe.

One commentator noted that the most important impact of the Marshall Plan was psychological. The plan "seriously damaged the Communist parties of Europe," provided support—because prosperity returned—to liberal and conservative political forces that resisted communist intrusions, and drew together the European countries in a common market. The dominant belief was that the American way of life, as represented by these goods and activities, was irresistible. The communists were losing in the struggle to capture the imaginations of western Europeans. Even in European countries, such as France and Italy, where the communist vote was high, "the very people who vote Communist are showing a preference for the American mode of living."[60] The Marshall Plan put the United States "firmly at the center of Europe," economically, politically, and culturally.[61]

As part of the plan, European participants had to agree to the dissemination within their borders of "information and news" on the workings of the ERP. This made it possible for the United States to engage in extensive selling of the American way of life. The ERP funded documentary films, radio programs, mobile cinemas, pamphlets, traveling exhibitions, concerts, contests, variety shows, calendars, postage stamps, cartoons, atlases, and traveling puppet shows all aimed at explaining the plan, encouraging European integration and greater productivity, and conveying U.S. accomplishments. Its overall efforts contributed to a "revolution of rising expectations" and enabled the United States to project "its power into Europe."[62]

The American way of life was spread most forcefully through U.S. consumer goods.[63] Europeans increasingly were replacing their family-run stores with supermarkets, their country lanes with superhighways, and their small hotels with motels. They were buying automobiles. Consumption was being made easier by the adoption of consumer credit and personal bank loans, of fixed-price selling rather than haggling, and of advertising. People were buying more labor-saving devices (such as blenders, vacuum cleaners, and washing machines), ready-to-wear clothing, home television sets, and packaged foods. American music (jazz and rock and roll), movies, and television spread the lifestyle that accompanied these products. A Swiss department store advertised a display of U.S. goods by admonishing its customers to "Live Like an American." American influence was, one journalist wrote, "creating a real revolution in the daily life of people."[64]

This influence also involved city planning and architecture. The Marshall Plan funded exhibits on U.S. construction techniques and planning paradigms. Architecture was exported to Europe in the form of American embassies and military bases, in shopping-mall design and (stretching the category) infrastructure such as oil refineries. One of the most significant, even if not the most common, of these endeavors was Hilton International, a wholly owned subsidiary of Hilton Hotels, whose purpose was to build modern hotels for international business travelers and tourists in the major cities of Europe and the Middle East. Hilton International often arranged its portion of the financing with the European Cooperative Administration, one component of the Marshall Plan. Moreover, Conrad Hilton, president of Hilton International, viewed the hotels as propaganda. He is quoted as having said that "an integral part of my dream was to show the countries most exposed to Communism the other side of the coin—the fruits of the free world." All of this was part of a longer-term flow from America to foreign countries of ideas and practices in architecture, city planning, and construction.[65]

The export of American ideas, goods, and customs was inseparable from the suburban dream. Supermarkets, motels, automobiles, and superhighways were all implicated in the parasitic urbanization that enabled postwar mass suburbanization and abetted the decline of the older, industrial cities. Televisions, washing machines, packaged foods, and consumer credit were primarily attributes of suburban living. Europeans adopted not simply isolated practices and products but an American way of life that was a suburban way of life. Correspondingly, Europeans had no need for American cities; their cities were older, more revered, and less dominated (with exceptions) by industrialization. When they embraced American ways, they also received, as part of that package, suburban images and the values of a suburban mentality. Put most bluntly, Americans made a "cultural assault on 'decadent' European values."[66]

Reinforcing the spread of U.S. popular culture into foreign lands was the constant stream of Cold War doctrine and cultural exchanges. As early as 1938, the Department of State had established a Division of Cultural Relations designed to counteract propaganda against the United States. The division was absorbed into the Office of War Information during World War II and later became the U.S. Information Agency (USIA) and the radio station Voice of America. To this conduit was added the Fulbright Act of 1946, which was designed to foster the exchange of artists and scholars in order to breed cultural understanding. In 1948, moreover, the Smith-Mundt Act authorized a peacetime overseas information program, thereby making information and cultural exchanges acknowledged instruments of foreign policy.[67]

The common objectives of these initiatives were to create a broad awareness of U.S. policy, negate the thrust of communist propaganda (especially that directed at casting the United States as imperialist and domestically oppressive), show a mutuality of interest among peoples and nations, and explain American values. The USIA hoped to make people from around the world friendlier toward the United States. Ideally, these efforts would "inculcate respect for, and if possible allegiance to, the democratic way of life."[68]

The divide between information and propaganda is undeniably thin, however. Consequently, the USIA and Voice of America often found themselves under attack from Cold War warriors—anticommunists to the core—who wanted more strident rhetoric directed against the Soviet Union and an approach that mimicked American advertising, that is, that was wholly positive and celebratory. Carl T. Rowan, the director of USIA, responded in a speech in 1964: "The easiest way to destroy USIA, to render it totally ineffective, would be to have it feed the world nothing but superlatives about America and the American way of life."[69]

In the early 1950s, Voice of America was broadcasting twenty-eight program hours a day in thirty-four different languages. The USIA daily press service delivered news items to 10,000 newspapers and regularly published twenty-five periodicals. In production were 466 reels of film footage. Additionally, the USIA set up 160 libraries and information centers around the world that were open to the public, and it was involved in numerous exhibitions and trade fairs.

For the most part, these different activities were meant to convey an evenhanded view of the United States. An American way of life was on display. Americans were portrayed as nice people, generous, altruistic, and cultured. The U.S. government was democratic and peace loving. The economy was characterized as a mixed economy generating a high standard of living for the great majority of people. The images were of skyscrapers, churches, factories, and suburbs. Although no one set of images or way of life dominated, the overall thrust was to convey the attainability of the American Dream.[70] The goal was a balanced portrayal. Yet the strong emphasis on the American standard of living, an emphasis supported by the Marshall Plan and amplified by the global reach of the U.S. economy, propelled U.S. proselytizing into the contentious realm of suburbanization and industrial-city decline.

No one event epitomizes the suburban quality of this postwar propaganda more than the famous, and now iconic, "kitchen debate" between Vice President Richard M. Nixon and Soviet premier Nikita Khrushchev in July 1959.[71] The debate took place at the American

National Exhibition in Sokolniki Park in Moscow. It followed a similar visit of dignitaries and an exhibition that the Soviets had held in New York City and came at a time when the Soviet premier was vociferous in his criticism of capitalist America. Cold War tensions were high, and Nixon looked forward with trepidation to his visit and first meeting with Khrushchev.

The exhibit covered 400,000 square feet and cost $5 million. It consisted of an exhibition hall containing 500 photographs of the United States, twenty-two American automobiles, sports and camping equipment, a supermarket display, and cosmetics and other commodities normally purchased by the American consumer. It also included a heart-lung machine and a computer (Ramac 305) preprogrammed to provide written answers to 3,500 questions about the people, land, institutions, history, and culture of the United States. Approximately 800 U.S. corporations were represented. In addition to the exhibition hall, a geodesic dome provided space for 5,000 people. In that space, American films were shown on Circlorama, a 360-degree movie screen, and events such as fashion shows were held.

Outside the hall was a detached, single-family, six-room, ranch-style house. This prefabricated model home would have cost $14,000 to build in the United States, and it contained $5,000 worth of furnishings including a color television, a built-in washing machine, an all-electric kitchen, and a home workshop. The house was billed as "within the price range of the average U.S. worker."[72]

Nixon opened the exhibit with a speech that stressed three themes: the importance of cultural understanding, the high U.S. living standard, and the commitment of the United States to domestic freedoms and international peace.[73] He gave statistics on home ownership and the purchase of cars, televisions, and radios and noted that all of these luxuries were affordable for the average American worker. U.S. workers, he said, "enjoy the highest standard of living of any people in the world's history." Nixon asserted that the United States "from the standpoint of distribution of wealth comes closest to the ideal of prosperity for all in a classless society." To balance his presentation, he called attention to such persistent problems as unemployment, support for the aged, labor strikes, and racial discrimination, but he quickly noted that they were being addressed.

Material progress, Nixon went on, was hardly worth praise if people were not free and their government not open. He pointed specifically to the freedoms of religion and travel, freedoms ostensibly absent in the Soviet Union, and followed that by saying that the United States would not impose its system of government on others. We want peace, Nixon proclaimed: War with the atomic bomb would destroy not only the victims but also the aggressor as radioactive fall-out drifted across the planet.

Relations between Nixon and Khrushchev were tense from the beginning. In a taped debate earlier that day, Khrushchev had accused Nixon of knowing "absolutely nothing about communism"—only fearing it—and had predicted that in seven years, the Soviet Union would surpass the United States economically.[74] The climax of their frank discussions came "when they went into a model American home— the home that Pravda (the Soviet news organ) had criticized as not representative and too expensive for the average American worker."[75] Walking through the house, and in front of reporters, Nixon encouraged Khrushchev to admire the kitchen, one like, he said, "those in our houses in California."[76] He pointed specifically to a built-in washing machine. Khrushchev responded: "We have such things." Nixon commented that such appliances made life easier for the American woman; Khrushchev retorted that the Russians did not share "the capitalist attitude toward women."

Nixon persisted. He explained that the model home was affordable, noting that veterans of World War II normally purchased homes in the range of $10,000 to $15,000. They debated how long the house would last, with the Soviet premier saying, "We build for our children and grandchildren," and Nixon replying that this house would last for more than twenty years, at which time Americans would then want a new kitchen and a new home. "The fact is," Khrushchev replied, "newly built Russian houses have all this equipment right now" and that moreover, in the Soviet Union one had a right to a home, unlike in America.

The debate then turned back to an earlier discussion they had had regarding missiles and who could destroy whom. Pointing to the washing machine, Nixon asked whether it was not better that the two world powers compete on the basis of consumer goods rather than with "machines of war such as rockets." Khrushchev responded as if threatened. "But your generals say: 'Let's compete in rockets.' In this respect we can also show you something." "We are both strong," Nixon replied and argued that neither side should engage in ultimatums. Khrushchev responded: "Who is giving an ultimatum?" After Nixon spoke, Khrushchev went on to say that he sensed he was being threatened: "We will answer threats with threats," and "We have the means to threaten too." As they moved away from the model home, the tension abated, and they agreed that peace was in both nations' interests.[77]

For standing up to the Soviet premier and doing so in front of an international audience of reporters, Nixon returned home as a "national hero." "He refuted Soviet propaganda, without making threats," noted *Life* magazine.[78] One month later, in a speech before the American Dental Association, the vice president commented on the "great battle of ideas going on in the world today" and declared that the United States "cannot stand silently by while the disciples of communism beat their drums in the world forum." In his book *Six Crises,* published in 1962, Nixon described his meeting with Khrushchev as one of the personal turning points of his career.[79]

The kitchen debate was a significant episode in the exchange of Cold War propaganda between the United States and the Soviet Union. It asserted in a very public and global way the values of American-style democracy and capitalism against Soviet-style communism and economic planning. The debate was also crucial in crystallizing the importance of a suburban way of life—and domesticity—to the selling of the American standard of living.

In an appliance-laden, suburban ranch house, as the historian Elaine May has observed, Nixon and Khrushchev argued over the relative merits of home appliances, the role of women as housewives, and the benefits of home ownership. The home—and the prosperity that enabled its purchase—anchored the core values of freedom and democracy. "Nixon insisted that American superiority in the cold war rested not on weapons but on the secure, abundant family life available in modern suburban homes."[80] Here was the American Dream in its quotidian form. This was what Nixon and myriad internationalists wanted people from other countries to admire. This was the image attached to the prepared foods, television sets, and automobiles and to the use of credit cards, supermarkets, and motels. And it was the image that people around the world absorbed when they bought and acted American.

All of these postwar goods and images and the lifestyle that went with them—the American way of life—were rooted firmly in the suburbs. "Suburbia would serve as a bulwark against communism and class conflict," blocking subversion and dissolving any lingering class divisions.[81]

Conclusion

At the center of the postwar global discourse—whether it was the Cold War rhetoric directed at the Soviet Union, the "information and news" aimed at the industrialized and industrializing democracies of western

Europe, or domestic policy debates laden with concern about international subversion—sat the suburban way of life. The suburbs symbolized the world's highest standard of living and focused the American Dream for both citizens and immigrants. While not every foreign citizen wanted to migrate to the United States and not every resident of the country wished to move to the suburbs, almost all wanted a piece of the suburban lifestyle: the freedom of the automobile, the convenience of home appliances, the benefits of consumer credit, and the choices offered by supermarkets.

The power of America's message was derived from a conflation of freedom and democracy with consumption and lifestyles.[82] When postwar apologists declared America the land of the free, they made reference to two quite different types of freedom: political freedom and freedom of consumer choice. The first was central to the allure that the United States projected to the rest of the world, especially communist countries and those increasingly under Soviet influence. But in the United States, people—more accurately, Caucasians—enjoyed civil rights. They could vote, speak freely, and congregate in public. What people did not enjoy were social rights: the right to a well-paying job, decent housing, health care, and adequate food. With welfare states emerging and becoming stronger in western Europe, these deficiencies were glaring.

Taking the place of social rights in the United States were prosperity and consumer choice. Prosperity made such rights seem redundant, while consumer choice made the uncertainties of capitalism seemingly manageable and more tolerable. People were free to work wherever and for whomever would hire them. Once paid, they were free to live where they wanted and consume what they desired. Riches were possible, and spending was virtually unconstrained. A wealth of consumer goods and services were available. People in the United States could even start their own businesses. Most importantly, they could live as they pleased. This was freedom.

The suburbs were the place where this freedom was most pronounced. In the city were the persistent problems of unemployment, poverty, and racial discrimination that Nixon had commented on in his speech opening the Moscow exhibit. Holding up the industrial cities as models to emulate would have served to publicize these embarrassments. With the cities becoming increasingly African American in the 1950s and with the country still unwilling to legislate against racial intolerance and spreading poverty, exposing the urban way of life was simply an invitation to the world's derision.

Cities were vulnerable to nuclear attack and were also seen as sites of potential subversion to which communists gravitated and where they fomented revolt and poisoned the minds of otherwise patriotic citizens. Considered the haunt of homosexuals, liberals, and intellectuals, cities were not to be trusted. Further disqualifying them from representing the preferred American way of life was their status as ground zero for atomic bombs—better to disperse the cities than praise them. Suburbanization was the antidote to the communist menace in the cities and the threat of nuclear attack; prosperity and rampant consumption were the antidote to communist propaganda.[83]

The suburban way of life thus enabled the United States to fight communism at home and to project its image across the globe. It marked the nation as unique. And suburbanization, "in its broadest sense, . . . promoted the expansion of American interests, activities, and power in other parts of the world."[84] The innovative nature of this new spatial form, and of the lifestyle associated with it, spoke to the technological and intellectual prowess of the country and the ability of its citizens to cast off the past in search of a better future. The physical and visual openness of the suburbs, with lawns surrounding each freestanding house, also contrasted with the density of the cities. The suburbs signaled a mixture of individualism and conformity, a democracy where people were equal and yet free to pursue their dreams. "Observing American happiness and prosperity, other nations would seek the same by adopting American methods."[85]

Suburbanization carried much of the burden of American claims to freedom and democracy and of its exceptionalism. The message embedded in these themes was convincing and powerful. The United States not only occupied the high moral ground against godless communism, but it also offered an alternative. Importantly, that alternative was within the grasp of peoples who adopted capitalist economies, opened themselves to world trade and foreign investment, and embraced democratic institutions that allowed civil rights and consumer choice.

Behind the short American Century and its peculiar pattern of urbanization was the force of the country's global project. By implicating the suburban way of life in postwar advances across the globe, the desirability of the cities was diminished. Dangerous in numerous ways, obsolete, and representing a time when labor toiled simply to survive, the industrial cities lacked the cultural weight to be considered seriously for extensive and fundamental redevelopment. It might have been cosmopolitan to be urban, but to be urban was no longer sensible. The suburbs were where people should want to be. It was there that the American Dream had relocated.

8

Identity and Urbanity

No historical period ever begins or ends abruptly. World War II marked the beginning of the short American Century and the onset of two events—industrial-city decline and mass suburbanization—that left the country's landscape, its dominant way of life, and what it meant to be an American irreparably changed. Neither event suddenly appeared as truce was declared. The recession of 1973–1975 marked the end. Yet the consequences of parasitic urbanization, postwar economic growth, and Cold War ideology linger.

Throughout those twenty-five years, the nation basked in its global dominance and enjoyed an unprecedented domestic prosperity. In the early 1970s, however, the triumvirate of suburban-style growth, widespread affluence, and international supremacy began to unravel. Productivity slowed, the economy faltered, and the United States became mired in Vietnam. The nation found itself economically and diplomatically challenged by a more organized western European community, by Japan, and by the Organization of Petroleum Exporting Countries (OPEC). The global responsibility that the country had taken on, seemingly as a matter of destiny, was now tainted. America could no longer sustain both prosperity at home and ascendance abroad.[1]

During the short American Century, citizens, corporations, and governments reaped a multitude of benefits. Incomes rose, consumer goods were abundant, housing production was robust, new communities were built, and life, for most people, was rewarding. The fascination with U.S. consumer goods and popular culture, interest in U.S. technology and know-how, and high levels of productivity allowed

American corporations to dominate world export markets. The capital at their disposal also led U.S. businesses to invest in western Europe, South America, and Asia. Local and state governments, with the exception of those in declining industrial cities, could count on expanding tax revenues, while the federal government grew in size and influence. The national government found itself at the center of world diplomacy; even if not directly consulted, it always figured in realpolitik calculations. America was at the center of the world.

Prosperity and global dominance permitted Americans—white Americans—to think of themselves as sharing a national destiny. The American identity seemed monolithic, built as it was on upward mobility and freedom. What America stood for and what it meant to be an American were relatively unquestioned. Dissent and deviance were ever present but were, nevertheless, pushed into the shadows. Consensus occupied center stage in the short American Century.

There were costs, and they were huge. Domestic prosperity and a global presence fed on the industrial cities, draining them of population and investment, weakening their governments, and consigning racial minorities and poor households to inner-city slums and chronic unemployment. In return for their contribution, the industrial cities were left with abandoned manufacturing zones, block after block of dilapidated housing, and blighted downtowns. The largest cities eventually became the shame of the nation, attended to when riots erupted but otherwise lamented and ignored.[2]

When Americans discarded the industrial cities, they also severed their connection to an urban way of life. The embrace of suburbia meant the rejection of an urbanity that had nurtured the coexistence of diverse peoples and life experiences from the early nineteenth century to the mid-twentieth century. The resultant pluralism had been central to the nation's identity. An urbanization that rejected density and social diversity impaired the moral ties that might have enabled the country to "save" its cities. First, commitment eroded as households fled to the suburbs and sprawling Sunbelt cities. Then, attachment diminished as the suburbs became self-sufficient. Finally, empathy waned as race and crime came to symbolize the central cities. A sense of national belonging was severely compromised. Cold War ideology only made matters worse.

With the end of the short American Century, dissatisfactions that had been kept on the margins became more and more pronounced. The result was a "collapse in American belief in a utopian national destiny."[3] Foundational narratives that anchored American thought and culture, focused its history, and legitimized its actions became less and less credible. Yet in another ironic twist of history, the cities that had suffered so ignominiously began to show signs of renewed energy. City life became desirable once again. Notwithstanding, what had been lost was not so easily recaptured.

Reprise

Just after World War II, the industrial cities of the United States, the cities that had ruled the economy and shaped the national consciousness for nearly a century, underwent a profound transformation. Whereas the large cities had experienced uninterrupted growth since the mid-nineteenth century, now they shed residents and cast off businesses at alarming rates. Although signs of this inauspicious turn had been visible decades earlier, persistent decline was unexpected. A few aberrant cities did lose population prior to the 1930s, and a significant number did so during the Depression of the 1930s. Their losses, however, were quickly recouped. The 1950s unleashed a deluge. Moreover, population and employment loss from the industrial cities became coupled with low-density development that took the form of mass-produced suburbs and Sunbelt-city sprawl. This was a sea change. A rupture had occurred in the underlying processes of urbanization.

The plight of the large manufacturing cities—places like St. Louis, Detroit, Philadelphia, Cleveland, and Buffalo—drew the greatest attention. There, the flight of predominantly white households and the closing of factories and downtown businesses left behind blighted areas and shrunken tax bases. The in-migration of blacks from the South, just when job opportunities were diminishing, accelerated the formation of slums and deepened poverty. It also ignited a racial tension between (nonwhite) cities and (white) suburbs that continues to plague older metropolitan areas. Although smaller industrial cities, many of them satellites of larger cities, received less national press, their demographic losses and social and economic problems were just as severe.

Whole regions suffered. Industrialization and urbanization had converged in the late nineteenth century in the northeastern quadrant of the country. There, the industrial cities flourished. Few cities outside this area were as reliant on manufacturing, and thus only a handful of them experienced the flight of people and capital that was the fate of their Rustbelt counterparts.

The investment in new homes, businesses, and infrastructure after World War II was impressive. Suburbs erupted everywhere, and small

Identity and Urbanity

towns in the West, Southwest, and South turned into low-density cities. The automobile was one of many factors that ignited a major building cycle. Little of this investment was channeled to the older, industrial cities, urban redevelopment notwithstanding. Yet suburban growth was not simply the counterweight to central-city decline. In this novel era of parasitic urbanization, disinvestment from the core contributed to national prosperity. Economic growth, suburban expansion, and industrial-city shrinkage were locked in a web of reciprocal influences.

From the late 1940s to the early 1970s, the country changed from urban to suburban. Even the emerging cities of the Sunbelt were suburban in form and lifestyle: low in density and dominated by acre after acre of single-family detached homes rather than by apartments and row houses. Their retailing was organized around shopping strips and regional malls, and their businesses were sited in industrial and office parks. An expanding middle class adopted a consumer-oriented and automobile-centered way of life, as the sidewalk-centered, high-density living of the city became less desirable. The postwar rupture in urbanization was more than a transformation in *where* people lived; it was also a transformation in *how* they lived.

Once, all of the country's cities had grown in parallel. Some grew at different rates than others, but none had to decline so others could grow. Urbanization had been distributive. Large cities added population on their edges and intensified their cores, often replacing existing buildings and functions with newer ones. New cities emerged when small towns and villages established a niche in the regional economy. Cities were essential to national growth: They anchored new territories, connected them (through commerce) to previously settled areas, and served as centers of economic activity.

After World War II, as another long wave of development formed, urbanization turned parasitic. The industrial cities had to decline for the suburbs and Sunbelt cities to expand. Negligible immigration, a cultural aversion to cities, the greater ease and profitability of new development (as compared with redevelopment), and immense demands on capital (especially for investment abroad) made flight from, and disinvestment in, the industrial cities seem unavoidable.

Historical conditions supported this shift from distributive to parasitic urbanization. The nearly fifteen years of disinvestment brought about by the paucity of capital during the Depression and its diversion to the war effort thereafter meant that the postwar cities were shabby and overcrowded. Moreover, once World War II ended, they were burdened by the need to replace a multitude of obsolete structures from office buildings to roadways. A dearth of housing was one of their most glaring deficiencies. The new suburbs suffered none of these problems.

Population flows turned against the cities. Since its European colonization, the country had expanded westward. Rural migrants and immigrants had flocked to the cities in the late nineteenth and early twentieth centuries and had replenished the residents lost to the lure of open space and the frontier. When distributive urbanization ruled, these flows had fed city growth. During the short American Century, they contributed to city decline. Immigration slackened considerably, and the westward movement of people siphoned households from industrial regions. The rural-to-urban migration of the postwar era consisted primarily of African Americans from the South who were ill-prepared to do well in a declining manufacturing economy. These migrants arrived in the industrial cities as jobs were leaving and as racial discrimination was on the rise. Their struggle to maintain a decent life in the face of numerous obstacles further tarnished any positive image the cities had retained. Redevelopment became even more problematic as the political will to fix the cities' problems evaporated. Federal and state governments were concerned, but their commitments stopped well short of reversing the decline.

Households, of course, had not moved westward alone. Industry and commerce had followed and, in certain times and places, had led. Through the late nineteenth and early twentieth centuries, manufacturing had consolidated in the cities: steel in Pittsburgh, chemicals in Buffalo, and automobile assembly in Detroit. Industries that used mass-production techniques to reach a national market and that required massive initial investments were major contributors to city growth. Some such industries (for example, wagon making) disappeared and others (such as iron manufacturing) shrank when new products took over their markets, but in all these instances, cities found other economic activities to take their place.

Political factors also made it difficult for the older cities to regain their earlier prosperity. As the suburbs developed, their influence in state legislatures increased. The suburbs were less and less interested in being annexed to the central cities. They crafted their tax bases to support infrastructure and to minimize dependency on the metropolitan cores. Moreover, they established the legal means to resist annexation. Cities could no longer capture the accretion that, with intensification, had allowed them continual growth. Hemmed in, facing deepening social and fiscal problems, and with little land for new development, they offered slight inducements to developers and investors.

After enduring the Depression and sacrificing so the country could defeat Japan and the Axis powers, Americans were ready for a return to the prosperity of the 1920s. They wanted families and babies, decent housing, and consumer goods. They also wanted college educations and secure jobs. In addition, people were impatient. No longer would gratifications be deferred. Consequently, Americans were not willing to wait for housing to be built in the cities, for the downtowns to be redeveloped, or for outmoded factories to be replaced by modern facilities. Better to go to the suburbs, where large numbers of affordable homes were quickly coming on the market, land was plentiful and relatively cheap, and everything—schools, roads, stores, and playgrounds—was new. The social costs seemed insignificant, even invisible in the bright light of personal rewards. In this environment, the decline of the industrial cities was simply another reason to abandon them.

With the industrial cities less necessary for social advancement and economic prosperity, ambivalence toward the cities became indifference and neglect. Most people could not imagine living the good life in the cities. Federal government policy was divided between programs that drained the cities of people and capital and those that attempted to improve them. City governments did the best they could with what people and resources they were given, but the former were shrinking and the latter were grudgingly distributed. One could hardly expect a different outcome, given the resurgence of a frontier capitalism that found sparsely developed places—metropolitan peripheries, Sunbelt states—irresistible.

Most important for the plight of the older cities was the shift in the international division of labor. Whereas the country's manufacturing firms had once enjoyed little competition in domestic and world markets and had mainly invested in U.S. factories, after World War II manufacturing spread to other countries, and foreign direct investment by U.S. firms soared. In addition, various foreign goods—jewelry, clothing, toys, automobiles, shoes—began to penetrate domestic markets. With corporations establishing plants in other countries, or moving them there, the United States lost both jobs and capital. Multinational corporations and their management benefited, but the shrinkage of domestic manufacturing irreparably harmed the industrial cities.

The world economy was in the throes of a major transformation. A long wave built on industrial agglomerations concentrated in a few countries was coming to an end. The United States and England no longer stood alone as industrial giants; serious challenges were being mounted. The spread of industrialization to other countries seemed inevitable. The United States responded by creating new industries (for example, the manufacturing of personal computers), taking on new activities (such as consumer credit management), and expanding old ones (such as automobile assembly and higher education). The U.S. economy grew. Falling demand for production workers and expansion of white-collar employment, though, meant that economic growth favored the kinds of people who were moving to the suburbs and penalized those left in, or who had migrated to, the industrial cities.

Abetting these changes was a national government intent on helping American corporations export to and invest in foreign markets. The Marshall Plan was one of the main conduits for doing so. Just as important were cultural products (for example, movies, books, music) that proselytized an American way of life and inflated the demand for American goods, technology, science and management, and advertising techniques. That many of these commodities came to be associated with a suburban lifestyle was a further blow to the prospects of the older cities.

As the United States took on the mantle of world leadership, projecting a positive image to foreign countries became even more necessary. America offered its way of life as an alternative to the purported constraints of communism. The images projected abroad focused on the freedom of choice Americans had in politics and markets. The two were connected. Political choice reinforced the commitment to a unique form of economic democracy, while consumer choice satisfied quotidian wants and desires and made people politically content. Suburban life epitomized and gave substantive weight to this connection.[4]

The older, industrial cities were swept up in the Cold War hysteria. Widespread fear of the atomic bomb led to calls for the deconcentration and decentralization of housing and industry. Limited-access interstate highways, a factor in the suburbanization that undermined the central cities, gathered political support in part for national defense reasons. Public housing benefited the cities by clearing slums and providing decent housing to low-income families, yet it was labeled communistic and was seen as the first step on the road to socialist serfdom.

All of these factors—from internal migration to world leadership—worked against the redevelopment of the industrial cores. The confluence of so many inhospitable forces suppressed any popular commitment to saving the older cities. Americans came to accept urban decline, although this era had seemingly come to an end by the mid-1970s. In retrospect, urban decline looks as if it had been preordained. Yet a whole host of conditions—demographic stasis, political neglect, cultural predispositions to progress and novelty, widespread automobile usage, trade surpluses, unprecedented domestic prosperity, the lure of development on open land—had to coincide for this to occur.

Once the shift from cities to suburbs was underway, once suburban growth literally took hold of the metropolitan periphery and the nation, an opportunity existed to broadcast the new American way of life across the globe. Suburbanization supported the political and foreign policy aspirations of the national government, the investment interests of multinational corporations, and the exports of U.S. businesses. Domestic prosperity and democratic freedoms came to play pivotal roles, not just as abstract values but as concrete realities, in the articulation of American dominance. Consumer goods, new production and management techniques, innovative retailing and financing strategies, novel building types such as tract housing and motels, sprawl-inducing highways, and new media such as television—all were defining qualities of the vaunted American way of life. Most significantly, they could not be imagined independently of suburban living. It will come as no surprise, then, that Luce, the outspoken advocate of the American Century, frequently used "the myth of suburbia to affirm the American way of life."[5]

The suburbs grounded life in postwar America; they gave it meaning and uniqueness both inside and outside the country. The cities, by contrast, were an embarrassment. By the 1980s, one commentator could observe that suburbia was "such a pervasive element of our culture that it requires an act of imagination to cast your mind back only a few decades to the time when a nation's way of life, and its landscape, was reinvented."[6]

The suburban way of life was swept up in a Cold War frenzy that further elevated the nation to superiority in world affairs and that spurred ideological conflict around an "over-heated nationalism."[7] As a consequence, American exceptionalism once again returned as a topic of intellectual, popular, and institutional concern. A major pillar of the postwar projection of American exceptionalism to the world was the suburban way of life. No other country had produced suburbs at this scale or made them so widely available. No other country could boast of its postwar domestic prosperity in the way that the United States could. Suburbs were not unique to the United States, but these types of suburbs were, and they made America exceptional.

In the propaganda wars, the suburbs proved to be a powerful resource. They not only distinguished the country from the centrally planned and massive new towns and housing developments in the

Soviet Union, but, even more importantly, they distanced the United States culturally from England and the countries of western Europe, "the standard from which all deviations are measured."[8] It was not just that these other places lacked mass suburbs. What was even more significant was that the mass suburbs enabled the United States to change the terms of the cultural comparison. For centuries, U.S. cities had never quite been able to overcome the history, urbanity, and civilizing image of European cities. Neither Boston, the country's strongest competitor, nor Philadelphia could match the cosmopolitanism of Paris or the cultural riches of St. Petersburg. Although the elites of Chicago and New York opted for commercialism, this did little to shift the cultural scales so as to favor the United States. The postwar suburbs did.[9]

What the postwar suburbs gave up in cosmopolitanism and intellectual and cultural depth, they more than made up in prosperity, freedom of choice, and opportunity. Living well was the American revenge on its European origins and was one of the nation's most potent weapons in the Cold War with the Soviet Union. Democracy—in markets and in local governments—amplified the differences. The United States had a new arrow in its quiver of exceptionalisms. During the short American Century, that arrow was used often.[10]

Nevertheless, Americans paid an enormous price for postwar affluence, global dominance, and this new cultural superiority. They turned their backs on the industrial cities that had made the country prosperous and powerful. They used the subsequent plight of the cities to marginalize African Americans in new ways. They shunned an urban way of life whose civic responsibility had kept ethnic, class, and religious distinctions from further deepening the inequalities endemic to American society. During the short American Century, the country reinvented itself. In doing so, Americans sacrificed the dense and diverse cities of an earlier era and the urbanity that they had spawned. In this, too, the United States was exceptional.

Urbanity Lost

In the postwar era, the decline of the industrial cities and mass suburbanization were pivotal to the restructuring of the national landscape. The rearrangement of population and investment, though, was the surface reality. When America turned its back on the industrial cities, much like when it embraced them a century earlier, it also cast aside a central feature of its national identity. Through a circuitous path, Americans began to question an idea that had earlier been sacrosanct:

that all within the country's boundaries shared a common ideology and a common destiny. In jettisoning these cities and the way of life that had brought them to such prominence, Americans undermined the ability to manage the pluralism that has been so central to the country's growth and development.[11]

Such a wrenching transformation in the dominant way of life, a way of life centered in large cities and factories, could not but affect how Americans imagined living the good life together and how they behaved as citizens. The question "Who are we?" engendered a much different answer in the mid-1970s than it had in the 1930s or even 1940s. Material life had been transformed, and the opportunities of which one could take advantage were barely comparable. People's basic values probably persisted, but their daily lives did not, and this altered how they thought of themselves and others. The reinvention of national identity subsequently filtered into public debates and influenced in numerous and undeniable ways the country's collective endeavors.

The fascination with national identity during the short American Century emerged from a variety of directions. One of the major influences was the change in the way people lived: buying their groceries at supermarkets along the highways rather than in corner stores, traveling more by automobile than by bus or trolley, living in houses surrounded by lawns rather than in tenements or apartment buildings, encountering in public fewer people unlike themselves. Americans were also anxious about maintaining status, being promoted at work, facing the perils of the atomic bomb, and surviving the often-frightening confrontations of the Cold War. As the period drew to a close, numerous events—the civil rights movement, women's liberation, environmentalism, antiwar protests—further undermined the sense of a shared destiny that had characterized the country from the 1930s until the early 1960s. The American identity was in flux.[12]

National identity, of course, is a volatile mixture of fiction and reality and is inherently paradoxical. Even in the most culturally monolithic societies where immigration has been absent, any attempt to define a sense of the nation is easily fractured by contrary understandings of the past as well as by the lingering suspicion that national boundaries are mere fictions in the containment of deeply held values, psychological traits, and social inclinations. "Who are we?" is a question so open-ended as to pull into its orbit not just shared memories but a vast and ever-changing array of differences. Accurate and stable representations are a delusion. Nonetheless, if a public culture can be said to exist in the United States, one of its tasks is to debate how contingent and multiple identities, diverse and fragmented histories, and events both tragic and joyous constitute a shared American identity.[13]

Like all national identities, the American identity is invented. It did not instantaneously take possession of the colonists. It was not already in place. Rather, those who came to the United States imagined and publicized traits that crystallized their aspirations and accomplishments. The American Revolution challenged the colonists' sense that they were English; the consolidation of the thirteen original colonies required thoughts of nationhood and citizenship. People were being asked to think of themselves not just as merchants in Boston or as farmers in the northwest territory but as citizens of a nation called the United States of America. The Civil War, industrialization, and massive immigration brought additions and modifications. Each major event constituted a challenge to prevailing views as to what it was to be, and who was, an American. The arrival of Irish, Italians, Russians, and Puerto Ricans in communities where previously there were none renewed, over and over again, public deliberations about national identity.

Wars and periods of ideological strife have often stirred up groups intent on imposing their preferred version of America. During the Cold War, one's ideological inclinations became a litmus test. To be an avowed member of the Communist Party was to be suspect, even to be stigmatized and denied employment. Throughout the country's history, suspicion of foreign sympathy or of a deficit of patriotism has constituted sufficient evidence to spark accusations of anti-Americanism. Native groups whose jobs and neighborhoods are ostensibly threatened by foreigners have also been quick to draw a clear line between being an American and not being one, the better to determine whose interests deserve priority. Nonetheless, the country has displayed a remarkable resilience, an ability to absorb conflict and differences and remain united.[14]

Given these qualities of national identity, one is hard-pressed to define what it means to be an American, much less to distinguish the core values of being an American from the ways in which numerous other nationalities imagine themselves—for example, as family oriented, peaceable, religious, open-minded, accomplished, or proud. There is "no indivisible Platonic essence of which America is the unique embodiment." These caveats notwithstanding, Americans have thought of themselves as exceptional, even if paradoxically so.[15] That these traits are often universalized (that is, equated with humanity generally) speaks to the destiny that Luce declared for the nation with his "American Century" and to the Cold War ideology in which it became embedded.[16]

Attempts to sum up the American identity often alight on allegiance to Enlightenment political principles. The reference brings to bear the colonists' flight from religious persecution, the Declaration of Independence, the Bill of Rights, and the commitment to freedom of choice in occupations, consumption, and places of residence. The principles evoked are those of freedom, equality, consent of the governed, and civil and political rights. The sustaining of democracy for over two centuries attests to a citizenship based on laws that underpin and supersede government and its elected leaders.[17]

Political freedoms, in turn, are viewed as essential for economic progress. The country's nearly unbroken history of growth and prosperity has characterized America within and abroad and has reinforced the allegiance of Americans to freedom, equality, and civil liberties. Americans are free to vote for whomever they want, live wherever they wish, freely take or refuse employment, move about the country unimpeded, speak their minds, and purchase whatever catches their fancy. Civic nationalism, "a belief in the universal values embedded in the Declaration of Independence and Constitution," is an integral part of the American identity. Of singular importance, political freedom and economic choice—including the choice of where to work, where to invest or save one's money, and whether or not to open a business—are often conflated.[18]

In theory, these political principles also support a commitment to tolerance, specifically tolerance of the pluralism that has characterized American society since the eighteenth century.[19] Only with difficulty can a belief in equality and liberty be confined to the few, particularly in a country where freedom of expression is vigorously pursued. Consequently, Americans have developed numerous ways to absorb and live with newcomers and have acclimated themselves to a continual rethinking of who is an American. Of course, intolerance and efforts to purify the American identity are never absent and at times become violent, while the country's particular brand of pluralism leaves some groups disadvantaged. The dominant sense, though, is of a country that has made diversity part of its identity.

This commitment to diversity is supported by a strong individualism that has always been a defining trait of the American character.[20] Americans think of themselves as self-made and self-defined. A common theme in reflections on American identity is that Americans are always in the process of "becoming." "What joins Americans . . . [is] their complicity in a shared work of imagination" that accommodates individual achievement and aspirations within a common matrix of opportunities.[21] This has not prevented Americans from also being highly conformist, fiercely defensive of group identities, and, at times, xenophobic and zealously patriotic. Nor has it blocked the periodic flourishing of civic virtue. When individualism intersects with freedom of movement, though, the resultant mobility erodes community involvement even as Americans attempt to maintain a sense of place.

From the time of the first European colonists, the tensions between individualism and civic virtue, between mobility and community, between the ideology and the reality, have been central to the development of the country.[22] The vastness of the American landscape and the seemingly ever-expandable frontier, the belief that nature's role was to serve society, and the commitment to profit-driven investment choices (with public investments mostly following rather than leading) have shaped the country's pattern of villages, towns, and cities. The embrace of mobility, whether it be trekking to the next wilderness or commuting by automobile to one's job, has amplified the tendencies to deconcentration and decentralization inherent to urbanization processes.

The unique geographical qualities of the country also contributed. Its vast land area and abundant natural resources absorbed immigrants and enabled people to pursue diverse forms of community and ways of life unencumbered by prevailing norms. The paucity of neighboring countries (compared to nations in Europe), whose presence would have required attention, enabled the national identity to evolve relatively autonomously. "Continental self-sufficiency" engendered a sense of uniqueness and difference—of exceptionalism—and allowed a singular destiny to take shape.[23]

National identity has a geographical quality and draws from and attaches to multiple, intersecting locales. Collective identity is layered. A sense of national space is important, but it is insufficient if people are to live well and craft complex understandings of who they are. Identity at this scale remains ill-defined. It needs to descend to the many, small worlds in which people carry on their daily lives. Citizenship is a good example. It involves national, state, and local affiliations, with local sentiments and experiences particularly important in the formation of a sense of self and nationhood.[24]

People develop strong attachments to specific places. They think of themselves and describe themselves to others as residents of Austin; Seattle; Scarsdale, New York; or Shaker Heights, Ohio. And almost always, they focus on an even more particular neighborhood: North Beach in San Francisco, the Garden District in New Orleans, or Federal

Hill in Providence. Who one is is often inseparable from where one lives or has lived. The fact that ethnicity, social status, and even cultural practices coalesce around place, as in a working-class Puerto Rican neighborhood or an affluent commuter suburb, further reinforces this connection between self and community.

The mobility unleashed by the decline of the industrial cities destabilized past identities. The Depression and World War II left behind vivid memories and scarred lives, but during these years, people, on the whole, stayed put. A few moved during the Depression, and many more were attracted into metropolitan areas to work in defense factories a few years later. Many entered the military and went overseas. However, the numbers who did so were relatively small, and the contribution of these movements to a changing national identity was minor. Not so for postwar migrations. People moved from southern farms to northern cities, from industrial cities to bedroom suburbs, and from the Rustbelt states to Sunbelt regions. This necessitated a detachment from one type of place and a reattachment to another. Such migrations were not the same as relocating from one industrial city to another (for example, from Milwaukee to Rochester) or from one suburb to another (say from Scarsdale to Bryn Mawr, Pennsylvania). In the latter instances, the new lifestyle is much like the old, the housing and stores familiar, and the neighbors generally of the same income and social background.

The parasitic urbanization of the postwar period unleashed the kinds of migrations that unsettled earlier identifications. The move from the Bronx to Levittown was part of and necessitated a rethinking of who one was and who one had become. The flight from the cities and the pursuit of a better life in the suburbs set personal and family identities in flux. Once one was in the suburbs and away from the city, the new way of life triggered a reimagining of identity, with changes in attitude and expectations both corresponding and precipitating.

During the short American Century, the American way of life was transformed. Many people decided to live differently. Their choice, though, was less informed than that statement implies. Few people understood what suburban living would be like or grasped in advance the burden of commuting, the isolation of housewives who stayed at home caring for the children, the new forms of neighborliness, the separation from extended families, or the pressure to consume. Although people were not particularly likely to change their values or political affiliations as a result of the move, their daily behaviors did change. In addition, the move brought about different attitudes toward the city, attitudes ranging from aversion to nostalgia.[25] America's urban ambivalence was clarified.

The change from an urban to a suburban way of life, a change that permeated American society, left behind a bourgeois urbanity that had made the cities of the late nineteenth and early twentieth centuries centers of cultural and intellectual accomplishment, social and political reform, and cosmopolitan tolerance.[26] Bourgeois urbanity, a set of values and behaviors specific to the expanding middle class of the late nineteenth century, engaged with the city as a place of opportunity, civic obligations, and cultural advancement. These cities, these crucibles of diversity, no longer exist. When World War II ended, white Americans made a choice to reject this way of life.

The late-nineteenth-century middle class—educated, professionalized, affluent, Protestant, and white—identified with the city.[27] They lived there and were involved in its businesses, government, civic and fraternal associations, and cultural activities. For this middle class, the city was a place of opportunities. Businesses thrived, professionals were in demand. One could earn enough to live well: taking up residence in the best neighborhoods, shopping in the new department stores, employing servants, strolling through the city's parks on holidays, and patronizing the theaters and museums. The bourgeoisie of the late nineteenth and early twentieth centuries lived a full urban life. If one aspired to the ranks of the bourgeoisie, the city was where that aspiration was realized.

Of course, the cities of this time were also places of polluting factories, inadequate sanitation, spreading slums, exploited and struggling immigrants, and political incompetence and corruption.[28] Instead of fleeing—nascent suburbs were beckoning—most of the bourgeoisie stayed in the cities. There, they became involved in various reform movements to improve housing for the working class and poor, to provide sanitation and public health, and to aid new residents in adjusting to city living. Much of their civic energy was directed at reforming local government with civil service regulations and improved technical capacities and steering it to provide public services from recreation to education. Many from the middle class, especially middle-class women, engaged in voluntary activities and established independently funded social service organizations.[29]

Civic virtue and the public realm were valued. Yet it was a civil society strongly linked to the social responsibilities of government. The bourgeoisie would share its wealth and provide leadership, but it also expected the government to do its part. Voluntary organizations thrived alongside an active public sector. From the late nineteenth century to the first decades of the twentieth century, and even into the 1950s for some commentators, bourgeois urbanity reigned in the cities and shaped American society. The bourgeoisie stood to benefit, and did. In doing so, though, they made the city a better place to live for everyone.

The bourgeoisie's efforts only began with social and political reform. Its civic obligations extended into the cultural realm as it established and funded natural history and art museums, symphonic orchestras, opera companies, botanical gardens, and universities.[30] Affluent families used their wealth to enrich the cultural life of the city. To them we are indebted for the Metropolitan Museum of Art in New York City, the Boston Public Library, the Chicago Symphony Orchestra, and the Carnegie Museum in Pittsburgh, cultural organizations that continue to support the cities as centers of "high" culture. Bourgeois urbanity encompassed a moral obligation to the city and to a national cultural identity.

With the postwar shift from an urban to a suburban way of life, this bourgeois urbanity was lost. More accurately, the urban middle class failed to reinvent it. Having languished during the Depression and the war, that urbanity would have required a commitment to a more diverse and geographically complex world. Instead, the white middle class—rapidly expanding—fled to the suburbs. Many of those who stayed behind withdrew from civic reform and cultural endeavors, leading to an "impoverishment of the public sphere."[31]

In the early postwar years, local governments were unable to respond effectively to the problems besetting industrial cities. The national government stepped in with urban renewal, public housing, and, later, a concerted effort to address poverty, but the impact of these programs was insufficient to stem the losses of residents, businesses, and stores. The assumption of responsibility by the federal government, of course, gave the middle class another reason to sever its obligations to the city and distance itself from those less favored. "Washington" would take care of the cities; the middle class merely had to focus on family and career. A bit later, in the late 1970s, and making matters worse, the rise of political conservatism turned people against government activism and toward personal solutions to social problems.[32]

With the loss of bourgeois urbanity and of faith in the government came a loss of civic virtue and a diminution of urban citizenship.[33] Such a citizenship recognizes the rights that people have to live as they wish in the city, to be protected from harm and suffering, and to engage in opportunities for advancement and expression. At the same time, an urban citizenship entails obligations to share public space, to be tolerant of diverse lifestyles and forms of expression, and to contribute to the democracy and cultural life that supports these rights and obligations. Such civic obligations, moreover, function as an important impetus for social reform.

An ideal citizenship, of course, has a strong, moral core. It is not simply an exchange—rights for obligations—but a commitment on the part of citizens to the cultural diversity, human celebrations and sufferings, and the continued integrity of the city itself. It is a commitment to a public realm and common concerns and to a life that transcends the daily pressures of work and survival. Consequently, where urban citizenship is embraced, civic virtue reigns. The city becomes a place where differences are tolerated and diversity is forged into a common identity. Under these conditions, a national identity and social reform can flourish. Absent them, the nation fragments and reform languishes.

No matter how far bourgeois urbanity was from this ideal, it was closer than what existed at the height of postwar suburbanization and central-city decline. During the short American Century, urbanity was ignored and allowed to wither. The suburbanity that replaced it, despite high levels of civic participation, lacked a moral center that would enable people to reach outside their communities and embrace diverse peoples; it lacked a widely shared sense of purpose. Citizenship reverted to calculation; socializing and conformity replaced empathy for others. In return for their taxes, suburbanites expected local governments to protect their property values and to defend them against a threatening city. They expected the national government to keep poverty, crime, and racial tensions encased within the boundaries of the cities. Suburbia was the hidden hand with a vengeance. Whatever public good that resulted would have to flow from individual pursuit of the good life.[34]

The flight to the suburbs produced a moral divide. It created a spatial separation between one group of people—white, relatively affluent—and another, mostly nonwhite and poor. The separation that enabled suburbanites to avoid urban problems and people unlike themselves reflected and exacerbated a moral disregard for the needs of those in the cities and a political reluctance to support a collective response. The national shame is this complex avoidance of the lingering racial discrimination, exploitation, and marginalization of the minorities and poor who live elsewhere. In such an environment, the cities had to struggle for a benign public presence. The consequences of parasitic urbanization and the loss of bourgeois urbanity narrowed the ways people's fates were connected.[35]

Given the changed metropolitan realities, any renewed urbanity would have to reappear at the regional scale and encompass the older, central cities, inner-ring suburbs, edge cities, and peripheral developments of all sorts. Contrarily, to the extent that the suburbs are "open," a new (sub)urbanity is available to all who make their way there. In the face of rigid political boundaries, continued racial discrimination, and the enduring inequalities of class, neither scenario seems imminent.

Nevertheless, in the early postwar period, the cities were still important to suburbanites. Many suburban households sent their primary wage earners into the cities, and the income earned there had a major impact on suburban living. Over the years, with businesses and investment leaving the cities and the suburbs attracting a greater and greater share of both, suburbanites had less and less need for the older, metropolitan cores. Satellite or edge cities concentrated jobs in the metropolitan periphery during the 1980s, and cross-commuting began to rival commuting from the suburbs to the centers. The cities maintained certain core functions in commercial banking and corporate services, but they were not the sole providers. Additionally, as families moved out and the suburbs developed a range of leisure and cultural facilities, reasons to go into the cities became fewer and fewer. Without a moral sense that the people of the cities and suburbs shared a common social space—that is, that their fates were intertwined and that people had moral obligations to each other—and without political coalitions that crossed municipal boundaries and could pressure state and federal governments to address the problems of the cities, the cities continued to stagnate.[36]

A national identity emerged in the postwar period that celebrated a suburban way of life, set the cities against the suburbs, and fostered a model of citizenship that devalued the public realm, life amid diversity, and care for those in need. This severely diminished the possibility of addressing the decline of the older cities. For the American identity to have been different, the landscapes of opportunities and hardships would have had to have been altered. Patterns of urbanization do not determine the lifestyles in which people engage, but when ruptured, they open up developmental possibilities. The subsequent impacts on how people live are often transformative.[37]

Crossing the Urban Divide

American social maps are layered with the erasures of conquered frontiers. The country reached its continental limits in the 1890s, crossed the urban boundary in the 1920s, and breached the crabgrass divide in the 1960s. And in the mid-twentieth century, it began its first tentative steps into outer space. America has been relentless in the quest to re-create itself. As frontiers have receded, new ones have been imagined in order to continue the quest for expansion, novelty, and connection. The American identity embraces the desire to be accomplished and praised. This, as much as the search for new places, fuels the frontier spirit.[38]

Relentless physical extension had spurred the spread of settlements westward and gave rise to cities from Pittsburgh to San Diego, extruded urban areas into the surrounding countryside, and continued unabated as edge cities in the late twentieth century enabled metropolitan development to sprawl further outward. Cities like Las Vegas, Nevada, and Phoenix pushed further and further into the fragile desert. In the 1990s, the city invaded the countryside as affluence underwrote vacation homes and tourist resorts in areas of Wyoming and Utah that heretofore had been considered impenetrable wilderness. Rather than remaining content with where they lived, Americans relentlessly searched out new places. Having always fled what was old and densely populated, they preferred to pursue ever-receding frontiers. In doing so after World War II, Americans diverted attention from the industrial cities.[39]

With the end of the short American Century came the possibility that, for America, there were limits. The President's Task Force on Suburban Problems of the late 1960s had cast the suburbs as "the burgeoning American frontier in the second half of the twentieth century," but its prophecy had become frayed by the mid-1970s.[40] The economy declined, foreign competitors invaded the national market, U.S. military might no longer deflected all challenges, and worldwide criticism of American cultural incursions multiplied. Inexorable expansion and mastery of geographical space became more unlikely. It seemed as if the United States could neither rest assured in its global dominance nor expect that domestic prosperity would persist. As its industrial cities had twenty-five years earlier, America seemed to be embarking on a long decline.[41]

The sorry state of the domestic economy—unprecedented double-digit inflation and unemployment, numerous factory closings, and excessively high interest rates that stifled new investment—became a national problem in the 1970s. The recessionary economy slowed suburbanization, further exacerbated the fiscal problems of the industrial cities, and even gave rise to a few short years of heightened migration to rural areas. The Northeast bore the brunt of this economic restructuring while migration to the Sunbelt accelerated.

America's share of manufacturing production was on the decline, and favorable trade balances were no longer a given. Foreign investors were buying U.S. companies and taking ownership of high-priced real estate. The failure to win the war in Vietnam and the inability to respond effectively to terrorism or to suppress regional conflicts were additional signs of America's weakness. The Iranian hostage crisis in the late 1970s was particularly embarrassing, given that Iran had once been a staunch ally. The United States, moreover, now had to consider Japan and a reinvigorated Germany, the two powers that it had vanquished in World War II, in its international calculations. The nation would no longer dominate world trade and foreign direct investment, be unchallenged militarily, or lead world diplomacy alone.

During the short American Century, the United States ended its isolationism and embraced an exalted global status. Throughout that quarter century, being international meant spreading American values, institutions, and the American way of life across the planet. Only when its global dominance began to crumble did it recognize the true implications of globalization. As dominance faded, it became increasingly apparent that America was neither in charge of, nor immune from, a changing world for which it was in part responsible. With the erosion of the country's hegemonic status and greater recognition of the irreconcilable social diversity within, claims to an American exceptionalism no longer resonated as strongly as they had during the short American Century. The United States had seemingly lost its exemption "from the constraints and contingencies of history."[42] Here was a cost that Cold War zealots had not factored into their strategic calculations.

How did this happen? What did it have to do with the decline of the industrial cities? Regrettably, most observers have ignored this line of investigation. Instead, they have opted to focus on the ways the world was changing. Japan and western European countries, previously blessed with strong economies, were finally recovering from the war. Development was spreading, industrialization in particular, and countries such as Brazil and South Korea began to produce for local markets and diminish their dependence on imports. Foreign direct investment by U.S. firms created new industrial complexes and stronger states. Coupled with the emergence of international investors, this bolstered foreign economies and made them more competitive in world markets. Hong Kong, Singapore, Japan, Korea, and Germany epitomized the challenges to America's global economic dominance.[43]

The debate over national decline, though, was not confined to global issues. There was also a turning inward to internal weaknesses.

Conservatives trod this path with great success.[44] For them, the 1960s had been a time of liberal indulgence. Universities had succumbed to the demands of campus radicals and liberal professors. The government had coddled the poor and distorted labor markets with affirmative action. The moral climate had deteriorated as more and more children were born to unwed mothers, religion was further distanced from public life, and a sense of tradition and a respect for authority were jettisoned. Multiculturalism displaced nationalism. Conservatives saw all of these as weaknesses and argued that a country internally weak could not be internationally strong. Such a nation would be less inclined to engage in realpolitik or to muster the will to intervene militarily.

In the 1970s, the national economy slowed, but so did the shedding of residents and jobs by the older, industrial cities. Urban decline abated in part because many households and businesses had already departed, leaving behind those less inclined to move, unable to do so, or committed to the cities. What was surprising was a surge in reinvestment. Residential gentrification initially and, a few years later, new commercial reinvestment fueled an urban renaissance in cities like Boston, Chicago, and New York.[45] Other cities—Akron, Cleveland, Buffalo, St. Louis, Louisville—continued to shed households and businesses and remained mired in a spiral of disinvestment.

The gentrification of the late 1970s was reinforced by a building boom in the 1980s that led to edge cities in the suburbs and to a new round of constructing office buildings, shopping malls, and entertainment complexes in the central cities. Driven by a federal relaxation of lending requirements, capital flowed into property development while new office buildings redefined skylines. The expansion of employment supported gentrification and attracted even more people to the older, urban centers. By the late 1990s, downtown retailing had been rejuvenated, though it still fell short of its past glory. In turn, urban tourism and entertainment were attracting suburbanites, foreign visitors, vacationers, and conventioneers from around the country.[46]

A rise in immigration added to the prosperity of some of the older cities. Immigrants took up low-wage service jobs in the new office towers, restaurants, and nightclubs. They became the carpenters, furniture makers, and house cleaners hired by affluent gentrifiers, and they rejuvenated low-wage manufacturing, specifically the garment industries in Los Angeles and New York City. The expansion of immigrant neighborhoods, with their ethnic restaurants and street festivals, became another tourist attraction.

All of this conferred a cachet on urban life. No longer was living

Identity and Urbanity

in the city viewed as foolhardy. City crime was down, opportunities for entertainment were abundant, and selected neighborhoods were once again attractive. Suburban growth was relentless, even if dampened, and white households persisted in their flight from the older cities. Yet for many of these cities, the future no longer looked bleak. A few places—Detroit, East St. Louis, and Buffalo—seemed immune to reinvestment and deeply rooted in decline; many other industrial cities were still struggling. Additionally, reinvestment was confined only to certain parts of the cities. Poverty and slums persisted, and numerous inner-ring suburbs, the suburbs of the 1920s and the late 1940s and 1950s, were showing signs of decay. In cities that had once been viewed as "lost causes," though, places like Newark, evidence of reinvestment was undeniable.

Ostensibly, Americans had conquered another frontier—the frontier between suburban prosperity and urban decay. By the end of the twentieth century, westward expansion had been exhausted and the cities of the Northeast—wild, untamed, and ripe for rediscovery and reinvestment—had become the country's new challenge. Parasitic urbanization seemed on the wane. For the former industrial cities to approximate their past glory, however, the American way of life would once more have to be reinvented, this time with the suburbs as the point of departure. No longer was the city ostracized; a fickle urban ambivalence had shifted again.

The renewed interest in cities unfolded simultaneously with a rethinking of the role of cities in national and global economies.[47] With the U.S. economy less competitive internationally, transnational corporations expanding in size and number, and financial markets becoming more and more global in scope, the nation, and nations generally, no longer stood as the central actors in the world economy. City-regions, dense nodes of economic activity and daily life that defy municipal boundaries, had superseded them. Places like New York City, Paris, London, and Tokyo became world cities that sat at key junctures in global commodity chains. Los Angeles reached across the Pacific Rim, Seattle linked the United States and Canada, and Miami was central to economic interdependencies throughout the Caribbean and South America. More and more, cities that prospered did so because they had become part of thriving regions and international networks.

Here was another frontier to be crossed. City-regions now had to be globally competitive if they wished to prosper. Regional competition—Houston with Galveston, for example, or Pittsburgh with Cleveland—gave way to international competitiveness. In this context, what was important was that cities and suburbs be understood as integral metropolitan units whose fates were linked. The antagonism between cities and suburbs would be forgotten, and cities would once again be the driving force of national prosperity.

Despite the resuscitation of the older, industrial cities, the antagonism between central cities and suburbs lingered. Poor African Americans and immigrants in the core still made suburbanites anxious. Moreover, suburbs were no more willing to take on the fiscal burdens and weak school systems of the central cities than they were to build at city densities. And rare was the big-city mayor who ventured into suburban municipalities in search of common ground. This frontier remained intact.

The end of the short American Century thus gave rise to two trends that favored the older cities and dampened their decline: the renewed interest in the city on the part of investors and households, and the casting of city-regions as the primary competitors in the global economy. The rise in immigration supported these trends and checked population loss, encouraged reinvestment, and improved local job opportunities. Relative to the suburbs, the older central cities were performing much better economically and demographically. Parasitic urbanization had abated.

Final Thoughts

Nearly 100 years ago, Henry James wrote of the development along the New Jersey shore that "there is too little history for dignity of ruin." Because of this, he suggested, Americans found it difficult to connect poverty and wealth to the workings of the larger society.[48] James could just as well have been referring to the wrenching problems faced by the cities of the time. His observation is also relevant to the decline of the industrial cities a half century later.

Once the industrial cities began to seem obsolete and no longer offered opportunities for wealth and fame, Americans forgot about them. Only unavoidable pleas for help or the possibility that their problems would overflow into the suburbs elicited assistance. For Americans, history is the past, and the past is that which has been discarded. The history of the country is a record of what has been achieved and thus of places and institutions that have served their purpose and are now no longer needed. This is how the industrial cities were treated after World War II. At best, their former glory became mere nostalgia. One can hardly expect more from "a culture of consumption and obsolescence."[49]

It was time to move on, and this is precisely what many Americans did. Investors encouraged and supported them; the national and state governments concurred.

A different way of thinking about history might have dampened disinvestment, the loss of people, and the multitude of social, economic, political, and fiscal problems that ensued. What if Americans were to consider their history as a record of what had to have been accomplished for the present to be possible? This would cast history as a continuum, not as the past in tension with the future but as the present as the source of both. From this point of view, flight from the city and the banishment of the urban way of life from a sense of collective identity makes little sense.

This failure to respect the past intersected with another American trait to deflect American attention from the postwar industrial cities. That trait is the tendency to think of the United States as being in control of its destiny. Unlike Canadians, who acknowledge the impact that their neighbor to the south has on their economy and culture, and unlike the Finns, who recognize that much of their history (and their major city, Helsinki) has been shaped by actions taken by Russia, Americans have little sense of their country as susceptible to outside influence. At best, Americans acknowledge external threats, such as the communist menace of the 1950s, Asian investments during the 1980s, or the terrorist attacks of September 11, 2001, but for the most part, they believe that they have accomplished alone what they have achieved.[50]

The American past, as one commentator has offered, has been "imagined in isolation, and Europe was considered only to present a contrast or to draw a moral."[51] Thus, when Americans asked themselves why the industrial cities declined and what it meant, they crafted a story that was partial and distorted, focused inward, confused change for progress, and ignored the wider world. In retrospect, we can see that this story was at odds with postwar realities.

The combination of historical amnesia and chauvinism has kept separate the four major events of the short American Century: the decline of the industrial city, mass suburbanization, domestic prosperity, and global dominance. These events were interconnected. The full force of postwar urbanization was deeply implicated in postwar domestic prosperity and integral to the fate of the industrial cities. In addition, the country's global project would have been more difficult, and quite different, in the absence of the suburban way of life—that great postwar exceptionalism—that carried American goods, behaviors, and values throughout the world.

The price the United States paid for its postwar affluence and global dominance was steep. Many people suffered, much of value was lost. Without an urban culture immersed in diversity and suffused with tolerance and compassion, society was diminished. In the short American Century, Americans lived differently than they had previously, and they lived well. They also turned away from a robust and compassionate public culture. This loss of urbanity was the burden imposed on the cities, and the shame of the suburbs.

Acknowledgments

The origins of this book extend back to one of the first courses I took in graduate school at Cornell University. Wonderfully stimulating and informative, the course was co-taught by Bill Goldsmith and Allan Feldt and focused on theories of urban and regional development. For many years, my research addressed other themes, but the knowledge that these two engaging teachers and scholars imparted lingered. In the mid-1980s, I became fascinated by redevelopment and gentrification and directed my energies to ideas learned in that course. My book *Voices of Decline: The Postwar Fate of U.S. Cities,* which discussed how troubled cities were publicly represented, began a quest for a more satisfactory understanding of postwar urban development in the United States and, specifically, of the decline of the industrial cities.

Eric Lampard's writings (which I had encountered first in that graduate course) were central to this quest. A fellowship at the Center for the Critical Analysis of Contemporary Culture at Rutgers University sensitized me to cultural perspectives. A visiting professorship at UCLA, intermittent teaching at the University of Helsinki, research trips to Johannesburg, and numerous international experiences broadened my perspective on cities of the United States. I benefited greatly from the seminar that Thomas Bender ran from 1997 to 2001 at New York University's International Center for Advanced Studies. Too few pages exist to list all of my intellectual debts.

Bob Lake and Daphne Spain deserve special thanks for their extraordinary efforts—each a perceptive reader whose critical remarks were both daunting and useful. Bob Fishman, Iris Young, and Larry Bourne offered helpful advice, as did audiences at presentations at the University of Toronto, Rutgers University, and the meetings of the Urban History Association and the Society for American City and Regional Planning History.

Simona Goldin provided research assistance in the early stages of the project and enabled me to build a historical database of U.S. cities. Nebahat Tokatli, before that, gathered data on Camden, as Linda Potter did for Philadelphia. Initially planned as case studies within the text, the two cities did not survive to the final version. Nonetheless, that research added immensely to my understanding of urbanization.

The book would not have been possible without the Urban Archives at Temple University and the libraries at New York University, Columbia University, Rutgers University, the University of Pittsburgh, and the University of Pennsylvania.

I thank Jason Weidemann, his assistant Heather Burns, Laura Westlund, and the rest of the very capable production staff at the University of Minnesota Press for their assistance and patience. Kathy Delfosse's editorial skills and numerous queries—greatly appreciated—significantly improved the text.

Finally, and once again, I thank Debra Bilow for her caring and for patience that I too seldom acknowledge.

APPENDIXES

A

DECENNIAL POPULATION LOSS FOR THE FIFTY
LARGEST U.S. CITIES, 1820–2000

B

DEMOGRAPHIC AND ECONOMIC COMPARISONS
ACROSS PERIODS OF URBANIZATION

C

MEASURES OF URBANIZATION FOR HISTORICAL
PERIODS

Appendix A

Decennial Population Loss for the Fifty Largest U.S. Cities, 1820–2000

| | Number of Cities | | Population Size | |
Years	Absolute Loss	Relative Loss	Largest City	Smallest City
1820–1830	3	33	123,706	3,545
1830–1840	5	29	202,589	5,566
1840–1850	1	32	312,710	7,887
1850–1860	1	31	515,547	14,257
1860–1870	1	27	813,669	18,266
1870–1880	2	20	942,292	26,766
1880–1890	0	28	1,206,299	35,629
1890–1900	3	16	1,515,301	57,478
1900–1910	1	26	3,437,202	78,961
1910–1920	0	28	4,766,883	100,253
1920–1930	0	23	5,620,040	132,358
1930–1940	15	22	6,930,446	156,492
1940–1950	2	29	7,454,995	167,402
1950–1960	24	29	7,891,957	203,486
1960–1970	24	28	7,781,984	261,685
1970–1980	33	26	7,895,563	277,714
1980–1990	18	26	7,071,639	284,413
1990–2000	12	23	7,322,564	328,123

Note: The fifty largest cities are recalculated for each decade as new cities join the rankings and other cities drop out of the category. An absolute loss is any net reduction in population, regardless of size; a relative loss involves a fall in ranking. Population size is for the first year of the period. For the entire time span, New York was the largest city; the smallest city varied from year to year, with York, Pennsylvania, occupying that position in 1820 and Buffalo, New York, in 1990.

Sources: U.S. Bureau of the Census population statistics for decennial years, plus Campbell Gibson, "Population of the 100 Largest Cities and Other Urban Places in the United States, 1790–1990," U.S. Bureau of the Census, Population Division, Working Paper 27 (Washington, D.C.: Government Printing Office, 1998).

Appendix B

Demographic and Economic Comparisons across Periods of Urbanization

	1890–1930	1950–1980
Average size of U.S. population (millions)	84.5	190.0
Percent change in U.S. population	95.2	50.3
Average household size	1890 = 4.96 1930 = 4.12	1950 = 3.47 1980 = 2.75
Average change per decade in number of households	4,303,750	13,170,333
Yearly average net natural increase per 1,000 population	13.4	11.0
Yearly average net immigration per 1,000 population	5.0	1.8
Percent of U.S. population in northeastern and north-central regions	1890 = 63.2 1930 = 59.3	1950 = 61.8 1980 = 54.0
Percent change in GNP	248.2	180.9

Note: Gross national product (GNP) is in constant 1958 dollars.

Sources: Data are from U.S. Department of Commerce, *Historical Statistics of the United States* (Washington, D.C.: Government Printing Office, 1975), and U.S. Bureau of the Census, *Statistical Abstract of the United States,* various years. Natural increase and immigration data for 1890–1930 and 1950–1980 are from table 1-10 in Donald T. Bogue, *Components of the Population of the United States, 1940–1950* (Miami, Fla.: Scripps Foundation for Research in Population Problems, 1985). See also Campbell Gibson, "Population of the 100 Largest Cities and Other Urban Places in the United States, 1790–1990," U.S. Bureau of the Census, Population Division, Working Paper 27 (Washington, D.C.: Government Printing Office, 1998).

Appendix C

Measures of Urbanization for Historical Periods

	1890–1930	1950–1980
Percent change in total urban population[a]	32.4	20.3
Percent change in urbanization rate	60.1	15.2
Percent change in central city population	38.5	13.5
Percent change in number of urban places	24.1	84.0
Percent change in number of places over 50,000 people	70.0	99.6
Percent change in number of places over 250,000 people[b]	236.4	36.6
Percent change in population in cities over 250,000 people[c]	316.2	16.3
Yearly average of new housing units started (thousands)[d]	429.4	1,569.8
Average land area in square miles for 25 largest cities[e]	1910 = 70.9	1950 = 96.7 1980 = 242.2
Average population density in population/ square mile for 25 largest cities	1910 = 10,129	1950 = 11,178 1980 = 6,594

Notes: [a] Unless otherwise noted, all numbers are decade averages.

[b] The number of new cities over 250,000 population was twenty-six for 1890–1930 and fifteen for 1950–1980.

[c] The actual change in raw numbers was 21,869,000 for 1890–1930 and 5,688,992 for 1950–1980.

[d] This includes both private and publicly built housing units.

[e] The year 1910 is the first date for which land area data are available. Data for Newark and Jersey City were unavailable and were excluded from this calculation.

Sources: Data are from U.S. Department of Commerce, *Historical Statistics of the United States* (Washington, D.C.: Government Printing Office, 1975), and U.S. Bureau of the Census, *Statistical Abstract of the United States,* various years. See also Campbell Gibson, "Population of the 100 Largest Cities and Other Urban Places in the United States, 1790–1990," U.S. Bureau of the Census, Population Division, Working Paper 27 (Washington, D.C.: Government Printing Office, 1998).

Notes

Preface

1. Here I quote the phrase "American way of life" from Daniel T. Rodgers, *Atlantic Crossings: Social Politics in a Progressive Age* (Cambridge, Mass.: Harvard University Press, 1998), 504. For an introduction to American exceptionalism, see Ian Tyrrell, "American Exceptionalism in an Age of International History," *American Historical Review* 96, no. 4 (1991): 1031–1055, and David W. Noble, *Death of a Nation: American Culture and the End of Exceptionalism* (Minneapolis: University of Minnesota Press, 2002).

2. The phrase "mass suburb" (from which I derive "mass suburbanization") is from John Palen, *The Suburbs* (New York: McGraw-Hill, 1995), 4.

3. One product of this interest is my *Voices of Decline: The Postwar Fate of U.S. Cities* (Oxford: Blackwell, 1993), whose second edition was published by Routledge in 2003.

4. Under the rubric "urban studies" I include all those endeavors, regardless of academic discipline or institutional affiliation, that take the city as an object of study.

5. One exception is Michael Peter Smith's *Transnational Urbanism* (Malden, Mass.: Blackwell, 2000). See also Rodgers, *Atlantic Crossings,* 112–208, and Joe Nasr and Mercedes Volait, eds., *Urbanism: Imported or Exported?* (Chichester, U.K.: Wiley-Academy, 2003). On empire, see Amy Kaplan, "'Left Alone with America,'" in *Cultures of United States Imperialism,* ed. A. Kaplan and D. E. Pease, 3–21 (Durham, N.C.: Duke University Press, 1993).

6. The quoted phrase is Daniel Rodgers's, from *Atlantic Crossings,* 2. On the necessity of a global perspective, see Thomas Bender, "Historians, the Nation, and a Plenitude of Narratives," in *Rethinking American History in a Global Age,* ed. T. Bender, 1–21 (Berkeley and Los Angeles: University of California Press, 2002). For a review of this emerging literature, see Shelley

Fisher Fishkin, "Crossroads of Culture: The Transnational Turn in American Studies," *American Quarterly* 57, no. 1 (2005): 17–57.

7. See Sharon Zukin's *The Cultures of Cities* (Cambridge, Mass.: Blackwell, 1995) for a start.

8. Robert A. Beauregard, "History in Urban Theory," *Journal of Urban History* 30, no. 4 (2004): 627–635.

9. On suburbanization and domestic prosperity, see Lizabeth Cohen, *A Consumers' Republic: The Politics of Mass Consumption in Postwar America* (New York: Knopf, 2003). On domestic prosperity and global dominance, see Donald W. White, *The American Century: The Rise and Decline of the United States as a World Power* (New Haven, Conn.: Yale University Press, 1996). Robert Fishman has attempted to place the suburbs in a global context; see his *Bourgeois Utopias: The Rise and Fall of Suburbia* (New York: Basic Books, 1987) and his "Global Suburbs" (paper presented at the First Biennial Conference of the Urban History Association, Pittsburgh, September 2002).

10. The quotation is from Benedict Anderson; he uses it to characterize his approach to community. See his *Imagined Communities* (London: Verso, 1983), 6. Peter Gay is another role model here. He accepts the elusiveness and variability of the bourgeoisie and yet refuses to declare it useless for understanding the nineteenth century. See his *Pleasure Wars: The Bourgeois Experience* (New York: Norton, 1998) and his *Schnitzler's Century: The Making of Middle-Class Culture, 1815–1914* (New York: Norton, 2002). And while I agree with James Patterson that "we cannot resurrect such a thing as an 'American character,'" that does not preclude its having discursive value. See his "America and the Writing of Twentieth Century United States History," in *Imagined Histories: American Historians Interpret the Past*, ed. A. Molho and G. S. Wood, 185–205 (Princeton, N.J.: Princeton University Press, 1998). The quotation is on page 197.

11. Dorothy Ross in 1995 wrote that "American exceptionalism remains a potential lure for any grand synthesis constructed around American national history, and the one sure-fire cure, transnational history, is as yet little practiced." "Grand Narratives in American Historical Writing: From Romance to Uncertainty," *American Historical Review* 100, no. 3 (1995): 676.

12. On the place of moral narratives in historical writing, see Charles S. Maier, "Consigning the Twentieth Century to History: Alternative Narratives for the Modern Age," *American Historical Review* 105, no. 3 (2000): 807–831.

13. See Anthony Molho and Gordon S. Wood, "Introduction," in Molho and Wood, *Imagined Histories*, 3–20.

14. The notion of a cognitive style comes from Albert O. Hirschman, "The Search for Paradigms as a Hindrance to Understanding," *World Politics* 22, no. 3 (1970): 329–343. See Bruno Latour on "things that gather" in his "Why Has Critique Run Out of Steam? From Matters of Fact to Matters of Concern," *Critical Inquiry* 30 (2004): 225–248.

15. Neil Fligston, *Going North: Migration of Blacks and Whites from the South, 1900–1950* (New York: Academic Press, 1981), 4.

1. The Short American Century

1. Henry R. Luce, "The American Century," *Life,* February 17, 1941, 63. Luce published *Time* and *Life,* two of the period's most popular mass-market magazines, in addition to the business journal *Fortune, Sports Illustrated,* and *Architectural Forum.* His company also produced news items for radio and cinema as part of its March of Time division.

2. Much like the twentieth century, which Eric Hobsbawm dates from 1914 to 1991, the American Century was abbreviated, lasting from approximately the late 1940s to the mid-1970s, after which a variety of factors (an energy crisis, renewed immigration, the war in Vietnam, and the civil rights and women's movements) dampened domestic prosperity, destabilized the nation's global dominance, and eroded any lingering sense of social cohesion. See Eric Hobsbawm, *The Age of Extremes* (New York: Vintage, 1996), 5–11. Olivier Zunz, in his *Why the American Century?* (Chicago: University of Chicago Press, 1998), argues that the ideology of the American Century was constructed before World War II but was only imposed on the world after the war had ended.

3. For overviews of postwar urban decline, see Carl Abbott, *Urban America in the Modern Age* (Arlington Heights, Ill.: Harlan Davidson, 1987), 117–125; Robert A. Beauregard, *Voices of Decline: The Postwar Fate of U.S. Cities,* 2nd ed. (New York: Routledge, 2003); Peter A. Gluck and Richard J. Meister, *Cities in Transition* (New York: New Viewpoints, 1979), 136–149; Jon C. Teaford, *The Twentieth-Century American City* (Baltimore: The Johns Hopkins University Press, 1986), 109–150; and Teaford, *The Rough Road to Renaissance* (Baltimore: The Johns Hopkins University Press, 1990), 10–43.

4. The reference is to Kenneth T. Jackson's comment in 1972 that "the decline of American cities is really an optical illusion; only a small part of the city is suffering while most of it is relatively prosperous." See his "Metropolitan Government versus Suburban Autonomy," in *Cities in American History,* ed. K. T. Jackson and S. K. Schultz, 442–462 (New York: Knopf, 1972). The quotation is on page 456. The descriptions of population loss are based on decennial U.S. Bureau of the Census data used to construct the data set used in chapter 2 below; see note 16 in that chapter.

5. For an introduction to the literature on urbanization, see Eric E. Lampard, "The Nature of Urbanization," in *The Pursuit of Urban History,* ed. D. Fraser and A. Sutcliffe, 3–52 (London: Edward Arnold, 1983), and Hope Tisdale, "The Process of Urbanization," *Social Forces* 20 (1942): 311–316.

6. On this perversity thesis and postwar urban decline, see Robert A. Beauregard, "Federal Policy and Postwar Urban Decline: A Case of Government Complicity?" *Housing Policy Debate* 12, no. 1 (2001): 129–151.

7. Lizabeth Cohen, *A Consumers' Republic: The Politics of Mass Consumption in Postwar America* (New York: Knopf, 2003), 193–289.

8. Rosalyn Baxandall and Elizabeth Ewen, *Picture Windows: How the Suburbs Happened* (New York: Basic Books, 2000), 175.

9. On this point, see Marshall Berman, *All That Is Solid Melts into Air* (New York: Penguin, 1982), 37–86. For a historical overview of how intellectuals in the United States have perceived the U.S. city, see Morton White and Lucia White, *The Intellectual versus the City* (New York: New American Library, 1962).

10. Michael Kammen, *People of Paradox* (New York: Knopf, 1972), 107 and 99. For a documented account of such tensions, see Robert N. Bellah, Richard Madsen, William M. Sullivan, Ann Swidler, and Stephen M. Tipton, *Habits of the Heart* (New York: Harper and Row, 1986). Urban theory shares these qualities; see Robert A. Beauregard, "Descendents of Ascendant Cities and Other Urban Dualities," *Journal of Urban Affairs* 15, no. 3 (1993): 217–229.

11. The phrase "the shame of the cities" is the title of Lincoln Steffens's famous condemnation of political corruption in the city of the late nineteenth and early twentieth centuries. His exposés focused on Pittsburgh, Philadelphia, St. Louis, Chicago, New York, and Minneapolis. See Steffens, *The Shame of the Cities* (New York: Hill and Wang, 1957; orig. pub. 1904).

12. James C. Scott's *Seeing Like a State: How Certain Schemes to Improve the Human Condition Have Failed* (New Haven, Conn.: Yale University Press, 1998) provides a thoughtful and substantive commentary on this perspective.

13. Joseph A. Schumpeter, *Capitalism, Socialism, and Democracy* (New York: Harper and Row, 1942), 81–86. Max Page uses the trope of creative destruction in his insightful history of city building in the late nineteenth and early twentieth centuries in New York City. See his *The Creative Destruction of Manhattan, 1900–1940* (Chicago: University of Chicago Press, 1999).

14. See Dorothy Ross's "Grand Narratives in American Historical Writing: From Romance to Uncertainty," *The American Historical Review* 100, no. 3 (1995): 651–677, and her discussion of "Cold War triumphalism" on page 661. The case for a global perspective on American history is made by Thomas Bender in his "Historians, the Nation, and the Plentitude of Narratives," in *Rethinking American History in a Global Age*, ed. T. Bender, 1–21 (Berkeley and Los Angeles: University of California Press, 2002).

15. The quotation is from Robert N. Bellah, Richard Madsen, William M. Sullivan, Ann Swidler, and Stephen M. Tipton, *The Good Society* (New York: Vintage, 1991), 53. For background on this period, see William H. Chafe, *The Unfinished Journey* (New York: Oxford University Press, 1986), 111–145; Michael French, *U.S. Economic History since 1945* (Manchester, U.K.: Manchester University Press, 1997), 196–207; Eric Hobsbawm, *The Age of Extremes: A History of the World, 1914–1991* (New York: Vintage,

1996), 257–286; James T. Patterson, *Grand Expectations: The United States, 1945–1974* (New York: Oxford University Press, 1996); Donald W. White, *The American Century: The Rise and Decline of the United States as a World Power* (New Haven, Conn.: Yale University Press, 1996); and Alan Wolfe, *America's Impasse: The Rise and Fall of the Politics of Growth* (New York: Pantheon, 1981), 13–18. Immanuel Wallerstein noted that this was not only a period of "U.S. hegemony and the incredible expansion of the world economy" but "the era as well of the triumph of the historical anti-systemic [national liberation] movements of the world-system." See his *The End of the World as We Know It* (Minneapolis: University of Minnesota Press, 1999). The quotation is on page 22.

16. Attempts to appropriate a century for national purpose are common. In 1905, the then prime minister of Canada Sir Wilfrid Laurier proclaimed that "as the nineteenth century had been the century of the United States, so the twentieth century would be the century of Canada." See Robert M. Hamilton and Dorothy Shields, eds., *The Dictionary of Canadian Quotations and Phrases* (Toronto: McClennand and Stewart, 1979), 909.

17. Luce, "The American Century." Quotations are on pages 63, 64, and 65, in that order.

18. Walter Lippman, "The American Destiny," *Life,* June 5, 1939, 47, 72–73. Quotations are on page 73. Saul K. Padover's "The American Century?" *American Scholar* 17, no. 1 (1947): 85–90, places the concept in its Cold War context. The description of this period as an era of self-congratulation is from Patterson, *Grand Expectations,* 188.

19. The first quotation is from Frieda Kirchwey, "Luce Thinking," *Nation,* March 1, 1941, 229, and the second is from Sean Wilentz, "That Century, Yet Again," *New Yorker,* November 9, 1998, 105. For White, see *The American Century,* 8–12.

20. William Appleman Williams, *The Contours of American History* (New York: New Viewpoints, 1973), 17–18. On the ideological suppression of an "American empire," see Amy Kaplan, "Left Alone with America: The Absence of Empire in the Study of American Culture," in *Cultures of United States Imperialism,* ed. A. Kaplan and D. E. Pease, 3–21 (Durham, N.C.: Duke University Press, 1993). Neil Smith positions these years as the tail end of the second effort by the United States to impose its brand of liberalism on the world. The first effort occurred in the late nineteenth and early twentieth centuries, and the third—the era of globalization—began in the late 1960s. See his *The Endgame of Globalization* (New York: Routledge, 2005).

21. See Chafe, *The Unfinished Journey;* French, *U.S. Economic History since 1945;* and Patterson, *Grand Expectations,* 311–320.

22. Charles A. Beard, *Contemporary American History* (New York: Macmillan, 1914), 90.

23. See Seymour Martin Lipset, *American Exceptionalism: A Double-Edged Sword* (New York: Norton, 1996), 31–39; Werner Sombert, *Why Is*

There No Socialism in America? (White Plains, N.Y.: Sharpe, 1976; orig. pub. 1906); and Zunz, *Why the American Century?* 73–92, 165. The quotation regarding world progress is from Ross, "Grand Narratives in American Historical Writing," 652.

24. The quotation is from George M. Fredrickson, "From Exceptionalism to Variability: Recent Developments in Cross-National Comparative History," *Journal of American History* 82, no. 2 (1995): 588. For a critique of the use of exceptionalism in the realm of urban theory, see Robert A. Beauregard, "City of Superlatives," *City & Community* 2, no. 3 (2003): 183–199. The point regarding resilience comes from Ian Tyrrell, "American Exceptionalism in an Age of International History," *American Historical Review* 96, no. 4 (1991): 1032.

25. Quoted in Max Silberschmidt, *The United States and Europe: Rivals and Partners* (New York: Harcourt Brace Jovanavich, 1972), 9.

26. For an introduction to these comparisons, see N. S. B. Gras, "The Development of Metropolitan Economy in Europe and America," *American Historical Review* 27, no. 4 (1922): 695–708; Frederick C. Howe, "The American and the British City—a Comparison," *Scribner's Magazine* 41, no. 1 (1907): 113–121; Sir Hugh Canon, "Critique of the Expanding Subtopia," *New York Times Magazine,* October 27, 1957, 31ff.; and Witold Rybcznski, *City Life: Urban Expectations in a New World* (New York: Scribner, 1995), esp. 15–83.

27. Fredrickson, "From Exceptionalism to Variability," 588. For additional discussion of the relationship of the United States to Europe, see Robert M. Crunden, *A Brief History of American Culture* (New York: Paragon House, 1994). On the centrality of Europe to American historiography, see Anthony Molho and Gordon S. Wood, "Introduction," in *Imagined Histories: American Historians Interpret the Past,* ed. A. Molho and G. S. Wood, 3–20 (Princeton, N.J.: Princeton University Press, 1998).

28. To this extent, I disagree with Liam Kennedy's claims that the city was the "privileged site of Americanization" and that it perpetuated the exceptionalist ideology. The former was the case only in the late nineteenth and early twentieth centuries, and the latter was never the case. Suburbanization is what enabled Americans to declare themselves exceptional in how they lived. See his *Race and Urban Space in Contemporary American Culture* (Edinburgh: Edinburgh University Press, 2000), 171.

29. See Frederick Jackson Turner, "The Significance of the Frontier in American History" (1893), in *The Early Writings of Frederick Jackson Turner,* ed. E. E. Edwards, 183–229 (Madison: University of Wisconsin Press, 1938), and David W. Noble, *The Death of a Nation: American Culture and the End of Exceptionalism* (Minneapolis: University of Minnesota Press, 2002).

30. The phrase is the title of Kenneth T. Jackson's well-known book on the suburbs *Crabgrass Frontier: Suburbanization of the United States* (New York: Oxford University Press, 1985).

31. Andrew Hacker, *Two Nations: Black and White, Separate, Hostile, Unequal* (New York: Scribner's, 1992).

32. See Gunnar Myrdal, *An American Dilemma: The Negro Problem and Modern Democracy* (New York: Harper and Row, 1944). Myrdal wrote that "the Negro Problem is a problem in the heart of America" (lxxix), a problem of moral conflict between the American Creed and the conditions under which the Negro lived.

33. From 1959 to 1975, the proportion of persons below the poverty line in the United States fell from 22.4 percent to 11.2 percent. See U.S. Bureau of the Census, *Statistical Abstract of the United States* (Washington, D.C.: Government Printing Office, 1979), 462, table 758. As for income disparities in the 1990s, the United States ranked ninth in the world in the percentage of the national income received by the richest 10 percent of the households: 46.9 percent. The United Kingdom ranked 83rd; Germany, 108th; Canada, 110th; and Sweden, 124th, at 18.6 percent. See George Thomas Kurian, ed., *The Illustrated Book of World Rankings* (Armonk, N.Y.: Sharpe, 2001), 102–103, table 7.6.

34. On the symbolic connection of race and urban decline, see Beauregard, *Voices of Decline*, 290–292. On slums as a dominant urban image, see Sam Bass Warner, "The Management of Multiple Urban Images," in Fraser and Sutcliffe, *The Pursuit of Urban History*, 383–394. For basic data, see Paul A. Jargowsky, *Poverty and Place* (New York: Russell Sage, 1997); Douglas S. Massey and Nancy Denton, *American Apartheid* (Cambridge, Mass.: Harvard University Press, 1993); and William Julius Wilson, *The Truly Disadvantaged* (Chicago: University of Chicago Press, 1987).

35. Molho and Wood, "Introduction," 10 and 15.

36. John A. Hall and Charles Lindholm claimed, quite myopically from my perspective, that "the argument that America must pay a dire price for its international leadership seems to be wrong." See their *Is America Breaking Apart?* (Princeton, N.J.: Princeton University Press, 1999), 72. They wrote prior to the terrorist attack on the Pentagon and the World Trade Center on September 11, 2001, and the onset of the "war on terrorism." On American global power and domestic decay, but with only passing reference to cities, see James Petras and Morris Morley, *Empire or Republic? American Global Power and Domestic Decay* (New York: Routledge, 1995).

2. Urbanization's Consequences

1. Michael P. Conzen, "American Cities in Profound Transition: The New City Geography of the 1980s," in *The Making of Urban America*, ed. R. A. Mohl, 227–289 (Wilmington, Del.: Scholarly Resources, 1988).

2. Robert A. Beauregard, *Voices of Decline: The Postwar Fate of U.S. Cities,* 2nd ed. (New York: Routledge, 2003), 125–178.

3. A survey sponsored by the Fannie Mae Foundation in the late 1990s

that involved 160 urban experts listed the "de-industrialization of central cities" as the third-most-significant influence on the American metropolis over the previous fifty years. The "mass-produced suburban tract house" was fifth and "Sunbelt-style sprawl" was eighth. See Robert Fishman, "The American Metropolis at Century's End: Past and Future Influences," *Housing Policy Debate* 11, no. 1 (2000): 199–213.

4. For the population data, see Ira Lowry, "The Dismal Future of the Central Cities," in *The Prospective City*, ed. A. P. Solomon, 161–203 (Cambridge, Mass.: MIT Press, 1980), 166–167. The quotation is from page 170. Population growth is a powerful measure of the prosperity of a city, and population loss is a good indicator of worsening social, economic, and fiscal problems. See Robert D. Ebel, "Urban Decline in the World's Developed Economies," *Research in Urban Economies* 5, no. 1 (1985): 1–19. Of course, cities are constantly adding and losing population, and the accurate statement of this is net growth or decline. The data reported for St. Louis in the text are net data and thus are underestimates of the actual out-migration.

5. Robert A. Beauregard, "Aberrant Cities: Urban Population Loss in the United States, 1820–1930," *Urban Geography* 24, no. 7 (2003): 672–690.

6. Adna F. Weber, "Growth of the Cities in the United States: 1890–1900," *Municipal Affairs* 5, no. 2 (1901): 370 and 373. See also W. Elliott Brownlee, *Dynamics of Ascent*, 2nd ed. (New York: Knopf, 1979), 280.

7. Quoted in M. A. Mikkelsen, "Have the Cities Reached Maturity?" *Architectural Record* 82, no. 6 (1937): 60. The National Resources Board was established in 1933 in the Public Works Administration to study urban distress and to develop proposals to remedy it. See Mark Gelfand, *A Nation of Cities* (New York: Oxford University Press, 1975), 83–98.

8. William F. Ogburn, *Social Characteristics of Cities* (Chicago: International City Managers' Association, 1937), 61.

9. The first quotation is from C. A. Dykstra, "The Future of American Cities," *American City* 49, no. 10 (1934): 53, and the second from Urban Land Institute, *Decentralization: What Is It Doing to Our Cities?* (Chicago: Urban Land Institute, 1940), 5.

10. These changes were calculated from the U.S. Bureau of the Census decennial population reports for 1930 and 1940. Large cities are those with over 250,000 residents, medium-size cities are those with over 100,000 residents and fewer than 250,000 residents, and small cities are those with between 50,000 and 100,000 residents.

11. Frank Fisher, "Rebuilding Our Cities," *Nation,* August 11, 1945, 130–132.

12. Homer Hoyt, "The Structure of American Cities in the Post-War Era," *American Journal of Sociology* 48, no. 4 (1943): 475.

13. The quotation is from Mabel Walker, "The American City Is Obsolescent," *Vital Speeches of the Day* 13, no. 22 (1947): 697. There were 412 cities with populations exceeding 25,000 residents in 1930.

14. The fourteen cities are Baltimore; Buffalo; Chicago; Cincinnati, Ohio; Cleveland; Detroit; Minneapolis; Newark; Philadelphia; Pittsburgh; Rochester, New York; St. Louis; Syracuse, New York; and Washington, D.C.

15. Michael Wegener, "The Changing Urban Hierarchy in Europe," in *Cities in Competition,* ed. J. Botchie, M. Batty, E. Blakely, P. Hall, and P. Newton, 139–160 (Melbourne: Longman, 1995). See the discussion in chapter 3 below also.

16. These observations are based on a data set that consists of the fifty largest cities by population size for each decade from 1820 to 2000, though the primary concern is with the period from 1950 to 1980. The data were drawn from the decennial censuses for these years and from Campbell Gibson, "Population of the 100 Largest Cities and Other Urban Places in the United States, 1790–1990," U.S. Bureau of the Census, Working Paper 27 (Washington, D.C.: Government Printing Office, 1998). To make the distinction between growth and decline, I use 0.0 percent as the dividing line rather than a range around zero that would account for measurement errors. On the quality of the enumeration procedures used to create the decennial census, see W. Stull Holt, *The Bureau of the Census* (Washington, D.C.: Brookings Institution, 1929); Barnes F. Lathrop, "History from the Census Returns," in *Sociology and History: Methods,* ed. S. M. Lipset and R. Hofstadter, 79–101 (New York: Basic Books, 1968); and Ann Herbert Scott, *Census USA* (New York: Seabury Press, 1968).

17. The manufacturing employment data, except for Baltimore, are from the fifty-city data set described in the previous note. For background on industrial decline in this period, see Barry Bluestone and Bennett Harrison, *The Deindustrialization of America* (New York: Basic Books, 1982). For Baltimore, see Bennett Harrison and Edward Hill, "The Changing Structure of Jobs in Older and Younger Cities," in *Central City Economic Development,* ed. B. Chinitz, 15–45 (Cambridge, Mass.: Abt Books, 1975). Also useful is George Sternlieb and James W. Hughes, "The Changing Demography of the Central City," *Scientific American,* August 1980, 48–53.

18. I use 1950–1980 to represent this period because of the war in the first half of the 1940s, the slight growth in the urban population in the late 1940s, and the fact that only two large cities lost population in that decade.

19. The range of population loss was 4 to 12 percent for the 1950–1980 decades and 5 to 7 percent for the 1830–1880 decades. The 12 percent for the postwar cities occurred in the 1970s. Of note, the declining cities of the 1870s were comparable to those of the 1970s—suffering a 13.2 percent population loss.

20. In this paragraph, the data refer to large, medium, and small cities as defined in note 10, this chapter.

21. David L. Birch, *The Economic Future of City and Suburbs* (New York: Committee for Economic Development, 1970), 14.

22. For background, see Richard M. Bernard and Bradley R. Rice, eds.,

Sunbelt Cities: Politics and Growth since World War II (Austin: University of Texas Press, 1983), 1–30; John M. Findlay, *Magic Lands: Western Cityscapes and Western Culture after 1940* (Berkeley and Los Angeles: University of California Press, 1992), 14–51; Michael French, *U.S. Economic History since 1945* (Manchester, U.K.: Manchester University Press, 1997), 54–80; Kirkpatrick Sales, "Six Pillars of the Southern Rim," in *The Fiscal Crisis of American Cities,* ed. R. E. Alcaly and D. Mermelstein, 165–180 (New York: Vintage, 1977); and Robert B. Vance and Nicholas J. Demerath, eds., *The Urban South* (Chapel Hill: University of North Carolina Press, 1954), esp. chaps. 1 and 2.

23. William K. Tabb, "Urban Development and Regional Restructuring: An Overview," in *Sunbelt/Snowbelt,* ed. L. Sawers and W. K. Tabb, 3–15 (New York: Oxford University Press, 1984), 7.

24. The data to support these claims were taken from U.S. Bureau of the Census, *Statistical Abstract of the United States,* various years.

25. These calculations were made from decennial census data. San Antonio had a population of 800,000 residents in 1980. Small cities are those with fewer than 100,000 residents.

26. U.S. Bureau of the Census, Population Estimate Program, Population Division, "Population Estimates for Cities with Populations over 100,000 and Greater, July 1, 1998" (Washington, D.C., June 30, 1999), and U.S. Bureau of the Census, "Table 2. Incorporated Places of 100,000 or More, Ranked by Population: 2000," Internet release, April 2, 2001.

27. These data and those in subsequent paragraphs are from the population analysis described in note 16, this chapter. The sixteen cities were Columbus; Dallas, Texas; El Paso; Honolulu, Hawaii; Houston; Jacksonville, Florida; Long Beach, California; Memphis, Tennessee; Miami; Nashville, Tennessee; Oklahoma City, Oklahoma; Phoenix; San Antonio; San Diego; San Jose; and Tulsa, Oklahoma.

28. William H. Frey, "The New Urban Revival in the United States," *Urban Studies* 30, nos. 4–5 (1993): 767, table 9, and Stephen A. Holmes, "Sunbelt Suburbs Set Pace for Fastest-Growing Cities," *New York Times,* November 19, 1997.

29. See William H. Frey and Alden Speare Jr., *Regional and Metropolitan Growth and Decline in the United States* (New York: Russell Sage Foundation, 1988), 50, table 3.4, and John D. Kasarda, "The Implications of Contemporary Redistribution Trends for National Urban Policy," *Social Science Quarterly* 61, no. 3 (1980): 373–400, particularly 375, table 1. In 1950, there were 162 metropolitan areas, and by 1980 there were 304. See Frey and Speare, *Regional and Metropolitan Growth and Decline in the United States,* 40, table 3.1.

30. See Gail Garfield Schwartz, *Retrospect and Prospects: An Urban Policy Profile of the United States* (Columbus, Ohio: Academy for Contemporary Problems, 1979), 2, table 2.

31. "Suburbs Cut Cities Down to Size," *Business Week,* June 18, 1960, 64.

32. This brief review of early suburbanization draws from Robert Fishman, *Bourgeois Utopias: The Rise and Fall of Suburbia* (New York: Basic Books, 1987), 116–154; Kenneth T. Jackson, *Crabgrass Frontier: The Suburbanization of the United States* (New York: Oxford University Press, 1985), 3–156; David Schuyler, *The New Urban Landscape* (Baltimore: The Johns Hopkins University Press, 1986), 149–163; Richard A. Walker, "The Transformation of Urban Structure in the Nineteenth Century and the Beginnings of Suburbanization," in *Urbanization and Conflict in Market Societies,* ed. K. R. Cox, 165–205 (Chicago: Maaroufa Press, 1978); and Sam Bass Warner Jr., *Streetcar Suburbs: The Process of Growth in Boston, 1870–1900* (Cambridge, Mass.: Harvard University Press, 1962). Dolores Hayden provides a useful chronology of types of suburbs in her *Building Suburbia: Green Fields and Urban Growth, 1820–2000* (New York: Pantheon, 2003).

33. Schuyler, *The New Urban Landscape,* notes that pre-1900, "the growth of the suburbs was part of the process of urbanization" (163).

34. Basil G. Zimmer, "The Urban Centrifugal Drift," in *Metropolitan America in Contemporary Perspective,* ed. A. H. Hawley and V. P. Rock, 23–91 (New York: Wiley and Sons, 1975), 31, table 1.4. For earlier data, see Paul Harlan Douglas, *The Suburban Trend* (New York: Century, 1925), 18.

35. See John D. Kasarda and George V. Redfern, "Differential Patterns of City and Suburban Growth in the United States," *Journal of Urban History* 2, no. 1 (1975): 54. The cities, by contrast, had almost one-third of the population in 1930. On suburban development in Los Angeles in the 1940s, see Greg Hise, "Home Building and Industrial Decentralization in Los Angeles," *Journal of Urban History* 19, no. 2 (1993): 95–125.

36. Donald T. Bogue, *The Population of the United States: Historical Trends and Future Projections* (New York: Free Press, 1985), 345. See also Thomas Muller, "Urban Growth and Decline," *Challenge* 19, no. 2 (1976): 10–13.

37. My description of postwar suburbanization relies on Rosalyn Baxandall and Elizabeth Ewen, *Picture Window: How the Suburbs Happened* (New York: Basic Books, 2000); Fishman, *Bourgeois Utopias;* Hayden, *Building Suburbia,* 128–120; Jackson, *Crabgrass Frontier;* William L. O'Neill, *American High: The Years of Confidence, 1945–1960* (New York: Free Press, 1993), 9–44; and John T. Palen, *The Suburbs* (New York: McGraw-Hill, 1995), 56–67. For an in-depth review of one metropolitan area's suburbanization, see Peter O. Muller, Kenneth G. Meyer, and Roman A. Cybriwsky, *Metropolitan Philadelphia: A Study of Conflicts and Social Cleavages* (Cambridge, Mass.: Ballinger, 1976).

38. The central-city share of the country's population went from 18.6 percent in 1890 to 30.0 percent in 1980 while the suburban share went from 4.2 percent to 44.8 percent. See Figure 4.

39. See Kasarda and Redfern, "Differential Patterns of City and Suburban Growth in the United States," 54, for 1900–1970, and Donald J. Bogue,

Population Growth in Standard Metropolitan Areas, 1900–1950 (Washington, D.C.: Government Printing Office, 1954); U.S. Bureau of the Census, *1990 Census Profile* (Washington, D.C.: U.S. Department of Commerce, 1991), number 3, figure 1; and U.S. Department of Commerce, *Metropolitan Districts: Population and Area* (Washington, D.C.: U.S. Superintendent of Documents, 1932). For contrary data on the 1980s, see Frey, "The New Urban Revival in the United States," 757, table 5. The 1960s were the first decade in which the number of whites failed to increase in the cities. See Reynolds Farley, "Components of Suburban Population Growth," in *The Changing Face of the Suburbs,* ed. B. Schwartz, 3–38 (Chicago: University of Chicago Press, 1976), 5.

40. On the suburbs' "milking" of the central cities in other ways (for example, siphoning off middle-class leadership), see Scott Donaldson, *The Suburban Myth* (New York: Columbia University Press, 1969), 114.

41. These comments on the changing central-city/metropolitan population ratio are based on data gathered for analysis of the fifty large cities. See also Phillip M. Hauser, "The Challenge of Metropolitan Growth," *Urban Land* 17, no. 11 (1958): 3–6.

42. David Birch, "From Suburbs to Urban Place," *Annals of the American Academy of Political and Social Science* 422 (1975): 28. See also Bogue, *The Population of the United States,* 345, and Alfred Nucci and Larry Long, "Spatial and Demographic Dynamics of Metropolitan and Nonmetropolitan Territory in the United States," *International Journal of Population Demography* 1 (1995): 170.

43. On the deconcentration of the 1970s, see William Alonzo, "Metropolis without Growth," *Public Interest* 53 (1978): 68–86; Brian J. L. Berry, "Urbanization and Counterurbanization in the United States," *Annals of the American Academy of Political and Social Science* 451 (1988):13–20; Larry Long and Diane DeAre, "The Slowing of Urbanization in the U.S.," *Scientific American,* July 1983, 33–41; and Larry Long and Alfred Nucci, "The 'Clean Break' Revisited: Is US Population Again Deconcentrating?" *Environment and Planning A* 29 (1997): 1355–1366.

44. In 1960, 12 percent of all central-city workers commuted whereas 37 percent of suburban workers did so. Advisory Commission on Intergovernmental Relations, *Metropolitan Social and Economic Disparities* (Washington, D.C.: Government Printing Office, 1965), 22. See also Birch, "From Suburbs to Urban Place," 29, table 4.

45. Birch, "From Suburbs to Urban Place," 26. See also J. Thomas Black, "The Changing Economic Role of Central Cities and Suburbs," in *The Prospective City,* ed. A. P. Solomon, 80–123 (Cambridge, Mass.: MIT Press, 1980).

46. Robert A. Beauregard, "Edge Cities: Peripheralizing the Center," *Urban Geography* 16, no. 8 (1995): 708–721; Joel Garreau, *Edge City: Life on the New Frontier* (New York: Doubleday, 1991); Hayden, *Building Suburbia,* 154–180; and Edward W. Soja, *Postmetropolis: Critical Studies of Cities and Regions* (Oxford: Blackwell, 2000), 233–263.

47. Ellis Cose, "Can American Cities Survive?" *Current*, March 1978, 27.

48. For the interrelationship of population loss with job loss and social problems, see Katherine L. Bradbury, Anthony Downs, and Kenneth A. Small, *Urban Decline and the Future of American Cities* (Washington, D.C.: Brookings Institution, 1982); Franklin James, "City Need and Distress in the United States: 1970 to the Mid-1980s," in *The Future of National Urban Policy*, ed. M. Kaplan and F. James, 13–31 (Durham, N.C.: Duke University Press, 1990); and Richard P. Nathan and Charles Adams, "Understanding Central City Hardship," *Political Science Quarterly* 91, no. 1 (1976): 47–62.

49. See Muller, "Urban Growth and Decline," 10–13, for a less succinct version of this scenario.

50. This description of Philadelphia is based on data from the U.S. Bureau of the Census's decennial population reports and *County & City Data Book* for various years. For general background, see Robert A. Beauregard, "The Spatial Transformation of Postwar Philadelphia," *Atop the Urban Hierarchy*, ed. R. A. Beauregard, 1–44 (Totowa, N.J.: Rowman and Littlefield, 1989).

51. On the competition between and among cities, see Daniel J. Boorstein, "The Businessman as an American Institution," in *American Urban History*, ed. A. B. Callow, 136–143 (New York: Oxford University Press, 1969); Michael A. Pagano and Ann O'M. Bowman, *Cityscapes and Capital* (Baltimore: The Johns Hopkins University Press, 1995); and Richard C. Wade, *The Urban Frontier* (Chicago: University of Chicago Press, 1959). Of course, rapid growth is unwelcome in some communities, particularly relatively affluent places, where the problems of growth—traffic congestion, environmental pollution, lagging provision of public services, rising home prices—spur a call for policies favoring slow or no growth.

3. Parasitic Urbanization

1. Bert F. Hoselitz deployed a similar distinction—generative and parasitic cities—but used it to distinguish cities that have a favorable impact on national economic development from those that have the opposite effect. See his "Generative and Parasitic Cities," *Economic Development and Cultural Change* 3 (1954–1955): 278–294. Jane Jacobs developed a different version in her *Cities and the Wealth of Nations* (New York: Vintage, 1985), 182–220. She argued that "transactions of decline" (for example, intergovernmental transfer payments, military procurement) create dependencies that prevent cities from relying on "one another's creativity and their volatile mutual trade" (207). David Harvey made a similar comment regarding cities that consume the social surplus through wasteful enterprise. See his *Social Justice and the City* (Baltimore: The Johns Hopkins University Press, 1973), 234. On the theoretical meanings of turning points and trajectories, see Andrew Abbott, "The Concept of Turning Point," in his *Time Matters: On Theory and Method*, 240–246 (Chicago: University of Chicago Press, 2001).

2. Lewis Mumford, *The City in History* (New York: Harcourt, Brace and World, 1961), 486.

3. "Urban" in this context refers to a relatively dense community of a certain size (over 2,500 people, according to the U.S. Bureau of the Census) and thus subsumes central cities, suburbs, and small towns outside metropolitan areas. According to the Bureau of the Census, the United States added 60 million people between 1890 and 1930 and 76 million people between 1950 and 1980. Unless otherwise stated, data are from the U.S. Bureau of the Census decennial population reports available in the various summaries and in the yearly *Statistical Abstract of the United States.*

4. On the lessened urbanization of the 1970s, see William Alonso, "Metropolis without Growth," *Public Interest* 53 (Fall 1978): 66–86; Brian J. L. Berry, "Urbanization and Counter-Urbanization in the United States," *Annals of the AAPSS*, no. 451 (September 1980): 13–20; and Larry Long and Diane DeAre, "The Slowing of Urbanization in the U.S.," *Scientific American,* July 1983, 33–41.

5. Frederick Jackson Turner, "The Significance of the Frontier in American History" (1893), in *The Early Writings of Frederick Jackson Turner,* ed. E. E. Edwards, 183–229 (Madison: University of Wisconsin Press, 1938). The quotation is on page 229.

6. The "largest economy" label is from David S. Landes, *The Wealth and Poverty of Nations* (New York: Norton, 1998), 307, and is for 1870 and thereafter. Interestingly, Allan Pred claimed that between 1860 and 1910, an incipient parasitic urbanization was underway as some cities grew at the expense of others. See his *The Spatial Dynamics of U.S. Urban-Industrial Growth, 1800–1914* (Cambridge, Mass.: MIT Press, 1966), 46–49.

7. The comparison presented in the following pages draws on the data in appendices B and C. I use the years 1890–1930 for the earlier period and 1950–1980 for the later period. These years do not correspond precisely with the estimated dates but represent the most appropriate dates for which data are available.

8. The data for 1920 are reported in David Ward, *Cities and Immigrants* (New York: Oxford University Press, 1971), 56, and those for the later period (1950 to 1980) appear in Donald T. Bogue, *The Population of the United States* (New York: Free Press, 1985), 17, table 1-10. On the urban destination of immigrants, see Ward, *Cities and Immigrants,* 75–81. For a general comparison of these periods, see Douglas S. Massey, "The New Immigration and Ethnicity in the United States," *Population and Development Review* 21, no. 3 (1995): 631–652.

9. Roger Waldinger, "Immigration and Urban Change," *Annual Review of Sociology* 15 (1989): 213.

10. On the early period, see Ward, *Cities and Immigrants,* 58, and Carl Abbott, *Urban America in the Modern Age* (Arlington Heights, Ill.: Harlan Davidson, 1987), 28–29. The comments on rural population decline and mi-

gration are from Lorraine Garkovich, *Population and Community in Rural America* (New York: Greenwood, 1989), 85–97. On the rates of rural-to-urban migration, see Eric E. Lampard, "The Evolving System of Cities in the United States," in *Issues in Urban Economics*, ed. H. S. Perloff and L. Wingo, 81–139 (Baltimore: The Johns Hopkins University Press, 1968), 112, table 3. To this extent, distributive urbanization also had a parasitic component, but not one that drained the cities.

11. On nonmetropolitan-to-metropolitan migratory streams, see Bogue, *The Population of the United States*, 346.

12. The data on black south-to-north migration are from Michael French, *U.S. Economic History since 1945* (Manchester, U.K.: Manchester University Press, 1997), 14, table 1.6. The quotation is from Abbott, *Urban America in the Modern Age*, 70. See also Gunnar Myrdal, *An American Dilemma: The Negro Problem and Modern Democracy* (New York: Harper and Row, 1944), 182–185, 191–197.

13. See U.S. Bureau of the Census, *Statistical Abstract of the United States 1995* (Washington, D.C.: Government Printing Office, 1995), 27. To tie demographics to economics, Eric E. Lampard has written that "over the 20th century's third quarter, the center of gravity of the U.S. economy finally moved away from the East Coast axis and its pivot the Empire City" (that is, New York City). See his "The New York Metropolis in Transformation," in *The Future of the Metropolis*, ed. H. Ewers, J. B. Goddard, and H. Matzerath, 27–110 (Berlin: de Gruyter, 1986). The quotation is on page 72.

14. The selection of regional boundaries is crucial here. For example, Lampard, "The New York Metropolis in Transformation," finds the Middle Atlantic region growing in population share in the first period. See his table 5 on page 68. The regional shifts picked up momentum after 1970. See John D. Kasarda, "The Implications of Contemporary Urbanization Trends for National Urban Policy," *Social Science Quarterly* 61, nos. 3–4 (1980): 373–400.

15. The following paragraphs draw on appendices B and C.

16. Department of Economic and Social Information and Policy Analysis, *Statistical Yearbook* (New York: United Nations, 1993), 75–76.

17. On the home-building industry, see Anthony Downs, "The Challenge of Our Declining Big Cities," *Housing Policy Debate* 8, no. 2 (1997): 372, table 4.

18. Data are from various years of the U.S. Bureau of the Census, *Statistical Abstract of the United States*. See also Gail Garfield Schwartz, *Retrospect and Prospect: An Urban Policy Profile of the United States* (Columbus, Ohio: Academy for Contemporary Problems, 1979), 2, table 2, which shows the decline in mean population density for central cities—11.0 persons per acre in 1900 to 8.5 persons per acre in 1973.

19. The quotation is from Ron Miller, Rita Seides Miller, and Stephanie Karp, *Brooklyn USA* (New York: Brooklyn College Press, 1979), 25. On the consolidation, see also David Ment, *The Shaping of a City* (Brooklyn, NY:

Brooklyn Educational and Cultural Alliance, 1979), and Kenneth T. Jackson, ed., *The Encyclopedia of New York City* (New Haven, Conn.: Yale University Press, 1995), 148–153.

20. See Francis G. Courares, *The Remaking of Pittsburgh* (Albany: State University of New York Press, 1984), and Stefan Lorant, *Pittsburgh* (Lenox, Mass.: Authors Editions, 1964).

21. Kenneth T. Jackson, "Metropolitan Government versus Suburban Autonomy," in *Cities in American History*, ed. K. T. Jackson and S. K. Schultz, 442–462 (New York: Knopf, 1972). The data are on page 453. This is the best documentation of the historical differences in annexations and consolidations between the nineteenth and twentieth centuries.

22. Jon C. Teaford, *City and Suburb: The Political Fragmentation of Metropolitan America, 1850–1970* (Baltimore: The Johns Hopkins University Press, 1979), 5–39, and Peter R. Gluck and Richard J. Meister, *Cities in Transition* (New York: New Viewpoints, 1979), 132–134 and 163–168. For the legal background, see Gerald E. Frug, *City Making* (Princeton, N.J.: Princeton University Press, 1999), 26–53.

23. See Jackson, "Metropolitan Government versus Suburban Autonomy," 454–456.

24. Jerome Ellison, "Relief for Strangled Cities," *Saturday Evening Post*, April 20, 1957, 38–39, 110, 111, 112–114. *The American City*, a magazine for municipal administrators, frequently reported on annexations.

25. Peter Dreier, John Mollenkopf, and Todd Swanstrom, *Place Matters: Metropolitics for the Twenty-first Century* (Lawrence: University Press of Kansas, 2001), 173–200.

26. This "elasticity" argument is made by David Rusk in his *Cities without Suburbs* (Washington, D.C.: Woodrow Wilson Center Press, 1993). Also, see his *Inside Game/Outside Game* (Washington, D.C.: Brookings Institution, 1999), where he argues that for central cities to thrive, metropolitan areas must halt sprawl, share the tax base, and institute metropolis-wide subsidized housing for low-income households.

27. On the continuity of urbanization, see Hope Tisdale, "The Process of Urbanization," *Social Forces* 20 (1942): 311–316, and Edward W. Soja, *Postmetropolis: Critical Studies of Cities and Regions* (Oxford: Blackwell, 2000). Soja, though, argues that a rupture in urbanization occurred in the late twentieth century that led to regional, rather than central city–based, agglomerations dominating the landscape. Urbanization, for Soja, had reached its limit.

28. On the contemporary change and continuity of urban form, see Robert A. Beauregard and Anne Haila, "The Unavoidable Continuities of the City," in *Globalizing Cities: A New Spatial Order?* ed. P. Marcuse and R. van Kempen, 22–36 (Oxford: Blackwell, 2000).

29. Eric E. Lampard, "Historical Aspects of Urbanization," in *The Study of Urbanization*, ed. P. M. Hauser and L. F. Schnore, 519–554 (New York: Wiley and Sons, 1965).

30. Eric E. Lampard, "The History of Cities in the Economically Advanced Areas," *Economic Development and Cultural Change* 3 (1955): 92.

31. Across countries, the ebbing of urbanization has usually begun when the urban population has reached 50 to 80 percent of the total population.

32. See David M. Gordon, "Capitalist Development and the History of American Cities," in *Marxism and the Metropolis,* ed. W. K. Tabb and L. Sawers, 25–63 (New York: Oxford University Press, 1978), as regards the first periodization, and Michael Dear and Steven Flusty, "Postmodern Urbanism," *Annals of the Association of American Geographers* 88, no. 1 (1998): 50–72; Edward W. Soja, *Postmodern Geographies* (London: Verso, 1989), 222–248; and Soja, *Thirdspace* (Oxford: Blackwell, 1996), 184–279, on postmodern cities. Also relevant here are Hoselitz, "Generative and Parasitic Cities," and Lampard, "The Evolving System of Cities in the United States," 109–118. Lewis Mumford also proposed a periodization of urbanization for the United States. See his "The Fourth Migration," *Survey* 54, no. 3 (1925): 130–133.

33. N. D. Kondratieff, "The Long Waves in Economic Life," *Review of Economic Statistics* 17, no. 6 (1935): 105–115. See also J. J. van Duijn, *The Long Waves in Economic Life* (London: George Allen and Unwin, 1983), 63, 68, and 163.

34. The centrality of technological advances and new fixed capital investment points to the role of propulsive sectors in long-wave development. This becomes particularly salient at the urban scale either as industrial specialization or as industrial districts. See Manuel Castells and Peter Hall, *Technopoles of the World* (London: Routledge, 1994).

35. Morris Abramovitz, *Evidence of Long Swings in Aggregate Construction since the Civil War* (New York: National Bureau of Economic Research, 1964); Morris Abramovitz, "Long Swings in Economic Growth," in *New Views on American Economic Development,* ed. R. Andreano, 377–434 (Cambridge, Mass.: Schenkman, 1965); Richard A. Easterlin, *Population, Labor Force, and Long Swings in Economic Growth* (New York: National Bureau of Economic Research, 1968); Manuel Gottlieb, *Long Swings in Urban Development* (New York: Columbia University Press, 1976); and John Randolph Riggleman, "Variations in Building Activity in United States Cities" (Ph.D. diss., The Johns Hopkins University, 1934).

36. A parallel and informative perspective on long swings and capital investment is provided by Karl Marx's notion of circuits of capital. See David Harvey, "The Urban Process under Capitalism," *International Journal of Urban and Regional Research* 2 (1978): 101–131. For an attempt to document these claims for the United States, see Robert A. Beauregard, "Capital Switching and the Built Environment: United States, 1970–1989," *Environment and Planning A* 26 (1994): 715–732. An outstanding spatial perspective on long waves can be found in John Agnew, *The United States in the World-Economy: A Regional Geography* (Cambridge: Cambridge University Press, 1987).

37. Walter Isard, "Transport Development and Building Cycles," *Quarterly*

Journal of Economics 57 (1942): 90–112, and Isard, "A Neglected Cycle: The Transport-Building Cycle," *Review of Economic Statistics* 24, no. 4 (1942): 149–158.

38. Jane Holtz Kay, *Asphalt Nation: How the Automobile Took Over America and How We Can Take It Back* (New York: Crown, 1997); Moshe Safdie, *The City after the Automobile* (New York: Basic Books, 1997); and S. B. Warner Jr., *The Urban Wilderness* (New York: Harper and Row, 1972), 113–149, on the development of Los Angeles and the automobile.

39. Homer Hoyt, *One Hundred Years of Land Values in Chicago* (Chicago: University of Chicago Press, 1933), 403.

40. Evidence of this appears in a comparison of trends in the value of nonresidential construction activity in the metropolitan areas of Los Angeles and New York City. In the late 1950s, the value of such activity in Los Angeles exceeded that of New York City for the first time and continued to do so through to the 1980s. New York City's metropolitan area was near its spatial limit, whereas that of Los Angeles was still expanding. See Robert A. Beauregard, "Capital Restructuring and the New Built Environment of Global Cities," *International Journal of Urban and Regional Research* 15, no. 1 (1991): 90–105. This phenomenon is also behind the emergence of edge cities.

41. For a claim that postwar cycles are more volatile, see Leo Grebler and Leland S. Burns, "Construction Cycles in the United States since World War II," *Journal of American Real Estate and Urban Economics Association* 10, no. 2 (1982): 125–151. On the postwar dampening of cycles, see Homer Hoyt, "The Urban Real Estate Cycle—Performances and Prospects," Technical Bulletin 38 (Washington, D.C.: Urban Land Institute, 1960), and, more generally, Christina A. Romer, "Is the Stabilization of the Postwar Economy a Figment of the Data?" *American Economic Review* 76, no. 3 (1986): 314–334.

42. Burnham O. Campbell, "Long Swings in Residential Construction," *American Economic Review: Papers and Proceedings* 53, no. 2 (1963): 508–518.

43. One might follow William Sites and characterize this period as one of primitive globalization whereby the destruction of the cities and the creation of mass suburbs set the stage for new regulatory structures and a repositioning of the nation in global markets. See his *Remaking New York: Primitive Globalization and the Politics of Urban Community* (Minneapolis: University of Minnesota Press, 2003), especially 11–15. On the regional shifts associated with this fourth wave, see Walt W. Rostow, "Regional Change in the Fifth Kondratieff Upswing," in *The Rise of the Sunbelt Cities,* ed. D. C. Perry and A. J. Watkins, 83–103 (Beverly Hills, Calif.: Sage, 1977).

44. The political biases attendant to parasitic urbanization are discussed in chapter 4. My argument parallels and draws on regulation theory and arguments noting the shift from Fordism to post-Fordism. (Notably, the period 1948–1973 is considered the golden age of Fordism.) However, I do not frame my argument in its terms. See Neil Brenner, *New State Spaces: Urban*

Governance and the Rescaling of Statehood (Oxford: Oxford University Press, 2004); Alain Lipietz, "New Tendencies in the International Division of Labor," in *Production, Work, Territory,* ed. A. J. Scott and M. Storper, 16–40 (Winchester, Mass.: Allen and Unwin, 1986); Gerry Stoker, "Regulation Theory, Local Government, and the Transition from Fordism," in *Challenges to Local Government,* ed. D. S. King and J. Pierre, 242–264 (London: Sage, 1990); and Adam Tickell and Jamie A. Peck, "Accumulation, Regulation, and the Geographies of Post-Fordism," *Progress in Human Geography* 16, no. 2 (1992): 190–218.

45. For an introduction to this literature on transnational influences, see Joe Nasr and Mercedes Volait, eds. *Urbanism: Imported or Exported?* (Chichester, U.K.: Wiley-Academy, 2003); Daniel Rodgers, *Atlantic Crossings: Social Politics in a Progressive Age* (Cambridge, Mass.: Harvard University Press, 1998), 112–208; and Stephen V. Ward, "The International Diffusion of Planning: A Review and a Canadian Case Study," *International Planning Studies* 4, no. 1 (1999): 53–77.

46. My claim is a general one. The statistical category of "cities" is not the same from country to country, making the comparison less than exact. In addition, both the elasticity of administrative boundaries and the cultural roles of cities present important distinctions.

47. Michael Wegener, "The Changing Urban Hierarchy in Europe," in *Cities in Competition,* ed. J. Brotchie, M. Batty, E. Blakely, P. Hall, and P. Newton, 139–160 (Melbourne: Longman, 1995).

48. The data were calculated from table B4 in B. R. Mitchell, ed., *European Historical Statistics: 1750–1975* (New York: Facts on File, 1981), 86–89.

49. From 1950 to 1990, London had a net loss of 1.54 million residents (19 percent). Liverpool had a net loss of 40 percent (about 315,000 residents); Manchester, 43 percent (about 300,000 residents); and Glasgow, 28 percent (about 303,000 residents).

50. These data are from David Clarke, *Urban Decline* (London: Routledge, 1989), 5, table 1; 17; 19, table 5; and 20. Also see John B. Parr, "The Metropolitan Area in Its Wider Setting," in *Urban Change in the United States and Western Europe,* ed. A. Summers, P. C. Cheshire, and L. Senn, 217–244 (Washington, D.C.: Urban Institute Press, 1993), 218.

51. Jens S. Dangschat, "Berlin and the German System of Cities," *Urban Studies* 30, no. 6 (1993): 1025–1051.

52. Of the other six Canadian cities that shed residents between 1971 and 1976, their losses were less than 10,000 in four cases and never exceeded 20,000 people. These data were calculated from Ira Robinson, *Canadian Urban Growth Trends* (Vancouver: University of British Columbia Press, 1981), 29, table 9. See also Larry S. Bourne, "Urban Geography in Transition: A Canadian Perspective on the 1980s and Beyond," *Urban Geography* 24, no. 4 (1993): 141–142.

53. See Larry S. Bourne, "Population Turnabout in the Canadian Inner

City," *Canadian Journal of Urban Research* 1, no. 1 (1992): 75, table 2, and Robinson, *Canadian Urban Growth Trends,* 31, table 11.

54. Chris Hamnett, *Unequal City: London in the Global Arena* (London: Routledge, 2003).

55. A comparative history of suburbanization and decentralization in the early postwar period has yet to be written. For a basic overview, constricted in time, for western Europe, see Paul White, *The Western European City* (London: Longman, 1984), 212–232. The three reasons for lesser suburbanization are on page 221. Peter Mieszkowski and Edwin S. Mills offer an economic analysis in their "The Causes of Metropolitan Suburbanization," *Journal of Economic Perspectives* 7, no. 3 (1993): 141–142. On the new towns, see Carol Corden, *Planned Cities: New Towns in Britain and America* (Beverly Hills, Calif.: Sage, 1977).

56. Robert Fishman, *Bourgeois Utopias: The Rise and Fall of Suburbia* (New York: Basic Books, 1987).

57. William C. Agpar Jr., "The Demographic Factor and Urban Decline: A Cross-National Comparison," *Research in Urban Economics* 5 (1985): 22.

58. Wegener, "The Changing Urban Hierarchy in Europe," 152.

59. Remy Prud'homme, "New Trends in the Cities of the World," in *Cities in a Global Society,* ed. R. V. Knight and G. Gappert, 44–57 (Newbury Park, Calif.: Sage, 1989), 51, table 2.1. Tokyo also had a significant rise in suburban growth.

60. Richard Harris, *Unplanned Suburbs: Toronto's American Tragedy, 1900 to 1950* (Baltimore: The Johns Hopkins University Press, 1996). In the early 1970s (1971–1976), the central cities lost 0.9 percent of their residents and the suburbs gained 15.1 percent. See Robinson, *Canadian Urban Growth Trends,* 30, table 10.

61. Alan Mabin, "Suburbs on the Veld" (unpublished manuscript, University of Witwatersrand, Johannesburg).

62. Teresa Caldeira, "Fortified Enclaves: The New Urban Segregation," *Public Culture* 8 (1996): 303–328, and Robert Fishman, "Global Suburbs" (paper presented at the First Biennial Conference of the Urban History Association, Pittsburgh, September 2002).

63. The quotation is from Kenneth T. Jackson, "Cities," in *The Columbia History of the 20th Century,* ed. R. W. Bulliet, 528–542 (New York: Columbia University Press, 1998), 531. See also Nancy Chen, Paolo Valente, and Hania Zlotnik, "What Do We Know about Recent Trends in Urbanization?" in *Migration, Urbanization, and Development,* ed. R. E. Bilsborrow, 59–88 (Norwall, Mass.: Kluwer Academic, 1998), and Nathan Keyfitz and Wilhelm Fliezer, *World Population Growth and Aging* (Chicago: University of Chicago Press, 1990), 3.

64. Instituto del Terler Mundo, *The World Guide 1997/98* (Oxford: New Internationalists, 1997), 40.

65. John J. Palen, *The Urban World* (New York: McGraw-Hill, 1992), 4.

66. George Thomas Kurian, *The Illustrated Book of World Rankings* (Armonk, N.Y.: Sharpe, 1977), 346.

67. T. G. McGee argues that Third World urbanization in the 1950s and 1960s was pseudo-urbanization, with city growth unhinged from national economic development and rural-urban migration. See his *The Southeast Asian City* (London: Bell and Sons, 1967), 15–28.

68. See Douglas S. Massey, "The New Immigration and Ethnicity in the United States," *Population and Development Review* 21, no. 3 (1995): 631–652, and Brian J. L. Berry, "Transnational Urbanward Migration, 1830–1980," *Annals of the Association of American Geographers* 83, no. 3 (1993): 389–405. Berry noted that urbanward transnational migration mainly bolstered urbanization in countries where urban growth was anemic.

69. Paul Kennedy, *Preparing for the Twenty-First Century* (New York: Vintage, 1993), 48, and Richard Peet, "The Geography of Class Struggle and the Relocation of the United States Manufacturing Industry," in *International Capitalism and Industrial Restructuring*, ed. R. Peet, 40–71 (Boston: Allen and Unwin, 1987), 22–23.

70. See Eric Hobsbawm, *The Age of Extremes: A History of the World, 1914–1991* (New York: Vintage, 1996), 302–310; Richard Peet, "Industrial Restructuring and the Crisis of International Capitalism," in Peet, *International Capitalism and Industrial Restructuring*, 22–23, table 2.2, and Peet, "The Geography of Class Struggle and the Relocation of the United States Manufacturing Industry," 62. The data on exports are from Herman Van der Wee, *Prosperity and Upheaval: The World Economy, 1945–1980* (Berkeley and Los Angeles: University of California Press, 1987), 265, table 31. On labor productivity, see Saskia Sassen, *The Mobility of Labor and Capital* (Cambridge: Cambridge University Press, 1988), 121.

71. John Agnew makes a similar point in reverse: "The history of American involvement in the world economy is also a history of regional [and urban] growth and decline" (*The United States in the World-Economy*, 89).

4. Culture and Institutions

1. James T. Patterson, *Grand Expectations: The United States, 1945–1974* (New York: Oxford University Press, 1996), 75. Levitt and Sons was one of the biggest suburban developers of the period, and the name itself has become emblematic of mass suburbanization.

2. Much has been written about the actors involved. Of the vast literature on urban redevelopment, see Robert A. Caro, *The Power Broker: Robert Moses and the Fall of New York* (New York: Knopf, 1974); Susan S. Fainstein, Norman I. Fainstein, Richard Child Hill, Dennis Judd, and Michael Peter Smith, *Restructuring the City*, rev. ed. (New York: Longman, 1986); Jeanne R. Lowe, *Cities in a Race with Time* (New York: Random House, 1968); and Jon C. Teaford, *The Rough Road to Renaissance* (Baltimore: The

Johns Hopkins University Press, 1990). On suburbanization, see Kenneth T. Jackson, *Crabgrass Frontier: The Suburbanization of the United States* (New York: Oxford University Press, 1985), and Rosalyn Baxandall and Elizabeth Ewen, *Picture Windows: How the Suburbs Happened* (New York: Basic Books, 2000).

3. In the late twentieth century in the United States, culture became an important factor in understanding economic growth and urban development. See David S. Landes, *The Wealth and Poverty of Nations* (New York: Norton, 1998), and Alexander J. Reichl, *Reconstructing Times Square* (Lawrence: University of Kansas Press, 1999).

4. Irving Kristol, "It's Not a Bad Crisis to Live In," *New York Times Magazine,* January 22, 1967, 11. More generally, see Robert A. Beauregard, *Voices of Decline: The Postwar Fate of US Cities* (Oxford: Blackwell, 1993), 159–216.

5. The quotation is from Walter Bern, "Thinking about the City," *Commentary* 56, no. 4 (1973), 74. Georg Simmel argued that ambivalence was intrinsic to city life. See Rolf Linder, *The Reportage of Urban Culture* (Cambridge: Cambridge University Press, 1996), 60.

6. The quotation is from Ruth Glass, *Clichés of Urban Doom and Other Essays* (Oxford: Blackwell, 1989), 45. See pages 41–50 for the larger discussion, as well as Raymond Williams, *The Country and the City* (New York: Oxford University Press, 1973). For the complexity of such attitudes in Japanese culture, see Paul Anderer, "Tokyo and the Borders of Modern Japanese Fiction," in *Visions of the Modern City,* ed. W. Sharpe and L. Wallock, 220–231 (Baltimore: The Johns Hopkins University Press, 1987). On Finnish culture, see Timo Cantell, *Helsinki and a Vision of Place* (Helsinki: City of Helsinki Urban Facts, 1999), 58–91, and Paul Tapani Karjalainen and Aissi Paasi, "Contrasting the Nature of the Written City," in *Writing the City,* ed. P. Preston and P. Simpson-Housley (London: Routledge, 1994), 59–79. On Germany, see Andrew Lees, *Cities, Sin, and Social Reform in Imperial Germany* (Ann Arbor: University of Michigan Press, 2002).

7. Robert N. Bellah, Richard Madsen, William M. Sullivan, Ann Swidler, and Stephen M. Tipton, *Habits of the Heart* (New York: Harper and Row, 1986), 29. See also Lee Schweninger, *John Winthrop* (Boston: Twayne, 1990), and for the sermon itself, see Massachusetts Historical Society, *Winthrop Papers,* ed. S. Mitchell, vol. 2, *1623–1630* (N.p.: Plimpton Press, 1931), 282–295.

8. Lewis Lapham, "City Lights," *Harper's Magazine,* July 1992, 4.

9. See Daniel Lazare, *America's Undeclared War* (New York: Harcourt, 2001), 1–26; Richard Lehan, *The City in Literature* (Berkeley and Los Angeles: University of California Press, 1998), 168–169; and Morton White and Lucia White, *The Intellectual versus the City* (New York: New American Library, 1962), 24–31. These themes of land and freedom are also part of Frederick Jackson Turner's frontier thesis. See his "The Significance of the Frontier in

American History" (1893), in *The Early Writings of Frederick Jackson Turner,* ed. E. E. Edwards, 183–229 (Madison: University of Wisconsin Press, 1938).

10. Ruth Glass wrote that "suburbia tamed [the] radicalism" (*Clichés of Urban Doom and Other Essays,* 46) of the working classes who left British cities in the late nineteenth century.

11. Thomas Bender, *The Unfinished City* (New York: New Press, 2002), 167–183; James L. Machor, *Pastoral Cities* (Madison: University of Wisconsin Press, 1987); Leo Marx, "The Puzzle of Anti-Urbanism in Classic American Literature," in *Literature and the Urban Experience,* ed. M. C. Jaye and A. C. Watts, 63–80 (New Brunswick, N.J.: Rutgers University Press, 1981); Leo Marx, *The Machine in the Garden* (London: Oxford University Press, 1964); David Schuyler, *The New Urban Landscape* (Baltimore: The Johns Hopkins University Press, 1986), 24–36; and Alan Trachtenberg, *The Incorporation of America* (New York: Hill and Wang, 1982), 101–115.

12. Robert Fishman, *Bourgeois Utopias: The Rise and Fall of Suburbia* (New York: Basic Books, 1987).

13. Beauregard, *Voices of Decline,* 13–17.

14. From the Civil War to 1910, farm production rose as a result of advances in technology and growing demand from an expanding population. Farm prices, however, fell and did not rise again until the mid-1890s. Throughout these years, farm employment increased in absolute terms but declined as a percentage of the labor force. See Ross M. Robertson, *History of the American Economy* (New York: Harcourt Brace Jovanovich, 1973), 305–310 and 384. William Cronon has provided a thoroughly informative and insightful study of these city-countryside relations in his *Nature's Metropolis: Chicago and the Great West* (New York: Norton, 1991).

15. See Lazare, *America's Undeclared War,* 104–105, and Daphne Spain, *How Women Saved the City* (Minneapolis: University of Minnesota Press, 200), 30–60. Gary Wills wrote in 1997 that "to become urban is to break the spirit of man" and attributed the American suspicion of the city to the separation of church and state in the United States. See his "American Adam," *New York Review of Books,* March 6, 1997, 30–33.

16. Lazare, in *America's Undeclared War,* 91–107, argued that this dynamic fueled the rise of the populist movement of the late nineteenth century. That movement was also antiurban.

17. Irving Kristol, "Common Sense about the Urban Crisis," *Fortune,* October 1967, 233–234, and "Not All This Country Is Tense, Troubled," *U.S. News & World Report,* August 7, 1967, 34–37. The latter noted that the strength of the United States lay with Americans "who live apart from crime-ridden and riot-plagued central cities" (37).

18. Margaret Weir, "Central Cities' Loss of Power in State Politics," *Cityscape* 2, no. 2 (1996): 23–40.

19. The quotation is from Gerald E. Frug, *City Making* (Princeton, N.J.: Princeton University Press, 1999), 143. Social isolation also contributes to the

loss of a sense of common fate. See Robert D. Putnam, *Bowling Alone* (New York: Simon and Schuster, 2000), 340, and Bellah et al., *Habits of the Heart,* esp. 177–181.

20. Thomas J. Sugrue's *The Origins of the Urban Crisis* (Princeton, N.J.: Princeton University Press, 1996) is very good on these conflicts, as is William Julius Wilson's *The Declining Significance of Race* (Chicago: University of Chicago Press, 1978), esp. 62–87. For a metropolitan perspective, see Robert O. Self, *American Babylon: The Struggle for Postwar Oakland* (Princeton, N.J.: Princeton University Press, 2003). Lest we forget the importance of race to urban development and antiurbanism prior to this time, it should be recalled that Yankee elites in communities outside Boston in the late 1800s resisted annexation in part to avoid mingling with the Irish who lived there. See Geoffrey Blodgett, "Yankee Leadership in a Divided City: Boston, 1860–1910," *Journal of Urban History* 8, no. 4 (1982): 371–396.

21. The quotation is from Max Ways, "The Deeper Shame of the Cities," *Fortune,* January 1968, 205. The crisis of the cities in the 1960s and 1970s eventually became the basis for a conservative critique and, surprisingly, for a pro-urban conservatism. See Fred Siegel, *The Future Once Happened Here* (New York: Free Press, 1997).

22. For a nostalgic view of this period, see Michael Johns, *Moment of Grace: The American City in the 1950s* (Berkeley and Los Angeles: University of California Press, 2003).

23. Beauregard, *Voices of Decline,* 246–275.

24. Frug, *City Making,* 155.

25. As background, see Timothy Barnekov, Robin Boyle, and Daniel Rich, *Privatism and Urban Policy in Britain and the United States* (New York: Oxford University Press, 1989), 14–37; Robert A. Beauregard, "Federal Policy and Postwar Urban Decline: The Case of Government Complicity," *Housing Policy Debate* 12, no. 1 (2001): 129–151; Beauregard, "Postwar Spatial Transformations," in *Atop the Urban Hierarchy,* ed. R. A. Beauregard, 1–44 (Totowa, N.J.: Rowman and Littlefield, 1989); Mark Gelfand, *A Nation of Cities* (New York: Oxford University Press, 1975); Paul Kantor, *The Dependent City* (Glenview, Ill.: Scott, Foresman, 1988); Raymond A. Mohl, "Shifting Patterns of American Urban Policy since 1900," in *Urban Policy in Twentieth Century America,* ed. A. R. Hirsch and R. A. Mohl, 1–45 (New Brunswick, N.J.: Rutgers University Press, 1993); and Carol O'Cleireacain, "Cities' Role in the Metropolitan Economy and the Federal Structure," in *Interwoven Destinies,* ed. H. Cisneros, 167–186 (New York: Norton, 1993).

26. Steven L. Elkin, *City and Regime in the American Republic* (Chicago: University of Chicago Press, 1987), and Kantor, *The Dependent City,* 34–162.

27. Robert M. Collins, *More: The Politics of Economic Growth in Postwar America* (New York: Oxford University Press, 2000), x.

28. Kristol, "It's Not a Bad Crisis to Live In," 70. On leadership, see also Lowe, *Cities in a Race with Time.*

29. The quotation is from the economist John Kenneth Galbraith and can be found in John Peter, "Cities: Who Can Save Them?" *Look,* June 11, 1968, 41. Also see Joseph S. Clark, "A Voice for the Cities," *Nation,* March 7, 1959, 199–201. While most city officials pursued federal aid, not all focused on the redevelopment of the central city. Officials in Atlanta, Georgia, for example, cast their lot with metropolitan growth. See Margaret Pugh O'Mara, *Cities of Knowledge: Cold War Science and the Search for the Next Silicon Valley* (Princeton, N.J.: Princeton University Press, 2005), 190–201.

30. Blake McKelvey, *The Emergence of Metropolitan America* (New Brunswick, N.J.: Rutgers University Press, 1968), 118–151.

31. Otis Graham, *Toward a Planned Society* (New York: Oxford University Press, 1976), and also O'Mara, *Cities of Knowledge.*

32. Dennis E. Gale, "Symposium: A Comparative View of National Urban Policy," *Journal of the American Planning Association* 48, no. 1 (1982): 5–66.

33. Marshall Kaplan and Franklin James, eds., *The Future of National Urban Policy* (Durham, N.C.: Duke University Press, 1990).

34. Robert L. Cook Benjamin, "From Waterways to Waterfronts," in *Urban Economic Development,* ed. R. D. Bingham and J. P. Blair, 23–45 (Beverly Hills, Calif.: Sage, 1984).

35. Martha Derthick, *New Towns In-Towns: Why a Federal Program Failed* (Washington, D.C.: Urban Institute Press, 1972). On Roosevelt Island, see Louis K. Lowenstein, "New York State Urban Development Corporation," *Journal of the American Institute of Planners* 44, no. 3 (1978): 261–273.

36. See Barnekov, Boyle, and Rich, *Privatism and Urban Policy in Britain and the United States,* 63–99; Gelfand, *A Nation of Cities;* Kenneth Fox, *Metropolitan America* (Jackson: University Press of Mississippi, 1986); Alison Isenberg, *Downtown America: A History of the Place and the People Who Made It* (Chicago: University of Chicago Press, 2004), 166–202; Dennis Judd and Todd Swanstrom, *City Politics* (New York: HarperCollins, 1994), 107–150; and John Mollenkopf, *The Contested City* (Princeton, N.J.: Princeton University Press, 1983), 47–138.

37. Briavel Holcomb and Robert A. Beauregard, *Revitalizing Cities* (Washington, D.C.: Association of American Geographers, 1981), 10–12. See also Beauregard, "Postwar Spatial Transformations," 21–24; Lowe, *Cities in a Race with Time;* and Teaford, *The Rough Road to Renaissance.*

38. Holcomb and Beauregard, *Revitalizing Cities,* 11, and Rachel Bratt, "Public Housing: The Controversy and Contribution," in *Critical Perspectives on Housing,* ed. R. G. Bratt, C. Hartman, and A. Meyerson, 335–361 (Philadelphia: Temple University Press, 1986), esp. 338–339. The respective dates are 1949–1974 for the demolitions and 1948–1973 for the new units.

39. Bratt, "Public Housing"; Arnold R. Hirsch, *Making the Second*

Ghetto (Cambridge: Cambridge University Press, 1983); and Lee Rainwater, *Behind Ghetto Walls* (Chicago: Aldine, 1970).

40. Roger E. Alcaly and David Mermelstein, eds., *The Fiscal Crisis of American Cities* (New York: Vintage, 1977). Federal aid to municipalities as a percent of the latter's own-source revenues peaked in 1978 and declined through the 1980s. In the 1950s and 1960s, it was relatively low, suggesting that the aid was in response mainly to the riots of the late 1960s and the fiscal crises of the 1970s. See Robert D. Reischauer, "The Rise and Fall of National Urban Policy," in Kaplan and James, *The Future of National Urban Policy,* esp. 227, table 12.2.

41. Beauregard, *Voices of Decline,* 219–245.

42. William Schneider, "The Suburban Century Begins," *Atlantic Monthly,* July 1992, 33–44.

43. The quotation is from Christopher Walker and Patrick Boxall, "Economic Development," in *Reality and Research,* ed. G. Galster, 13–27 (Washington, D.C.: Urban Institute Press, 1996), 19. See also Beauregard, "Federal Policy and Postwar Urban Decline," 129–151, and Charles Abrams, *The City Is the Frontier* (New York: Harper and Row, 1965).

44. Jackson, *Crabgrass Frontier,* 190–218.

45. These data were drawn from U.S. Department of Commerce, *Historical Statistics of the United States* (Washington, D.C.: Government Printing Office, 1975), Series N273-284, 648–649. The data are in constant 1958 dollars.

46. Kenneth T. Jackson, "Race, Ethnicity, and Real Estate Appraisal," *Journal of Urban History* 6, no. 4 (1980): 419–452.

47. The home-ownership statistic is from Jackson, *Crabgrass Frontier,* 205, and the data on new, nonfarm private housing are from U.S. Department of Commerce, *Historical Statistics of the United States,* Series N156-169, 639–640.

48. These data were taken from U.S. Department of Commerce, *County and City Data Book* (Washington, D.C.: Government Printing Office) for various years from 1972 to 1983, and from U.S. Department of Commerce, *State and Metropolitan Area Data Book* (Washington, D.C.: Government Printing Office, 1986). Philadelphia's population was falling and houses were being demolished, but the number of dwelling units still increased partly because of a fall in the average size of households. See Peter O. Muller, Kenneth G. Meyer, and Roman Cybriwsky, *Metropolitan Philadelphia* (Cambridge, Mass.: Ballinger, 1976), 36.

49. Frug, *City Making.*

50. In 1967, the central cities of the fifty largest metropolitan areas had 65.2 percent of the jobs in the region. In 1977, they had 55.7 percent. See Robyn S. Phillips and Avis C. Vidal, "Restructuring and Growth Transitions of Metropolitan Economies," in *Local Economies in Transition,* ed. E. M. Bergman, 59–83 (Durham, N.C.: Duke University Press, 1986). In the 1950s

and 1960s, annual job growth in manufacturing and retailing was negative in the central cities and positive in the suburbs. See T. M. Stanback, *The New Suburbanization* (Boulder, Colo.: Westview Press, 1991), 9, table 1.3.

51. On the number of urban miles, see Beauregard, "Federal Policy and Postwar Urban Decline," 139, table 1.

52. U.S. Department of Commerce, *Historical Statistics of the United States*, 718.

53. Thomas W. Hanchett, "U.S. Tax Policy and the Shopping Center Boom of the 1950s and 1960s," *American Historical Review* 101, no. 4 (1996): 1082–1110.

54. William H. Whyte Jr., "Urban Sprawl," *Fortune*, January 1958, 102–109ff. In the cities, the need was for maintaining the existing infrastructure, not for new construction. In fact, maintenance would have to come from general tax revenues. In 1958 dollars, total public expenditures on new construction went from $5.9 billion in 1948 to $20.8 billion in 1973. See U.S. Bureau of the Census, *Statistical Abstract*, various years.

55. O'Mara, *Cities of Knowledge*.

56. "Troubled Cities—and Their Mayors," *Newsweek*, March 13, 1967, 43.

57. Chalmers Johnson, ed., *The Industrial Policy Debate* (San Francisco: ICS Press, 1984), and Michael L. Wachter and Susan M. Wachter, eds., *Toward a New U.S. Industrial Policy?* (Philadelphia: University of Pennsylvania Press, 1981). More generally, see Milton J. Esman, *Government Works: Why Americans Need the Feds* (Ithaca, N.Y.: Cornell University Press, 2000), 62, 81–83. On the federal government as a weak state, see Steven D. Krasner, *Defending the National Interest* (Princeton, N.J.: Princeton University Press, 1976), 55–70.

58. "Rural and Urban Growth," *New Republic*, September 25, 1971, 13.

59. The comment is by James W. Rouse, a major real estate developer of the 1960s and 1970s. He was calling for government regulation to eliminate risk from the market. See "Can Today's Big Cities Survive?" *U.S. News & World Report*, November 6, 1967, 55.

60. Witold Rybczynski, *City Life* (New York: Scribner, 1995), 78. Historically, see Lisa M. Benton and John Rennie Short, *Environmental Discourse and Practice* (Oxford: Blackwell, 1999), 27–59.

61. William Appleman Williams, "The Frontier Thesis and American Foreign Policy," *Pacific Historical Review* 24 (1955): 379–395, and Neil Smith, "Gentrification, the Frontier, and the Restructuring of Urban Space," in *Gentrification of the City*, ed. N. Smith and P. Williams, 15–34 (Boston: Allen and Unwin, 1986).

62. Of the multitude of basic sources on capitalism that could be mentioned, the reader might start with David Harvey, *The Limits to Capital* (Chicago: University of Chicago Press, 1982); Joseph A. Schumpeter, *Capitalism, Socialism, and Democracy* (New York: Harper and Row, 1942); and Michael

Peter Smith, *City, States, and Markets* (New York: Blackwell, 1988). The quotation is from David Harvey, *Social Justice and the City* (Baltimore: The Johns Hopkins University Press, 1973), 249.

63. On different types of investors, see Anne Haila, "Four Types of Investment in Land and Property," *International Journal of Urban and Regional Research* 15, no. 3 (1991): 343–365. On profit-product cycles, see Ann Markusen, *Profit Cycles, Oligopoly, and Regional Development* (Cambridge, Mass.: MIT Press, 1985), 27–62. The restriction on profits as more investors enter a market is not as inevitable in financial markets.

64. Neil Smith, *Uneven Development* (Oxford: Blackwell, 1985); and Harvey, *The Limits to Capital,* 373–412. The stock market often develops its own dynamics independent of firm profitability, and this exacerbates the volatility of investment decisions, particularly when large construction and real estate entities (such as real estate investment trusts) are publicly traded.

65. The quotation is from Thad Williamson, David Imbroscio, and Gar Alperovitz, *Making a Place for Community* (New York: Routledge, 2002), 16. The classic texts on these two points are Max Weber's *The Protestant Ethic and the Spirit of Capitalism* (New York: Scribner's Sons, 1930) and Karl Polanyi's *The Great Transformation* (New York: Farrar and Rinehart, 1944). For an application of this point of view to property markets, see Robert A. Beauregard, "The Textures of Property Markets: Downtown Housing and Office Conversions in New York City," *Urban Studies* 43, no. 1 (2006): 2431–2445.

66. Barnekov, Boyle, and Rich, *Privatism and Urban Policy in Britain and the United States,* 14–26; James O'Connor, *The Fiscal Crisis of the State* (New York: St. Martin's, 1973); and Alan Wolfe, *America's Impasse* (New York: Pantheon, 1981).

67. See Nicholas Dagen Bloom, *Merchant of Illusion: America's Salesman of the Businessman's Utopia* (Columbus: Ohio State University Press, 2004); Pietro S. Nivola, *Laws of the Landscape: How Policies Shape Cities in Europe and America* (Washington, D.C.: Brookings Institution, 1999); and Goran Thernborn, *European Modernity and Beyond* (London: Sage, 1996).

68. William H. Chafe, *The Unfinished Journey* (New York: Oxford University Press, 1986), 79–110.

69. Richard D. Lamm, "Is Bigger Also Better?" *New Republic,* June 5, 1971, 17–19.

70. Claus Offe, "The Theory of the Capitalist State and the Problem of Policy Formation," in *Stress and Contradiction in Modern Capitalism,* ed. L. N. Lindberg, R. Alford, C. Crouch, and C. Offe, 125–144 (Lexington, Mass.: Lexington Books, 1975); Chafe, *The Unfinished Journey,* 92–97; and Graham, *Toward a Planned Society.* The quotation is on page 10 of Wolfe's *America's Impasse.*

71. Frug, *City Making;* Gelfand, *A Nation of Cities,* 157–197; Sidney Plotkin, *Keep Out: The Struggle for Land Use Control* (Berkeley and Los Angeles: University of California Press, 1987); and Daniel T. Rodgers, *Atlantic*

Crossings: Social Politics in a Progressive Age (Cambridge, Mass.: Harvard University Press, 1998), 160–208.

72. John Delafons, *Land-Use Controls in the United States* (Cambridge, Mass.: MIT Press, 1962); John Logan and Harvey Molotch, *Urban Fortunes* (Berkeley and Los Angeles: University of California Press, 1987); Paul E. Peterson, *City Limits* (Chicago: University of Chicago Press, 1981); and Sam Bass Warner Jr., *The Private City* (Philadelphia: University of Pennsylvania Press, 1968).

73. Robert J. Ellis, "The American Frontier and the Contemporary Real Estate Advertising Magazine," *Journal of Popular Culture* 27, no. 3 (1993): 124.

74. William Leach, *Country of Exiles* (New York: Vintage, 2000), 9. See also James Howard Kunstler, *The Geography of Nowhere* (New York: Simon and Schuster, 1993), 10, and Putnam, *Bowling Alone*, 204–215.

75. Robert D. Kaplan, *An Empire Wilderness* (New York: Random House, 1998), 26.

76. Rybczynski, *City Life*, 83. In the quotation, I replaced "cities" with "communities" for the sake of clarity.

77. Adam W. Rome, "Building on the Land: Toward an Environmental History of Residential Development in American Cities and Suburbs, 1870–1990," *Journal of Urban History* 20, no. 3 (1994): 416, and "Why Land Values Keep Rising," *U.S. News & World Report*, July 6, 1956, 86–87.

78. Rome, "Building on the Land," 415.

79. Whyte Jr., "Urban Sprawl." In 1960, 79.5 percent of all new private homes were single-family dwellings. See U.S. Bureau of the Census, *Statistical Abstract of the United States* (Washington, D.C.: Government Printing Office, 1968), 702, table 1077.

80. "Pull of the Suburbs Is Stronger: Buyers, Taxpayers Move Out," *U.S. News & World Report*, June 30, 1950, 11.

81. Harold H. Martin, "Our Urban Revolution, Part One: Are We Building a City 600 Miles Long?" *Saturday Evening Post*, January 2, 1960, 78. For a contemporary perspective, see Lazare, *America's Undeclared War*, 203–205 and 213–242.

82. The first quotation is from "Spiraling Land," *Time*, March 13, 1964, 92, and the second from "Why the Price of Land Is Soaring," *U.S. News & World Report*, February 17, 1964, 74. For an international perspective, see Charles Abrams, "The Uses of Land in Cities," in *Cities: Their Origin, Growth, and Human Impact*, ed. Scientific American, 225–231 (San Francisco: Friedman, 1973).

83. See Paul Harlan Douglas, *The Suburban Trend* (New York: Century, 1925), 123–163; Anthony Downs, *New Visions for Metropolitan America* (Washington, D.C.: Brookings Institution, 1994); and Joseph Persky and Wim Wiewel, *When Corporations Leave Town* (Detroit: Wayne State University Press, 2000).

84. Bernard J. Frieden and Lynn B. Sagalyn, *Downtown, Inc.* (Cambridge, Mass.: MIT Press, 1989), and Teaford, *The Rough Road to Renaissance.*

85. Mel Scott, *American City Planning since 1890* (Berkeley and Los Angeles: University of California Press, 1969), 452–456, and Marc Weiss, *The Rise of the Community Builders* (New York: Columbia University Press, 1987).

86. Barry Checkoway, "Large Builders, Federal Housing Programs, and Postwar Suburbanization," in *Marxism and the Metropolis,* ed. W. Tabb and L. Sawers, 152–173 (New York: Oxford University Press, 1984).

87. Neil Smith, *The New Urban Frontier* (London: Routledge, 1996).

88. Lizabeth Cohen, "Is There an Urban History of Consumption?" *Journal of Urban History* 29, no. 2 (2003): 87–106. The quotation in the paragraph is from "Flight to the Suburbs," *Time,* March 22, 1954, 102.

89. William F. Ogburn, *Social Characteristics of Cities* (Chicago: International City Managers' Association, 1937), 51–55, and Anthony Orum, *City Building in America* (Boulder, Colo.: Westview Press, 1995).

90. "Big City Troubles—Is There an Answer?" *U.S. News & World Report,* March 22, 1966, 79.

91. This aspect of postwar urbanization will be discussed in more detail in chapter 5.

92. Council of Economic Advisors, *Economic Report of the President* (Washington, D.C.: Government Printing Office, 1979), 184, table B.2. Industrial investment refers to nonresidential fixed investments in structures and producers' durable equipment.

93. C. W. Griffin Jr., "Specialists Diagnose the Stricken American City," *Saturday Review,* August 3, 1963, 23.

5. Domestic Prosperity

1. The phrase "affluent society" was coined by the economist John Kenneth Galbraith. See his critique of the postwar revival of a market ideology in *The Affluent Society* (Boston: Houghton Mifflin, 1969).

2. John Agnew, *The United States in the World Economy: A Regional Geography* (Cambridge: Cambridge University Press, 1987).

3. Robert M. Collins, *More: The Politics of Economic Growth in Postwar America* (New York: Oxford University Press, 2000), 41.

4. The first quotation is from William E. Leuchtenburg, *A Troubled Feast: American Society since 1945* (Boston: Little, Brown, 1973), 5. The second quotation appears in Thomas J. McCormick, *America's Half-Century: United States Foreign Policy in the Cold War* (Baltimore: The Johns Hopkins University Press, 1989), 99.

5. For general background on domestic prosperity in the postwar period, see Robert Brenner, *The Boom and the Bubble: The US in the World Economy* (London: Verso, 2002), 9–15; William H. Chafe, *The Unfinished Journey* (New

York: Oxford University Press, 1986), 112–117; Michael French, *U.S. Economic History since 1945* (Manchester, U.K.: Manchester University Press, 1997); Leuchtenburg, *A Troubled Feast;* and James T. Patterson, *Grand Expectations: The United States, 1945–1974* (New York: Oxford University Press, 1996). The respective growth rates for the economy are 3.9 percent for 1948–1973, 2.4 percent for 1929–1948, and 1.8 percent for 1973–1979. Edward F. Denison, *Trends in American Economic Growth, 1929–1982* (Washington, D.C.: Brookings Institution, 1985), 1–5. The population increased by 60 percent during the postwar period.

6. U.S. Department of Commerce, *Construction Reports* for various years. All statistics are based on constant dollars unless otherwise noted. The GNP growth rates per decade were calculated from U.S. Department of Commerce, *Historical Statistics of the United States* (Washington, D.C.: Government Printing Office, 1975) and various volumes of U.S. Bureau of the Census, *Statistical Abstract of the United States* (Washington, D.C.: Government Printing Office, various years).

7. See French, *U.S. Economic History since 1945,* 199, table 10.1, and Herman Van der Wee, *Prosperity and Upheaval: The World Economy, 1945–1980* (Berkeley and Los Angeles: University of California Press, 1987), 51, table 4. The data on gross world product are from Christopher K. Chase-Dunn, "The World-System since 1950: What Has Really Changed?" in *Labor in the Capitalist World-Economy,* ed. C. Bergquist (Beverly Hills, Calif.: Sage, 1984), 92–94, table 3.1.

8. On world trade, see Harold G. Vatter, *The U.S. Economy in the 1950s* (New York: Norton, 1963), 266, and on the Marshall Plan, see French, *U.S. Economic History since 1945,* 197. The data on the Marshall Plan are for the 1948–1951 period.

9. French, *U.S. Economic History since 1945,* 200.

10. On military spending, see Ann Markusen, Peter Hall, Scott Campbell, and Sabina Deitrick, *The Rise of the Gunbelt* (New York: Oxford University Press, 1991), 10. The numbers are in 1982 constant dollars. Between 1953 and 1961, military aid constituted nearly half of all foreign aid. See French, *U.S. Economic History since 1945,* 198–199.

11. In 1940, federal government expenditures accounted for 9.9 percent of GNP, and in 1980 they accounted for 22.3 percent. See French, *U.S. Economic History since 1945,* 22, table 2.1. The employment estimate is from Markusen et al., *The Rise of the Gunbelt,* 19. On military research and development expenditures and suburbanization, see Margaret Pugh O'Mara, *Cities of Knowledge: Cold War Science and the Search for the Next Silicon Valley* (Princeton, N.J.: Princeton University Press, 2005).

12. Regarding the doubling of productivity, see Manuel Castells, *The Economic Crisis and American Society* (Princeton, N.J.: Princeton University Press, 1980), 97, table 7. Using a different measure of productivity, David Gordon and his coauthors claim a fivefold increase in the core manufacturing

sector. See David Gordon, Richard Edwards, and Michael Reich, *Segmented Work, Divided Workers* (Cambridge: Cambridge University Press, 1982), 196, table 5.3. Productivity was well above that for the western European countries, Japan, and Canada in the 1950s, 1960s, and early 1970s. See Angus Maddison, *Phases of Capitalist Development* (Oxford: Oxford University Press, 1982), 212, table C10. On the consumer society, see Patterson, *Grand Expectations,* 343–374.

13. On productivity growth comparisons, see Castells, *The Economic Crisis and American Society,* 111, table 9, and Angus Maddison, *The World Economy in the 20th Century* (Paris: Development Centre of the Organization for Economic Co-operation and Development, 1989), 35, table 3.2. The work stoppages figures were calculated from the data in table 6 on page 92 of Castells's book.

14. See Van der Wee, *Prosperity and Upheaval, 77.* The U.S. unemployment rate for 1975 was 8.5 percent.

15. The actual ratios are 18.8 percent in 1945 and 30.7 percent in 1975. The data were calculated using Council of Economic Advisors, *Economic Report of the President, 1998* (Washington, D.C.: Government Printing Office, 1998), 300, table B-16; U.S. Department of Commerce, *Historical Statistics of the United States;* and, for employment data as well, U.S. Bureau of the Census, *Statistical Abstract of the United States,* various years.

16. French, *U.S. Economic History since 1945,* 84, table 5.3, and Gordon, Edwards, and Reich, *Segmented Work, Divided Workers,* 211, table 5.7/5.8.

17. Lizabeth Cohen, *A Consumers' Republic: The Politics of Mass Consumption in Postwar America* (New York: Knopf, 2003), 196. The home-ownership rates are on page 195. The estimated percentage of middle-class families is from Frank Levy, *The New Dollars and Dreams: American Incomes and Economic Change* (New York: Russell Sage Foundation, 1998). On advertising and the planning for postwar consumption, see Victor J. Visor, "Winning the Peace: American Planning for a Profitable Postwar World," *Journal of American Studies* 35 (2001): 111–126. The GI Bill also contributed to rising rates of home ownership. See Michael Bennett, *When Dreams Come True: The GI Bill and the Making of Modern America* (McLean, Va.: Brassey's, 1996).

18. Castells, *The Economic Crisis and American Society,* 157, table 18. On the growth in the value added to manufacturing, see various years of the U.S. Bureau of the Census, *Statistical Abstract of the United States.*

19. See Paul Kennedy, *Preparing for the Twenty-First Century* (New York: Vintage, 1993), 48, table 1.

20. The income data are from Council of Economic Advisors, *Economic Report of the President, 1979* (Washington, D.C.: Government Printing Office, 1979), 192, table B.8. The data supporting the other claims come from U.S. Department of Commerce, *Historical Statistics of the United States,*

and U.S. Bureau of the Census, *Statistical Abstract of the United States,* various years.

21. Thomas Hine, *Populuxe* (New York: Knopf, 1986), 23.

22. David Harvey, *Social Justice and the City* (Baltimore: The Johns Hopkins University Press, 1973), 27.

23. Rosalyn Baxandall and Elizabeth Ewen, *Picture Windows: How the Suburbs Happened* (New York: Basic Books, 2000), 137. See also Lizabeth Cohen, "Is There an Urban History of Consumption?" *Journal of Urban History* 29, 2 (2003): 92; Cohen, *A Consumers' Republic,* 114–129; and "Family Utopia," *Life,* November 25, 1960, 58–60.

24. The ratio data are from Homer Hoyt, "The Housing Market in the United States since World War II," *Real Estate Issues* 8, no. 1 (1983): 2. The other data are from U.S. Bureau of the Census, *Statistical Abstract of the United States,* various years. Private residential investment went from $16.5 billion to $36.8 billion in 1958 dollars between 1948 and 1973. The national discussion regarding mass-produced housing began in the 1930s.

25. Kenneth T. Jackson, *Crabgrass Frontier: The Suburbanization of the United States* (New York: Oxford University Press, 1985), 234–235.

26. Cohen, *A Consumers' Republic,* 73.

27. Expenditure data are from U.S. Bureau of the Census, *Historical Statistics of the United States,* 639, table N156-169, and U.S. Bureau of the Census, *Statistical Abstract: 1985* (Washington, D.C.: Government Printing Office, 1985), table 1301, 727. Real estate capital averaged 22.3 percent of GNP from 1948 to 1965. After that time, and to 1975, it dropped to 20.4 percent. See National Realty Committee, *America's Real Estate* (Washington, D.C.: National Realty Committee, 1989), 73, table 1.2. These are 1958 dollars.

28. See Michael E. Stone, "Housing and the Dynamics of U.S. Capitalism," in *Critical Perspectives on Housing,* ed. R. Bratt, C. Hartman, and A. Meyerson, 41–67 (Philadelphia: Temple University Press, 1986), 51. The percentage for residential mortgage debt in 1946 was 13.5.

29. Calculated from U.S. Bureau of the Census, *Statistical Abstract of the United States 1973* (Washington, D.C.: Government Printing Office, 1973), 343, table 564.

30. Reuben J. Ellis, "The American Frontier and the Contemporary Real Estate Advertising Magazine," *Journal of Popular Culture* 27, no. 3 (1993): 119–133.

31. Cohen, "Is There an Urban History of Consumption?" 96. See also Gerald E. Frug, *City Making* (Princeton, N.J.: Princeton University Press, 1999).

32. In 1950, 7 percent of households owned one automobile. In 1967, 25 percent did. The data in this paragraph come from various years of the U.S. Bureau of the Census, *Statistical Abstract of the United States.*

33. Ann Markusen, *Profit Cycles, Oligopoly, and Regional Development* (Cambridge, Mass.: MIT Press, 1985), 163.

34. The data on expenditures are from the U.S. Department of Commerce, *Historical Statistics of the United States,* Series G416-469, 316–318, and Council of Economic Advisors, *Economic Report of the President, 1998* (Washington, D.C.: Government Printing Office, 1998), 300, table B-16. The job ratio is from Markusen, *Profit Cycles, Oligopoly, and Regional Development,* 164.

35. See U.S. Bureau of the Census, *Statistical Abstract of the United States,* selected years.

36. The quotation is from Cohen, *A Consumers' Republic,* 123, and the data on debt are from Ernest Mandel, *The Second Slump* (London: Verso, 1980), 29, and Stone, "Housing and the Dynamics of U.S. Capitalism" for private debt in general; U.S. Department of Commerce, *Historical Statistics of the United States,* Series N278-290, 649, for mortgage loans; and Council of Economic Advisors, *Economic Report of the President, 1998,* tables B-75 and B-77, for mortgage and automobile debt, respectively. Private debt went from 74 percent to 150 percent of GNP.

37. See Eva Jacobs and Stephanie Shipp, "How Family Spending Has Changed in the United States," *Monthly Labor Review* 113, no. 3 (1990): 20–27. For the prewar roots of postwar consumerism and suburbanization, see Roger Miller, "Selling Mrs. Consumer: Advertising and the Creation of Suburban Socio-Spatial Relations, 1910–1930," *Antipode* 23, no. 3 (1991): 263–306.

38. See David S. Evans, *Paying with Plastic* (Cambridge, Mass.: MIT Press, 1999), 61–84, and Lewis Mandall, *The Credit Card Industry* (Boston: Twayne, 1990), 11–21. Consumer credit was 4 percent of GNP in 1946. See Stone, "Housing and the Dynamics of U.S. Capitalism," 51.

39. On television consumption, see French, *U.S. Economic History since 1945,* 189, and for the other data see the *Statistical Abstract of the United States* for various years and Council of Economic Advisors, *Economic Report of the President, 1979* (Washington, D.C.: Government Printing Office, 1979), table B-13, 198. Household operating costs as a proportion of personal consumer expenditures went from 5.4 percent to 6.2 percent.

40. The share data are from Thomas Muller, "Regional Malls and Central City Retail Sales: An Overview," in *Shopping Centers: USA,* ed. G. Sternlieb and J. W. Hughes, 177–199 (New Brunswick, N.J.: Center for Urban Policy Research, 1981), 180. The share was 13 percent in 1967. On the number of shopping centers, see Ann Satterthwaite, *Going Shopping: Consumer Choices and Community Consequences* (New Haven, Conn.: Yale University Press, 2001), 52.

41. See Satterthwaite, *Going Shopping,* 52, on retail sales. The quotation is from George Sternlieb, "Is Business Abandoning the City?" *Harvard Business Review* 39, no. 1 (1961): 7. See also Cohen, *A Consumers' Republic,* 268, and Jon C. Teaford, *The Rough Road to Renaissance* (Baltimore: The Johns Hopkins University Press, 1990), 129–131. As regards the social consequences of this shift, see Alison Isenberg, *Downtown America: A History*

of the Place and People Who Made It (Chicago: University of Chicago Press, 2004), 166–254.

42. Council of Economic Advisors, *Economic Report of the President, 1977,* 263, table B-69, and 270, table B-75. On GNP, see French, *U.S. Economic History since 1945,* 22, table 2.1. State and local government expenditures went from $16.4 billion to $132.8 billion.

43. Council of Economic Advisors, *Economic Report of the President, 1979,* 270, table B-75, and Ann Fetter Friedlaender, *The Interstate Highway System* (Amsterdam: North-Holland, 1965), 59, table 3.12.

44. One approach to documenting these expenditures can be found in assessments of the costs of sprawl. See Real Estate Research Corporation, *The Costs of Sprawl: Environmental and Economic Costs of Alternative Residential Development Patterns at the Urban Fringe* (Washington, D.C.: Government Printing Office, 1974), and Robert W. Burchell, Anthony Downs, Sahan Mukheri, and Barbara McCann, *Sprawl Costs: Impacts of Unchecked Development* (Washington, D.C.: Island Press, 2005).

45. The data were calculated from Donald T. Bogue, *The Population of the United States* (New York: Free Press, 1985), 129. The Philadelphia data are reported in Fred K. Vigman, *Crisis of the Cities* (Washington, D.C.: Public Affairs, 1955), 62.

46. Dolores Hayden, *Building Suburbia: Green Fields and Urban Growth, 1820–2000* (New York: Pantheon, 2003), 128. David Harvey has argued that suburbanization and the growth of the South and West in the 1950s and 1960s absorbed surplus capital generated by prosperity. See his *The New Imperialism* (Oxford: Oxford University Press, 2003), 113.

47. For the business cycle peaks between 1948 and 1964, exports ranged between 4.7 and 6.6 percent of GNP. Exports peaked (8.4 percent) in 1973 as the short American Century came to an end.

48. Calculated from Council of Economic Advisors, *Economic Report of the President, 1979,* 199, table B-14.

49. Chafe, *The Unfinished Journey,* 119.

50. Industrial construction expenditures in Philadelphia's suburbs were over three times larger and commercial construction expenditures about one-third larger, with the lower ratio for the latter mainly due to the concentration of office activities in the city. For every three dwelling units built in the city, seven were built in the suburbs. Data are from U.S. Department of Commerce, *Construction Reports* (Washington, D.C.: Government Printing Office, various years).

51. Calvin P. Bradford and Leonard S. Rubinowitz, "The Urban-Suburban Investment-Disinvestment Process: Consequences for Older Neighborhoods," *Annals of the AAPSS,* no. 422 (1975): 77–86.

52. On the urban renewal and public housing programs, see H. Briavel Holcomb and Robert A. Beauregard, *Revitalizing Cities* (Washington, D.C.: Association of American Geographers, 1981), 10–11. On Newark, see George

Sternlieb and Robert W. Burchell, *Residential Abandonment: The Tenement Landlord Revisited* (New Brunswick, N.J.: Center for Urban Policy Research, 1973), Exhibit 1-23, 24. On Philadelphia, see Robert A. Beauregard, "The Turbulence of Housing Markets: Investment, Disinvestment, and Reinvestment in Philadelphia, 1963–1986," in *The Restless Urban Landscape,* ed. P. L. Knox, 55–82 (Englewood Cliffs, N.J.: Prentice-Hall, 1993), 67.

53. Paul Harlan Douglas, *The Suburban Trend* (New York: Century, 1925), 127.

54. See Albert Berggsen and Chintamani Sahoo, "Evidence of the Decline of American Hegemony in World Production," *Review* 8, no. 4 (1985): 595–611; Paul Kennedy, "Fin-de-Siècle America," *New York Review of Books,* June 28, 1990, 31–40; Jeff Madrick, "The End of Affluence," *New York Review of Books,* September 21, 1995, 13–17; and Kenneth W. Thompson, "The Literature of Decline," *Ethics and International Affairs* 3 (1989): 303–315.

55. Robert A. Beauregard, *Voices of Decline: The Postwar Fate of US Cities* (Oxford: Blackwell, 1993), 219–275.

6. Ways of Life

1. Quoted in Rosalyn Baxandall and Elizabeth Ewen, *Picture Windows: How the Suburbs Happened* (New York: Basic Books, 2000), 131. The notion of an "American way of life" was a theme heavily mined by the U.S. advertising industry beginning in the 1930s. See Jackson Lears, *Fables of Abundance: A Cultural History of Advertising in America* (New York: Basic Books, 1994), 124.

2. The concepts *urban* and *suburban* are used here not as categorical distinctions but as references to meanings that connect place, behavior, values, and identity. In this way, I hope to avoid the ideological misrepresentations famously discussed by Manuel Castells in his *The Urban Question* (Cambridge, Mass.: MIT Press, 1977). For a debate over whether suburbs have become more urban in the late twentieth century, see the symposium in the *American Quarterly* 46, no. 1 (1994): 1–61. And for an earlier rejection of a strong urban-suburban distinction, see Herbert Gans, "Urbanism and Suburbanism as Ways of Life: A Re-evaluation of Definitions," in *People and Plans,* ed. H. Gans, 34–52 (New York: Basic Books, 1968).

3. Since 1920, the majority of the U.S. population has lived in urban areas. The official definition of urban, however, is so broad as to subsume almost all of a metropolitan area, including the suburbs. On urban culture and influence, see Thomas Bender, *The Unfinished City: New York and the Metropolitan Idea* (New York: New Press, 2002), 81–100.

4. Bennett M. Berger, "Suburbia and the American Dream," *Public Interest* 2 (1966): 82. The reference to a "suburban ethos" is from Eric Avila, "Popular Culture in the Age of White Flight," *Journal of Urban History* 31, no. 1 (2004): 3–22.

5. Daniel J. Elazar, "Are We a Nation of Cities?" *Public Interest* 4 (1966): 46. See also "Pull of Suburbs Is Stronger: Buyers, Taxpayers Move Out," *U.S. News & World Report,* June 30, 1950, 11–13. All of this is prelude to thinking about the postwar suburbs as a cultural project. See Amy Maria Kenyon, *Dreaming Suburbia: Detroit and the Production of Postwar Space and Culture* (Detroit: Wayne State University Press, 2004), 1–2.

6. On small-town America and social cohesion, see Robert Putnam, *Bowling Alone: The Collapse and Revival of American Community* (New York: Simon and Schuster, 2000), 204–215.

7. Gail Radford, *Modern Housing for America* (Chicago: University of Chicago Press, 1996), 51–53.

8. Clifford E. Clark Jr., "Ranch-House Suburbia: Ideals and Realities," in *Recasting America,* ed. L. May, 171–191 (Chicago: University of Chicago Press, 1989), and Clark Jr., *The American Family Home, 1800–1960* (Chapel Hill: University of North Carolina Press, 1986), 217–243. The quotation is from Neil P. Hurley, "The Case for Suburbia," *Commonweal* 70, no. 18 (1959): 441.

9. For general background, see Robert N. Bellah, Richard Madsen, William M. Sullivan, Ann Swidler, and Stephen M. Tipton, *Habits of the Heart* (New York: Harper and Row, 1986), 177–181; William H. Chafe, *The Unfinished Journey: America since World War II* (New York: Oxford University Press, 1986), 117; Clark Jr., "Ranch-House Suburbia"; Landon Y. Jones, *Great Expectations: America and the Baby Boom Generation* (New York: Ballantine, 1980); William L. O'Neill, *American High: The Years of Confidence, 1945–1960* (New York: Free Press, 1986), 33–44; and Lynn Spigel, *Welcome to the Dream House: Popular Media and Postwar Suburbs* (Durham, N.C.: Duke University Press, 2001). The quotation is from Bellah et al., *Habits of the Heart,* 180.

10. Baxandall and Ewen, *Picture Windows,* 143.

11. On this point, see "Live in the City or the Suburbs?" *Changing Times,* April 1958, 7–11. To wit: "In cold fact, however, many families have fled to the suburbs simply because there was no other place to go" (8). The quotation in the text is from Penn Kimball, "'Dream Town'—Large Economy Size," in *American Society since 1945,* ed. W. L. O'Neill, 37–44 (Chicago: Quadrangle Books, 1969), 40.

12. Lisle A. Rose, *The Cold War Comes to Main Street* (Lawrence: University Press of Kansas, 1999), 11.

13. The quotations, respectively, are from "Suburbs Cut Cities Down to Size," *Business Week,* June 18, 1960, 64; "Suburbia Regnant," *Time,* July 6, 1970, 6; and "Report of the President's Task Force on Suburban Problems," in *The End of Innocence: A Suburban Reader,* ed. C. M. Haar, 13–18 (Glenview, Ill.: Scott, Foresman, 1973), 15.

14. Herbert J. Gans, *The Levittowners: Ways of Life and Politics in a New Suburban Community* (New York: Vintage, 1967), 286. For a general

overview of life in the suburbs, see Michael Johns, *Moment of Grace: The American City in the 1950s* (Berkeley and Los Angeles: University of California Press, 2003), 91–118. For an argument that the family was being changed by the move, see E. Gartly Jaco and Ivan Belknap, "Is a New Family Form Emerging in the Urban Fringe?" *American Sociological Review* 18, no. 5 (1953): 551–557.

15. Dolores Hayden, *Redesigning the American Dream: The Future of Housing, Work, and Family Life* (New York: Norton, 1984), 40–41.

16. Daphne Spain, *Gendered Spaces* (Chapel Hill: University of North Carolina Press, 1992), 109–140, and Gwendolyn Wright, *Building the Dream: A Social History of Housing in America* (New York: Pantheon, 1981), 252–255.

17. Ann Satterthwaite, *Going Shopping: Consumer Choices and Community Consequences* (New Haven, Conn.: Yale University Press, 2001), 75. See also 64–117. Lizabeth Cohen links the transformation of shopping to the decline of downtowns in her "Is There an Urban History of Consumption?" *Journal of Urban History* 29, no. 2 (2003): 87–106.

18. The number of national corporations with fifty or more stores increased from eight in 1966 to thirty-one in 1977. See Satterthwaite, *Going Shopping,* 90.

19. Between 1948 and 1964, the number of motel rooms in the United States went from 304,000 to 1.0 million while the number of hotel rooms (city-based accommodations) declined from 1.55 million to 1.45 million. See James T. Patterson, *Grand Expectations: The United States, 1945–1974* (New York: Oxford University Press, 1996), 334.

20. Avila, "Popular Culture in the Age of White Flight."

21. Gans, *The Levittowners,* 151–302.

22. Clark Jr., *The American Family Home, 1800–1960,* 235.

23. Putnam, *Bowling Alone,* 209.

24. Patterson, *Grand Expectations,* 334.

25. Jones, *Great Expectations,* 23.

26. For a critical perspective on the American pursuit of success, see Jennifer L. Hochschild, *Facing Up to the American Dream: Race, Class, and the Soul of the Nation* (Princeton, N.J.: Princeton University Press, 1995), 15–38. See also Barbara Ehrenreich, *Fear of Falling: The Inner Life of the Middle Class* (New York: Pantheon, 1989).

27. On property and class identity, see Reuben J. Ellis, "The American Frontier and the Contemporary Real Estate Advertising Magazine," *Journal of Popular Culture* 27, no. 3 (1993): 119–133.

28. Nicholas Dagen Bloom, *Merchant of Illusion: America's Salesman of the Businessman's Utopia* (Columbus: Ohio State University Press, 2004), 34.

29. See Baxandall and Ewen, *Picture Windows,* 171–190; Dolores Hayden, *Building Suburbia: Green Fields and Urban Growth, 1820–2000* (New York: Pantheon, 2003), 196–197; Hayden, *Redesigning the American*

Dream, 55–59; Kenneth T. Jackson, *Crabgrass Frontier: The Suburbanization of the United States* (New York: Oxford University Press, 1985), 241.

30. Thomas Hine, *Populuxe* (New York: Knopf, 1986), 23.

31. John J. Palen, *The Suburbs* (New York: McGraw-Hill, 1995), 4.

32. Margaret Pugh O'Mara, *Cities of Knowledge: Cold War Science and the Search for the Next Silicon Valley* (Princeton, N.J.: Princeton University Press, 2005). O'Mara has claimed that to the extent that this added economic diversity, the suburbanization of science "helped to *urbanize* American suburbs" (4, her emphasis).

33. "Crisis in the City," *Senior Scholastic,* October 5, 1960, 8–11.

34. Peter O. Muller, *Contemporary Suburban America* (Engelwood Cliffs, N.J.: Prentice-Hall, 1981), 148–162.

35. Gans, "Urbanism and Suburbanism as Ways of Life."

36. This is the theme of Johns, *Moment of Grace.*

37. Jon C. Teaford, *The Rough Road to Renaissance: Urban Revitalization in America, 1940–1985* (Baltimore: The Johns Hopkins University Press, 1990), 10–121.

38. Jane Jacobs, *The Death and Life of Great American Cities* (New York: Vintage, 1961). For an assessment of her work, see David R. Hill, "Jane Jacobs's Ideas on Big, Diverse Cities," *American Planning Association Journal* 54, no. 3 (1988): 302–314. For a more general portrayal of life in cities, see David A. Karp, Gregory P. Stone, and William C. Yoels, *Being Urban: A Sociology of Urban Life* (New York: Praeger, 1991).

39. Alan Ehrenhalt, *The Lost City: Rediscovering the Forgotten Virtues of Community in the Chicago of the 1950s* (New York: Basic Books, 1995).

40. Arnold R. Hirsch, *Making the Second Ghetto: Race and Housing in Chicago, 1940–1960* (Cambridge: Cambridge University Press, 1983).

41. Douglas Massey and Nancy Denton, *American Apartheid: Segregation and the Making of the Underclass* (Cambridge, Mass.: Harvard University Press, 1993), 16–59.

42. Herbert J. Gans, *The Urban Villagers: Group and Class in the Life of Italian-Americans* (New York: Free Press, 1962), and Daniel J. Monti Jr., *The American City: A Social and Cultural History* (Malden, Mass.: Blackwell, 1999), 279–318.

43. Howard S. Becker and Irving Louis Horowitz, "The Culture of Civility," in *Culture and Civility in San Francisco,* ed. H. S. Becker, 4–19 (New Brunswick, N.J.: Transaction Books, 1971); George Chauncey, *Gay New York: Gender, Urban Culture, and the Making of the Gay Urban World, 1890–1940* (New York: Basic Books, 1994); Edward F. Delaney, *New York's Greenwich Village* (Barre, Mass.: Barre Publishers, 1967); and Herbert Gold, *Bohemia: Digging the Roots of the Cool* (New York: Simon and Schuster, 1993).

44. Daniel Fusfeld and Timothy Bates, *The Political Economy of the Ghetto* (Carbondale: Southern Illinois University Press, 1984); Lee Rainwater, *Behind Ghetto Walls: Black Family Life in a Federal Slum* (Chicago: Aldine,

1970); Carlo Rotella, *October Cities: The Redevelopment of Urban Literature* (Berkeley and Los Angeles: University of California Press, 1998); Sam Bass Warner Jr., "The Management of Multiple Urban Images," in *The Pursuit of Urban History*, ed. D. Fraser and A. Sutcliffe, 383–394 (London: Edward Arnold, 1983).

45. Hirsch, *Making the Second Ghetto;* Nicholas Lemann, *The Promised Land: The Great Black Migration and How It Changed America* (New York: Knopf, 1991); Allan H. Spear, *Black Chicago: The Making of a Negro Ghetto* (Chicago: University of Chicago Press, 1967); and William Julius Wilson, *The Declining Significance of Race* (Chicago: University of Chicago Press, 1978), 122–143.

46. Robert A. Beauregard, *Voices of Decline: The Postwar Fate of U.S. Cities,* 2nd ed. (New York: Routledge, 2003), 127–149.

47. Douglas W. Rae declared the end of urbanism in the postwar period and celebrated its revitalization in the early twentieth century. See his *City: Urbanism and Its End* (New Haven, Conn.: Yale University Press, 2003).

48. Jerry Herron, *AfterCulture: Detroit and the Humiliation of History* (Detroit: Wayne State University Press, 1993).

49. The intellectual critique of the suburbs began in the 1930s. See Catherine Jurca, *White Diaspora: The Suburb and the Twentieth-Century American Novel* (Princeton, N.J.: Princeton University Press, 2001).

50. See Scott Donaldson, *The Suburban Myth* (New York: Columbia University Press, 1969); O'Neill, *American High,* 22–28; Palen, *The Suburbs,* 68–100; and Samuel G. Freedman, "Suburbia Outgrows Its Image in the Arts," *New York Times,* February 28, 1999, Section 2. For a powerful fictional version of these observations, see Richard Yates, *Revolutionary Road* (New York: Random House, 1961).

51. Herbert Gans points to this critique in *The Levittowners,* xvi. See also Andrew Jamison and Ron Eyerman, *Seeds of the Sixties* (Berkeley and Los Angeles: University of California Press, 1995), 30–63; Jackson, *Crabgrass Frontier,* 272; and Patterson, *Grand Expectations,* 337–338. The quotation is from Lewis Mumford, *The City in History* (New York: Harcourt, Brace and World, 1961), 486.

52. John Keats, "Compulsive Suburbia," *Atlantic Monthly,* April 1960, 47–50. The quotations are on pages 47 and 48. On female dissatisfaction with the suburbs, see Alison Isenberg, *Downtown America: A History of the Place and the People Who Made It* (Chicago: University of Chicago Press, 2004), 183–187.

53. Keats, "Compulsive Suburbia," 50.

54. Baxandall and Ewen, *Picture Windows,* 158–167, and Ruth Rosen, *The World Split Open: How the Modern Women's Movement Changed America* (New York: Viking, 2000). Lynn Spigel, in *Welcome to the Dream House,* writes of the "long-term American romance with the detached family home" (3) that complicated the subordination of suburban women.

55. Ehrenreich, *Fear of Falling,* and Richard Sennett, *The Uses of Disorder: Personal Identity and City Life* (New York: Vintage, 1970).

56. Catherine Jurca makes middle-class malaise the core theme of her book *White Diaspora.*

57. Hayden, *Redesigning the American Dream,* 42–45; Hayden, *Building Suburbia,* 128, 148–151; and Jackson, *Crabgrass Frontier,* 236–238.

58. See "Live in the City or the Suburbs?"; "More People and Problems," *Newsweek,* August 28, 1950, 59ff.; and "Suburbs Cut Cities Down to Size," 64.

59. Hurley, "The Case for Suburbia," 439–441.

60. Phyllis McGinley, "Suburbia: Of Thee I Sing," *Harper's Magazine,* December 1949, 82.

61. Larry R. Ford, *Cities and Buildings: Skyscrapers, Skidrows, and Suburbs* (Baltimore: The Johns Hopkins University Press, 1994), 164. See also Lears, *Fables of Abundance.*

62. O'Neill, *American High,* 77–83.

63. Baxandall and Ewen, *Picture Windows,* 167. For the view that the choice of the suburbs was coerced, see "Live in the City or the Suburbs?" The perspective that developers and investors defined the choices of consumers rather than vice versa is also presented in Barry Checkoway, "Large Builders, Federal Housing Programs, and Postwar Suburbanization," in *Marxism and the Metropolis,* ed. W. Tabb and L. Sawers, 152–173 (New York: Oxford University Press, 1984).

64. The phrase is from Karp, Stone, and Yoels, *Being Urban,* 231.

65. Johns, *Moment of Grace,* 118, emphasis mine. See also James Gilbert, *Another Chance: Postwar America, 1945–1985* (Chicago: Dorsey Press, 1986), 107. From a more contemporary observer: "New York has saved itself in part by becoming the very thing it had always claimed to despise: suburban." Paul Goldberger, "The Malling of Manhattan," *Metropolis* 20, no. 7 (2001): 135.

66. Robert N. Bellah, Richard Madsen, William M. Sullivan, Ann Swidler, and Stephen M. Tipton, *The Good Society* (New York: Vintage, 1991), 54.

67. Herron, *AfterCulture,* 37.

68. Lizabeth Cohen, *A Consumers' Republic: The Politics of Mass Consumption in Postwar America* (New York: Knopf, 2003), 197. Alison Isenberg writes that during this period the "consumer culture lost its urban foundations." See her *Downtown America,* 324, endnote 12.

69. The first quotation is from Jurca, *White Diaspora,* 136, and the second is from William Sharpe and Leonard Wallock, "Bold New City or Built-Up 'Burb? Redefining Contemporary Suburbia," *American Quarterly* 46, no. 1 (1994): 17. For a physical-determinist position on these issues, see Harold H. Martin, "Our Revolution, Part One: Are We Building a City 600 Miles Long?" *Saturday Evening Post,* January 2, 1960, 74.

7. America's Global Project

1. James T. Patterson, *Grand Expectations: The United States, 1945–1974* (New York: Oxford University Press, 1996), vii.

2. Patterson, *Grand Expectations,* vii. The historian Henry Steele Commanger agreed: "Americans emerged from the war less self-centered and more conscious of the economic interdependence of all nations and of their responsibilities for the maintenance of sound international economy." See his *The American Mind: An Interpretation of American Thought and Character since the 1880s* (New Haven, Conn.: Yale University Press, 1950), 432. David Harvey made a similar point in relation to American cultural imperialism in his *The New Imperialism* (Oxford: Oxford University Press, 2003), 56–57. Neil Smith, in *The Endgame of Globalization* (New York: Routledge, 2005), 44, commented on an empire detached from geography.

3. Sir Hugh Casson, "Fairest Cities of Them All," *New York Times Magazine,* January 24, 1960, 10ff., and Homer Hoyt, "The Structure and Growth of American Cities Contrasted with the Structure of European and Asiatic Cities," *Urban Land* 18, no. 8 (1959): 245–250.

4. Thomas Borstelmann, *The Cold War and the Color Line: American Race Relations in the Global Arena* (Cambridge, Mass.: Harvard University Press, 2001), 75.

5. "New 'Hearts' for Our Cities," *Newsweek,* March 29, 1954, 74.

6. William H. Whyte Jr., "Are Cities Un-American?" *Fortune,* September 1957, 123ff. Thirty-five years later, Thomas Bender answered Whyte's question by noting the historical tenacity of the claim that cities are un-American and yet the necessity of cities for sustaining democracy. See his "Are Cities American?" *CultureFront* 1, no. 2 (1992): 4–11.

7. Ben Kocivar, "All-American Cities," *Look,* February 4, 1958, 35–37, and Robert A. Beauregard, *Voices of Decline: The Postwar Fate of U.S. Cities,* 2nd ed. (New York: Routledge, 2003), 226–228.

8. The Thurmond quotation is from "The Cities: What Next," *Time,* August 11, 1967, 11. That same article reports that the House Un-American Activities Committee had received a staff study that blamed the riots on extremists and communists.

9. The Katzenback quotation is from "Cities: The Bonfire of Discontent," *Time,* August 26, 1966, 10, and the conclusion of the National Commission is on page 9 of its report, U.S. Riot Commission, *Report of the National Commission on Civil Disorders* (New York: Bantam Books, 1968).

10. Thomas J. McCormick, *America's Half Century: United States Foreign Policy in the Cold War* (Baltimore: The Johns Hopkins University Press, 1989), 192.

11. The first quotation is from Paul Boyer, *By the Bomb's Early Light: American Thought and Culture at the Dawn of the Atomic Age* (New York: Pantheon, 1985), 279. The second quoted phrase is from Mark Gelfand, *A Nation of Cities* (New York: Oxford University Press, 1975), 166–167. A na-

tionwide Gallup poll in 1950 asked respondents, "What do you think is the most important problem facing the country today?" War was mentioned by 40 percent, the economy by 15 percent, unemployment by 10 percent, and communism by 8 percent. In 1975, as the short American Century came to an end, the same question elicited a different list: high cost of living (60 percent), unemployment (20 percent), dissatisfaction with government (7 percent), and the energy crisis (7 percent). See "What's the Problem?" This Week in Review, *New York Times,* August 1, 1999. On the geopolitical aspects of city-suburban distinctions in this period, see Matthew Farish, "Disaster and Decentralization: American Cities and the Cold War," *Cultural Geographer* 10 (2003): 125–148.

12. See "The City under the Bomb," *Time,* October 2, 1950, 12.

13. "The City under the Bomb," 13. See also "A-Bombs on a U.S. City," *Life,* February 27, 1950, 81ff.; "How U.S. Cities Can Prepare for Atomic War," *Life,* December 18, 1950, 77–82; "Naked City," *Time,* November 28, 1949, 66; and "What an Atomic Bomb Might Do to Your City," *American City,* March 1948, 83–84. In "Mist of Death over New York," *Reader's Digest,* April 1947, 7–10, a fictional atomic bomb was detonated at night deep in the city's harbor, creating a radioactive mist that spread over the city and killed 389,104 people within six weeks.

14. "The City under the Bomb," 12.

15. The quotation is from Elaine Tyler May, "Explosive Issues: Sex, Women, and the Bomb," in *Recasting America: Culture and Politics in the Age of the Cold War,* ed. L. May, 154–170 (Chicago: University of Chicago Press, 1989), 161. On the "Family Radiation Kit," see "The People: Ready to Act," *Time,* September 29, 1961, 13–15.

16. Margot A. Henriksen, *Dr. Strangelove's America: Security and Culture in the Atomic Age* (Berkeley and Los Angeles: University of California Press, 1997), 204–205.

17. "A-Bombs on a U.S. City," 89. The advertisement is reproduced in Boyer, *By the Bomb's Early Light,* 311.

18. R. E. Lapp, *Must We Hide?* (Cambridge, Mass.: Adison-Wesley, 1949), 8 and 85. See also Lisle A. Rose, *The Cold War Comes to Main Street* (Lawrence: University Press of Kansas, 1999), 106. For useful discussions of decentralization and the atomic bomb, see Michael Quinn Dudley, "Sprawl as Strategy: City Planners Face the Bomb," *Journal of Planning Education and Research* 21, no. 1 (2001): 52–63; Farish, "Disaster and Decentralization"; and Margaret Pugh O'Mara, *Cities of Knowledge: Cold War Science and the Search for the Next Silicon Valley* (Princeton, N.J.: Princeton University Press, 2005), 28–45. During and just after World War II, federal policy concerning defense industries and related worker housing was one of decentralization. See Greg Hise, *Magnetic Los Angeles: Planning the Twentieth-Century Metropolis* (Baltimore: The Johns Hopkins University Press, 1997), 49–55, and Arnold L. Silverman, "Defense and Deconcentration: Defense Industrialization after

World War II and the Development of Contemporary American Suburbs," in *Suburbia Re-examined,* ed. Barbara M. Kelly, 157–163 (New York: Greenwood, 1989).

19. "Asserts Dispersal Best Bomb Protection," *American City,* February 1955, 24. For a review of the role of city planning in proselytizing "defensive dispersal," see Dudley, "Sprawl as Strategy."

20. Slyvian G. Kindall, *Total Atomic Defense* (New York: Richard Smith, 1952), 83–119.

21. "How U.S. Cities Can Prepare for Atomic War," 85.

22. See Tracy B. Augur, "Planning Cities for the Atomic Age," *American City,* August 1946, 75–76, 123. Richard Gerstell, in his *How to Survive an Atomic Bomb* (New York: Bantam Books, 1950), argued that dispersal was a "silly idea" and that while cities were more vulnerable to attack, they also had more protective shelters. See Boyer, *By the Bomb's Early Light,* 323–325.

23. "Moves Are to Cities," *Science News Letter* 64, no. 24 (December 12, 1953): 373. Of course, "to the cities" meant to metropolitan areas and not necessarily to the central cities.

24. Quotation is from "How U.S. Cities Can Prepare for Atomic War," 85. See also Augur, "Planning Cities for the Atomic Age," 75, and Lapp, *Must We Hide?* 9.

25. Kindall, *Total Atomic Defense,* 87–88.

26. As Michael Quinn Dudley wrote, "The efforts of the dispersal advocates were sincerely—if naively—directed toward maintaining economic functionality after a nuclear attack and to save lives; yet, they consistently failed to identify dispersal's inherent futility" ("Sprawl as Strategy," 62).

27. Henriksen, *Dr. Strangelove's America,* 96.

28. See Dudley, "Sprawl as Strategy"; Gelfand, *A Nation of Cities,* 222–234; and Helen Leavitt, *Superhighway-Superhoax* (Garden City, N.Y.: Doubleday, 1970).

29. The funding formula was later changed to 90:10, federal to state.

30. Augur, "Planning Cities for the Atomic Age," 75.

31. Henriksen, *Dr. Strangelove's America,* 75. For general background on public housing, see Rachel Bratt, "Public Housing: The Controversy and Contribution," in *Critical Perspectives on Housing,* ed. R. Bratt, C. Hartman, and A. Meyerson, 335–361 (Philadelphia: Temple University Press, 1986).

32. Catherine Bauer, "Freedom of Choice," *Nation,* May 15, 1948, 533–537.

33. On this effort, see Rosalyn Baxandall and Elizabeth Ewen, *Picture Windows: How the Suburbs Happened* (New York: Basic Books, 2000), 87–105; Richard O. Davies, *Housing Reform during the Truman Administration* (Columbia: University of Missouri Press, 1966), 67–72; and Nathan Strauss, *Two-Thirds of a Nation* (New York: Knopf, 1952), 256–257.

34. Quoted in Strauss, *Two-Thirds of a Nation,* 263.

35. Davies, *Housing Reform during the Truman Administration,* 18.

A similar ideological attack was mounted against national health insurance during these years. See Jacob S. Hacker, *Divided Welfare State: The Battle over Public and Private Social Benefits in the United States* (Cambridge: Cambridge University Press, 2002), 224–225.

36. Cited in Kenneth T. Jackson, *Crabgrass Frontier: The Suburbanization of the United States* (New York: Oxford University Press, 1985), 231.

37. The first quotation is from Davies, *Housing Reform during the Truman Administration,* 68, and the other two quotations are from Baxandall and Ewen, *Picture Windows,* 91 and 93, respectively. In 1952, Congress passed the Gavin Amendment. It stipulated that "no housing built under the [Housing Administration] Act was to be occupied by any current member of any organization listed by the Attorney General as subversive." A number of local public housing authorities attempted to enforce the amendment, but by 1956, after failing a number of court challenges, the federal government withdrew its commitment to enforcement. See David Caute, *The Great Fear: The Anti-Communist Purge under Truman and Eisenhower* (New York: Simon and Schuster, 1978), 181–182.

38. The subsequent Housing Act of 1954 contained a section (910) that encouraged the provision of housing "in a manner that will facilitate progress in the reduction of vulnerability of congested urban areas to enemy attack" (see Dudley, "Sprawl as Strategy," 59).

39. The Truman quotation is from Davies, *Housing Reform during the Truman Administration,* 96, and the Strauss quotation is from Strauss, *Two-Thirds of a Nation,* 265.

40. Henriksen, *Dr. Strangelove's America,* 96.

41. See Elaine May, "Cold War—Warm Hearth: Politics and the Family in Postwar America," in *The Rise and Fall of the New Deal Order,* ed. S. Fraser and G. Gerstle, 153–181 (Princeton, N.J.: Princeton University Press, 1989); May, "Explosive Issues"; and Anne M. Boylan, "Containment on the Home Front: American Families during the Cold War," *Reviews in American History* 17, no. 2 (1989): 301–305.

42. May, "Cold War—Warm Hearth," 175.

43. John D'Emilio, *Sexual Politics, Sexual Communities: The Making of a Homosexual Minority in the United States* (Chicago: University of Chicago Press, 1983), 40–53.

44. May, "Explosive Issues." Sexual fears were also, as they had been for decades, connected to race, specifically to miscegenation involving black men and white women.

45. May, "Cold War—Warm Hearth," 153–181.

46. Quotation is from Clifford E. Clark Jr., "Ranch-House Suburbia: Ideals and Realities," in May, *Recasting America,* 171. See also Vera Michaels Dean, "U.S. Foreign Policy in the Atomic Age," *American Scholar* 17, no. 1 (1947): 81–85. William W. Goldsmith argued that the racial divides in postwar cities had a significant influence on U.S. foreign policy. His argument is

rudimentary but very suggestive. See his "The Metropolis and Globalization," *American Behavioral Scientist* 41, no. 3 (1997): 299–310.

47. On the political side of the American Dream—citizenship, civil rights, and civic virtues—see Michael Walzer, *What It Means to Be an American* (New York: Marsilio, 1992).

48. By contrast, Hollywood was portraying the cities of the time as a nightmare, particularly in the film noir genre that explored crime, sexuality, and even communism. See Nicholas Christopher, *Somewhere in the Night: Film Noir and the American City* (New York: Holt, 1977), 33–65.

49. Emily S. Rosenberg, *Spreading the American Dream: American Economic and Cultural Expansion, 1890–1945* (New York: Hill and Wang, 1982), 201.

50. Andrew Jamison and Ron Eyerman, *Seeds of the Sixties* (Berkeley and Los Angeles: University of California Press, 1994), 5. The "world dominance" seems a bit extreme. See also Rose, *The Cold War Comes to Main Street*, 297.

51. Henriksen, *Dr. Strangelove's America*, 13. See also Robert Dalleck, "The Postwar World: Made in the USA," in *Estrangement: America and the World*, ed. S. J. Ungar, 27–49 (New York: Oxford University Press, 1985), and David S. Landes, *The Poverty and Wealth of Nations* (New York: Norton, 1998), 459–460.

52. On the turn from isolationism to global engagement, see McCormick, *America's Half Century*, 17–124; Patterson, *Grand Expectations*, 82–104; and Donald W. White, *The American Century: The Rise and Decline of the United States as a World Power* (New Haven, Conn.: Yale University Press, 1996), 159–271.

53. Rosenberg, *Spreading the American Dream*, 234. See also Eric Hobsbawm, *The Age of Extremes: A History of the World, 1914–1992* (New York: Vintage, 1996), 234, where he wrote of this period that "the U.S.A. was a power representing an ideology, which most Americans sincerely believed to be the model for the world."

54. White, *The American Century*, 211–242. On "America's market empire" and its impact on Europe, see Victoria de Grazia, *Irresistible Empire: America's Advance through 20th Century Europe* (Cambridge, Mass.: Belknap Press, 2005).

55. Quoted in Patterson, *Grand Expectations*, 129. On the Marshall Plan, see Hobsbawm, *The Age of Extremes*, 240–241; Scott Jackson, "Prologue to the Marshall Plan: The Origins of an American Commitment for a European Recovery Program," *Journal of American History* 65, no. 4 (1979): 1043–1068; McCormick, *America's Half Century*, 78–86; Charles L. Mee Jr., *The Marshall Plan: The Launching of Pax Americana* (New York: Simon and Schuster, 1984); White, *The American Century*, 201–205; Robin W. Winks, *The Marshall Plan and the American Economy* (New York: Simon and Schuster, 1960); and Herman Van der Wee, *Prosperity and Upheaval: The World*

Economy, 1945–1980 (Berkeley and Los Angeles: University of California Press, 1987), 42–47.

56. The first quotation is from Winks, *The Marshall Plan and the American Economy,* 25, and the second is from Edmond Wright, *The America Dream: From Reconstruction to Reagan* (Cambridge, Mass.: Blackwell, 1996), 339.

57. The quotations are from David Ellwood, "'You Too Can Be Like Us': Selling the Marshall Plan," *History Today* 48, no. 10 (1998): 34 and 33, respectively. See also Wright, *The American Dream,* 339.

58. White, *The American Century,* 204. The trade data can be found in Wright, *The American Dream,* 339.

59. The data in this paragraph were taken from U.S. Department of Commerce, *Historical Statistics of the United States* (Washington, D.C.: Government Printing Office, 1975), and U.S. Bureau of the Census, *Statistical Abstract of the United States* (Washington, D.C.: Government Printing Office, various years). All data are in 1958 dollars.

60. "Is the World Going American?" *U.S. News & World Report,* March 23, 1959, 74. At the same time, European intellectuals held American culture in contempt, much like the contempt that American intellectuals had for the suburbs.

61. Mee Jr., *The Marshall Plan,* 263. Later, the Marshall Plan became an ideal in the debate over the redevelopment of U.S. cities. In 1960, an advisory committee to the Democratic Party, in a report on cities and suburbs, wrote that "just as the Marshall Plan restored the cities of western Europe from the devastation of war, so our program will restore urban America from the ravages of spreading slums and disorderly growth" (quoted in Gelfand, *A Nation of Cities,* 290).

62. Ellwood, "'You Too Can Be Like Us,'" 33.

63. Olivier Zunz commented in *Why the American Century?* (Chicago: University of Chicago Press, 1998) that mass consumption was "the basis for American democracy" and was "emblematic of the 'American Century' as liberals saw it" (90). To this extent, noted Nicholas Dagen Bloom, "the government and the mass media exported the image of the commodious suburban house" as well as that of the shopping mall. Bloom, *Merchant of Illusion: James Rouse, America's Salesman of the Businessman's Utopia* (Columbus: Ohio University Press, 2004), 12 and 125. The invasion of Europe by American consumer goods actually began just after World War I. See Daniel Rodgers, *Atlantic Crossings: Social Policies in a Progressive Age* (Cambridge, Mass.: Harvard University Press, 1998), 370–372, and Peter J. Taylor, "Locating the American Century: A World-Systems Analysis," in *The American Century: Consensus and Coercion in the Projection of American Power,* ed. D. Slater and P. J. Taylor, 3–16 (Oxford: Blackwell, 1999).

64. "Is the World Going American?" 82. See also William E. Leuchtenburg, *A Troubled Feast: American Society since 1945* (Boston: Little, Brown,

1973), 55–57, where, on page 55, he mentioned the Swiss department store advertisement.

65. The Hilton quotation is from Annabel Jane Wharton, *Building the Cold War: Hilton International Hotels and Modern Architecture* (Chicago: University of Chicago Press, 2001), 8. More generally on this topic, see Jeffrey W. Cody, *Exporting American Architecture, 1870–2000* (London: Routledge, 2003), 128–135, and Stephen Ward, "Learning from the U.S.: The Americanization of Western Urban Planning," in *Urbanism: Imported or Exported?* ed. J. Nasr and M. Volait, 83–106 (Chichester, U.K.: Wiley-Academy, 2003). On the domestic impact of Cold War ideas in architecture and city planning, see Timothy Mennel, "Victor Gruen and the Construction of Cold War Utopias," *Journal of Planning History* 3, no. 2 (2004): 116–150.

66. Harvey, *The New Imperialism,* 55.

67. Richard M. Barsam, *Nonfiction Film: A Critical History,* rev. and expanded ed. (Bloomington: Indiana University Press, 1992), 276–280; Leo Bogart, *Premises for Propaganda: The United States Information Agency's Operating Assumptions* (New York: Free Press, 1976); Ronald T. Rubin, *The Objectives of the U.S. Information Agency* (New York: Praeger, 1966); George N. Shuster, "The Nature and Development of United States Cultural Relations," in *Cultural Affairs and Foreign Relations,* ed. R. Blum, 8–40 (Englewood Cliffs, N.J.: Prentice-Hall, 1963); White, *The American Century,* 236–242; and Reinhold Wagnleiter, "Propagating the American Dream: Cultural Politics as Means of Integration," *American Studies International* 24, no. 1 (1986): 60–84.

68. Shuster, "The Nature and Development of United States Cultural Relations," 13. The Voice of America was "the nation's ideological arm of anti-communism." See David F. Krugler, *The Voice of America and the Domestic Propaganda Battles, 1945–1953* (Columbia: University of Missouri Press, 2000), 1.

69. Quoted in Rubin, *The Objectives of the U.S. Information Agency,* 79. See Krugler, *The Voice of America and the Domestic Propaganda Battles, 1945–1953* on frictions around Voice of America between liberal internationalists and conservative isolationists. The difficulties of promoting a single vision of the United States are discussed in Paul Swann, "The Little State Department: Washington and Hollywood's Rhetoric of the Postwar Audience," in *Hollywood to Europe: Experience of a Cultural Hegemony,* ed. D. W. Ellwood and R. Kroes, 176–195 (Amsterdam: VU University Press, 1994).

70. Bogart, *Premises for Propaganda,* xii and 89–90; White, *The American Century,* 238. In its involvement with the motion-picture industry and the exporting of movies, the State Department usually objected to three types of films: those depicting race relations (which it believed foreign audiences had too little knowledge to contextualize), gangster films, and horror movies. The first two can be associated with cities. See Swann, "The Little State Department." For a case study of efforts to export American culture to Austria, see

Reinhold Wagnleitner, "The Irony of American Culture Abroad," 285–301, in May, *Recasting America*.

71. For brief overviews of the debate, see de Grazia, *Irresistible Empire,* 454–456, and White, *The American Century,* 231–233. The cultural clash between the United States and the Soviet Union was part of international trade fairs during these years and was a major aspect of the Brussels World's Fair of 1958. See Johne Findling, ed., *Historical Dictionary of World's Fairs and Exhibitions, 1851–1988* (New York: Greenwood, 1990), 311–318. The Brussels World's Fair had a model of the city of Philadelphia that flipped over to replace a slum with a modern city center, thereby recognizing the country's problems but demonstrating its ability to solve them. See Robert H. Haddow, *Pavilions of Plenty: Exhibiting American Culture Abroad in the 1950s* (Washington, D.C.: Smithsonian Institution Press, 1997), 108.

72. This description of the exhibition is based on "At the Fair, Fascinated Russians Flock to U.S. Exhibits," *Life,* August 10, 1959, 28ff.; "When Nixon Took on Khruschchev," *U.S. News & World Report,* August 3, 1959, 36–39; and White, *The American Century.* The quotation is from "When Nixon Took on Khruschchev," 39.

73. The full text of the speech can be found in "Setting Russia Straight on Facts about the U.S.," *U.S. News & World Report,* August 3, 1959, 70–72.

74. "Nixon-Khrushchev Moscow Debate," August 24, 1959. Video recording 306.2520, records of the U.S. Information Agency, Research Group 306. National Archives at College Park, College Park, Md.

75. Harrison E. Salisbury, "Nixon and Khrushchev Argue in Public as U.S. Exhibit Opens," *New York Times,* July 25, 1959.

76. California was both Nixon's birthplace and the state that epitomized postwar suburban development.

77. The quotations are taken from "Encounter," *Newsweek,* August 3, 1959, 17–18; Salisbury, "Nixon and Khrushchev Argue in Public as U.S. Exhibit Opens," 1–2; and "When Nixon Took on Khruschchev," 36–39.

78. "A Barnstorming Masterpiece," *Life,* August 10, 1959, 22–25. The quotation is on page 22.

79. The quotation is cited in "Nixon, Once Soviet Guest, Becomes Top Soviet Target," *U.S. News & World Report,* September 28, 1959, 60. Richard M. Nixon, *Six Crises* (New York: Doubleday, 1962), 235–291. Nixon would later have another major crisis when in August 1974 he resigned from the presidency, the only president to do so, in the face of probable impeachment for obstruction of justice.

80. May, "Cold War—Warm Hearth," 158.

81. Ibid. See also Daniel Lazare, *America's Undeclared War: What's Killing Our Cities and How to Stop It* (New York: Harcourt, 2001), 243–249.

82. On the politics of mass consumption, see Lizabeth Cohen, *A Consumers' Republic: The Politics of Mass Consumption in Postwar America* (New York: Knopf, 2003), esp. 124–129, and Ruth Rosen, *The World Split*

Apart: How the Modern Women's Movement Changed America (New York: Viking, 2000), 14.

83. Despite this, "cold war tensions induced a terrible self-doubt and ambiguity" about the American Dream. See Thomas Schaub, "Without Fanfare or Foucault: The Cold War and the Loss of a Defining Narrative," *Clio* 26, no. 1 (1996): 104.

84. Wayne S. Cole, *An Interpretive History of American Foreign Relations* (Homewood, Ill.: Dorsey Press, 1968), 482. I have replaced Cole's "urbanization" with "suburbanization." Better than either would be "parasitic urbanization."

85. William L. O'Neill, *American High: The Years of Confidence, 1945–1960* (New York: Free Press, 1986), 4. On the openness of suburbs and their democratic qualities, see Amy Maria Kenyon, *Dreaming Suburbia: Detroit and the Production of Postwar Space and Culture* (Detroit: Wayne State University Press, 2004), 55–59. Promoting American interests abroad also siphoned energy and political will from solving domestic problems. One commentator noted in 1969 that "perhaps our generation is so taken up with America's global supremacy that local concerns seem provincial and picayune." See Kenneth E. Fry, "Central Cities Fight Back," *Nation's Business,* September 1969, 60.

8. Identity and Urbanity

1. See John A. Hall and Charles Lindholm, *Is America Breaking Apart?* (Princeton, N.J.: Princeton University Press, 1999), 61–78; Eric Hobsbawm, *The Age of Extremes: A History of the World, 1914–1991* (New York: Vintage, 1996), 403–432; and James Petras and Morris Morley, *Empire or Republic? American Global Power and Domestic Decay* (New York: Routledge, 1995).

2. Writing in 1967, Guy Debord, a central figure in the revolutionary movements of the 1960s, noted that "we already live in an era of the self-destruction of the urban environment." See his *The Society of the Spectacle* (New York: Zone Books, 1995; orig. pub. 1967), 123.

3. Mike Davis, *Ecology of Fear* (New York: Metropolitan Books, 1998), 354. See also Tom Engelhardt, *The End of Victory Culture: Cold War America and the Disillusioning of a Generation* (New York: Basic Books, 1995), and Thomas Schaub, "Without Fanfare or Foucault: The Cold War and the Loss of a Defining Narrative," *Clio* 26, no. 1 (1996): esp. 98.

4. "The United States was involved in a global 'war,' yet Americans were militarily un-menaced. The economy was churning out the most peaceable and the most warlike of big ticket items, and both were being sold to audiences migratory to the suburbs, intent on creating a carefree world of basement playrooms and backyard barbecues. The country was re-imaging itself as a magic kingdom, a cornucopic mechanism for turning out the world's play toys and pleasure environments" (Engelhardt, *The End of Victory Culture,*

87). See also Lizabeth Cohen, *A Consumers' Republic: The Politics of Mass Consumption in Postwar America* (New York: Knopf, 2003).

5. Bennett M. Berger, "Suburbia and the American Dream," *Public Interest* 2 (1996): 82. I would disagree with the characterization of suburbia as a myth—mythical, maybe, but also very real.

6. Thomas Hine, *Populuxe* (New York: Knopf, 1986), 37.

7. The phrase is from Leo Marx, "Thoughts on the Origins and Character of the American Studies Movement," *American Quarterly* 31, no. 3 (1979): 400. See also George M. Fredrickson, "From Exceptionalism to Variability: Recent Developments in Cross-National Comparative History," *Journal of American History* 82, no. 2 (1995): 587–604.

8. Fredrickson, "From Exceptionalism to Variability," 593.

9. On U.S. urban development versus that in the Soviet Union and western Europe, see Nicholas Dagen Bloom, *Merchant of Illusion: James Rouse, America's Salesman of the Businessman's Utopia* (Columbus: Ohio State University Press, 2004).

10. On the Cold War and American exceptionalism, see Anthony Molho and Gordon S. Wood, "Introduction," in *Imagined Histories: American Historians Interpret the Past,* ed. A. Molho and G. S. Wood, 3–20 (Princeton, N.J.: Princeton University Press, 1988), 10–16.

11. For a theoretical reflection on the relation between space and identity, see Kian Tajbakhsh, *The Promise of the City: Space, Identity, and Politics in Contemporary Thought* (Berkeley and Los Angeles: University of California Press, 2001).

12. My interest is in national identity and not national character. The former has to do with collective perceptions, and the latter with inherent qualities. Moreover, I emphasize the influence of social forces on national identity rather than the reverse. Richard Rorty uses national pride and national identity to center the American Left in political discourse. See his *Achieving Our Country* (Cambridge, Mass.: Harvard University Press, 1998). The urge to connect the suburbs and American identity continued beyond the postwar period. See, for example, David Brooks, "Our Sprawling, Supersize Utopia," *New York Times Magazine,* April 4, 2004, 46–51. On America's bewilderment and incapacitation *after* the short American Century, see Sanford J. Ungar Jr., "The Roots of Estrangement," in *Estrangement: America and the World,* ed. S. J. Ungar Jr., 3–25 (New York: Oxford University Press, 1985), and David A. Hollinger, "How Wide the Circle of 'We'? American Intellectuals and the Problem of the Ethos since World War II," *American Historical Review* 98, no. 2 (1993): 317–337.

13. On how to think about national character and identity, see Henry Steele Commager, *The American Mind: An Interpretation of American Thought and Character since the 1880s* (New Haven, Conn.: Yale University Press, 1950), 406–443; Michael Kammen, *People of Paradox* (New York: Knopf, 1972), 273–298; and Rupert Wilkinson, *American Social Character: Modern*

Interpretations from the '40s to the Present (New York: HarperCollins, 1992), 1–14. The point about public culture is based on Thomas Bender, "Venturesome and Cautious: American History in the 1990s," *Journal of American History* 81, no. 3 (1994): esp. 995. Numerous commentators have used a single trait to define the national identity, culture, or character. See, for example, Michael A. Bellesiles, *Arming America: The Origins of a National Gun Culture* (New York: Knopf, 2000).

14. Hall and Lindholm, *Is America Breaking Apart?*

15. The quotation is from Ralph Barton Perry, *Characteristically American* (New York: Knopf, 1949), 5. The antipodal notion of national identity works against any observer's conclusions. This is also the case here. See Kammen, *People of Paradox,* and Sheldon Hackney, "The American Identity," *Public Historian* 19, no. 1 (1997): 19. On religion as a marker of identity, see Robert D. Putnam, *Bowling Alone: The Collapse and Revival of American Community* (New York: Simon and Schuster, 2000), 65–79.

16. The use of American values to justify a world destiny has been common throughout U.S. history, particularly as regards territorial expansion and military intervention. See David Slater, "Locating the American Century: Themes for a Post-Colonial Perspective," in *The American Century: Consensus and Coercion in the Projection of American Power,* ed. D. Slater and P. J. Taylor, 17–31 (Oxford: Blackwell, 1999).

17. William R. Brock, "Americanism," in *The United States: A Companion to American Studies,* ed. D. Welland, 59–88 (London: Methuen, 1974). Amy Maria Kenyon has pointed out that American citizenship and suburban residence came to be equated. See her *Dreaming Suburbia: Detroit and the Production of Postwar Space and Culture* (Detroit: Wayne State University Press, 2004), 21.

18. The quotation is from Hackney, "The American Identity," 18. On the political aspects of consumption, see Cohen, *A Consumers' Republic.*

19. Michael Walzer, *What It Means to Be an American* (New York: Marsilio, 1992).

20. See Robert Bellah, Richard Madsen, William M. Sullivan, Ann Swidler, and Stephen M. Tipton, *Habits of the Heart* (New York: Harper and Row, 1986); Milton J. Esman, *Government Works: Why Americans Need the Feds* (Ithaca, N.Y.: Cornell University Press, 2000), 38; and Perry, *Characteristically American.* The contemporary partner of individualism is a suspicion of public authority.

21. Lewis Lapham, "Who and What Is American," *Harper's Magazine,* January 1992, 48. See also William Leach, *Country of Exiles: The Destruction of Places in American Life* (New York: Vintage, 2000), 26–30.

22. Jennifer L. Hochschild, *Facing Up to the American Dream* (Princeton, N.J.: Princeton University Press, 1995); Leach, *Country of Exiles;* Sharon Zukin, *Landscapes of Power: From Detroit to Disneyworld* (Berkeley and Los Angeles: University of California Press, 1991).

23. The phrase "continental self-sufficiency" is from Perry, *Character-istically American,* 18. Along these lines, Sanford Ungar Jr., in his "The Roots of Estrangement," 15, focused on self-confidence as a key aspect of the national ideology. He also set his argument in an international context.

24. On the place-based qualities of citizenship, see Richard Dagger, *Civic Virtues* (New York: Oxford University Press, 1997), 154–172, and James Holston, ed., *Cities and Citizenship* (Durham, N.C.: Duke University Press, 1999).

25. Jerry Herron has offered a pro-urban interpretation: "Although most people chose to live elsewhere, they haven't been able to abandon the city imaginatively, whether out of nostalgia or guilt or a combination of the two." See his *AfterCulture: Detroit and the Humiliation of History* (Detroit: Wayne State University Press, 1993), 24.

26. To this extent, I disagree with Henry Steele Commager's assessment that from the 1890s to the 1950s, "American civilization was urban, but it was not yet an urbane civilization" (Commager, *The American Mind,* 406). The "loss of urbanity" theme became a staple of urban scholarship in the 1990s, with particular attention being given to public space and democracy. See Alison Isenberg, *Downtown America: A History of the Place and the People Who Made It* (Chicago: University of Chicago Press, 2004); Don Mitchell, *The Right to the City: Social Justice and the Fight for Public Space* (New York: Guilford Press, 2003); Douglas Rae, *City: Urbanism and Its End* (New Haven, Conn.: Yale University Press, 2003); and Michael Sorkin, ed., *Variations on a Theme Park* (New York: Hill and Wang, 1992). Liam Kennedy also makes the loss of urbanity a central theme in his *Race and Urban Space in Contemporary American Culture* (Edinburgh: Edinburgh University Press, 2000), esp. 3–4.

27. For background on this period, see Stuart M. Blumin, *The Emergence of the Middle Class* (Cambridge: Cambridge University Press, 1989); T. J. Jackson Lears, *No Place of Grace* (New York: Pantheon, 1981); John Tomisch, *A Genteel Endeavor: American Culture and Politics in the Gilded Age* (Stanford, Calif.: Stanford University Press, 1971); and Alan Trachtenburg, *The Incorporation of America* (New York: Hill and Wang, 1982).

28. See M. Christine Boyer, *Dreaming the Rational City* (Cambridge, Mass.: MIT Press, 1983).

29. Daphne Spain, *How Women Saved the City* (Minneapolis: University of Minnesota Press, 2000).

30. Helen Leflowitz Horowitz, *Culture and the City* (Lexington: University Press of Kentucky, 1976).

31. Bellah et al., *Habits of the Heart,* 299. In this way, the loss of bourgeois urbanity reinforced the momentum of parasitic urbanization.

32. Robert N. Bellah, Richard Madsen, William M. Sullivan, Ann Swidler, and Stephen M. Tipton, *The Good Society* (New York: Vintage, 1991), 10–12 and 60–64. On the conservative turn and cities, see Fred Siegel, *The Future Once Happened Here* (New York: Free Press, 1997).

33. On urban citizenship, see Robert A. Beauregard and Anna Bounds, "Urban Citizenship," in *Democracy, Citizenship, and the Global City,* ed. E. Isin, 243–256 (London: Routledge, 2000), and Thomas Bender, "Cities and Citizenship," *The Unfinished City: New York and the Metropolitan Ideal* (New York: New Press, 2002), 199–217.

34. For debate on these issues, see Robert Fishman, "Urbanity and Suburbanity: Rethinking the 'Burbs," *American Quarterly* 46, no. 1 (1994): 35–39, and William Sharpe and Leonard Wallock, "Bold New City or Built-Up 'Burb? Redefining Contemporary Suburbia," *American Quarterly* 46, no. 1 (1994): 1–30. See also Gerald E. Frug, *City Making: Building Communities without Building Walls* (Princeton, N.J.: Princeton University Press, 1999).

35. See Frug, *City Making,* 115–142; Hackney, "The American Identity," 15; Sharon Zukin, *The Cultures of Cities* (Cambridge, Mass.: Blackwell, 1995), 263–271. Robert Putnam, in *Bowling Alone,* wrote that "metropolitans are less engaged [civically] because of where they are, not who they are" (206).

36. As Robert Bellah and his coauthors wrote in the 1990s, U.S. institutions "do not challenge us to use all our capacities so that we have a sense . . . of contributing to the welfare of others" (Bellah et al., *The Good Society,* 49).

37. Neil P. Hurley wrote in 1959: "Not only is the American landscape and traditional way of life of the U.S. in a state of 'becoming' but the national character as well." See his "The Case for Suburbia," *Commonweal* 70, no. 18 (August 25, 1959): 441. Simon Parker goes a bit far when he claims, in *Urban Theory and the Urban Experience* (London: Routledge, 2004), that a "suburban mentality" became "the authentic folk identity of post-war America" (81).

38. The closing of the continental frontier was announced by Frederick Jackson Turner in 1893, while the country's population (according to census records) became more than 50 percent urban in 1920. Kenneth Jackson's *Crabgrass Frontier: The Suburbanization of the United States* (New York: Oxford University Press, 1985) is the suburban reference. President Truman once supposedly commented that "the future itself is America's new frontier." See William Appleman Williams, "American Century: 1914–1957," *Nation,* November 2, 1957, 299. In the context of U.S. foreign policy, the frontier also functions as an impetus for territorial expansion. See Slater, "Locating the American Century," 25, and William Appleman Williams, "The Frontier Thesis and American Foreign Policy," *Pacific Historical Review* 24 (1955): 379–395.

39. Joel Garreau, *Edge City: Life on the New Frontier* (New York: Doubleday, 1991); Robert D. Kaplan, *An Empire Wilderness: Travels into America's Future* (New York: Random House, 1998); Leach, *Country of Exiles;* and Henry Nash Smith, "The Myth of the Garden and Turner's Frontier Thesis," in *A Cultural Studies Reader,* ed. J. Monns and G. Rajan, 216–224 (London: Longman, 1995).

40. "Report on President's Task Force on Suburban Problems," in *The End of Innocence: A Suburban Reader,* ed. C. M. Haar, 13–18 (Glenview,

Ill.: Scott, Foresman, 1972), 13. For the historian Robert Fishman, the history of the suburbs came to an end with the rise of mass suburbanization. See his *Bourgeois Utopias: The Rise and Fall of Suburbia* (New York: Basic Books, 1987), 182–186.

41. Ernest Mandel, *The Second Slump* (London: Verso, 1980); Donald W. White, *The American Century: The Rise and Decline of the United States as a World Power* (New Haven, Conn.: Yale University Press, 1996), 339–438.

42. The quoted phrase is from Molho and Wood, "Introduction," 15. See also Hollinger, "How Wide the Circle of 'We'?"

43. On globalization and cities, see Peter Marcuse and Ronald van Kempen, eds., *Globalizing Cities: A New Spatial Order?* (Oxford: Blackwell, 2000); Saskia Sassen, *The Global City: New York, London, Tokyo* (Princeton, N.J.: Princeton University Press, 1991); and Michael Peter Smith, *Transnational Urbanism: Locating Globalization* (Malden, Mass.: Blackwell, 2000).

44. Sara Diamond, *Roads to Dominion: Right-Wing Movements and Political Power in the United States* (New York: Guilford Press, 1995), 178–227.

45. On this turn in the fortunes of cities, specifically the older, industrial cities, see Robert A. Beauregard, *Voices of Decline: The Postwar Fate of U.S. Cities,* 2nd ed. (New York: Routledge, 2003), 181–233; Larry Bennett, *Fragments of Cities: The New American Downtowns and Neighborhoods* (Columbus: Ohio University Press, 1990); Edward Relph, *The Modern Urban Landscape* (Baltimore: The Johns Hopkins University Press, 1987), 211–251; Neil Smith, *The New Urban Frontier: Gentrification and the Revanchist City* (London: Routledge, 1996); and Jon C. Teaford, *The Rough Road to Renaissance* (Baltimore: The Johns Hopkins University Press, 1990), 253–313.

46. On the late-twentieth-century city as a site for consumption and entertainment, see John A. Hannigan, *Fantasy City: Pleasure and Profit in the Postmodern Metropolis* (London: Routledge, 1998), and Dennis R. Judd and Susan S. Fainstein, eds., *The Tourist City* (New Haven, Conn.: Yale University Press, 1999).

47. See Paul L. Knox, "Globalization and Urban Change," *Annals of the AAPSS,* no. 551 (1997): 17–27, and Hank V. Savitch, "What Is New about Globalization and What Does It Portend for Cities?" *International Social Science Journal* 172 (2002): 179–189.

48. The quotation is from Henry James, *The American Scene* (Bloomington: Indiana University Press, 1907), 9. On the necessity of memory, see Avishai Margalit, *The Ethics of Memory* (Cambridge, Mass.: Harvard University Press, 2002).

49. The phrase is from Andreas Huyssen, *Present Pasts: Urban Palimpsests and the Politics of Memory* (Stanford, Calif.: Stanford University Press, 2003), 10.

50. David Harvey argued that the U.S. responses to terrorism in 2002

and 2003, including the invasions of Afghanistan and Iraq, were indicators of a renewed American empire and thus a return to the arrogance of the short American Century. See his *The New Imperialism* (Oxford: Oxford University Press, 2003).

51. Brock, "Americanism," 66.

Index

London, 61, 63, 65–66, 103, 193
Long Island (New York), 94
long swings of development. *See*
  development, long waves of
long waves. *See* development, long
  waves of
Look, 146
Los Angeles, 28, 45, 47, 111, 148,
  192–93
Louisiana Purchase, 73
Louisville (Kentucky), 26, 192
Luce, Henry, 1, 11, 13, 161, 179,
  182, 209n1

Madrid, 145
Malaysia, 67
Manchester (England), 62, 63, 65
Manifest Destiny, 12. *See also*
  empire
manufacturing, 24–26, 68, 98,
  105–6, 145, 173, 176–77; world-
  wide, 67
Marshall, George C., 162
Marshall Plan, xiii, 10, 104, 162–65,
  178, 253n61
Marx, Leo, 73
mass society, 138
May, Elaine Tyler, 158, 169
McCarthy, Joseph, 156
McCarthyism, 156, 158
McGinley, Phyllis, 140
McKeesport (Pennsylvania), 33
megacities, 66
men: in suburbs, 126–27, 158–59
metropolitan areas, 5, 34, 45, 47;
  districts, 33; economies, 2;
  growth of 30–31, 35; metropolitanization, 40, 50
Mexicans, 29
Mexico, 67, 149
Mexico City, 66
Miami (Florida), 29, 193
middle class, 13, 24, 34, 103, 107,
  124, 131, 187; *embourgeoise-*

ment, 13. *See also* bourgeois
  urbanity
migration, internal U.S., 3, 35, 176;
  to cities, 21, 34; from cities,
  20–21, 23, 33–34, 35–36, 38,
  47, 59, 188; rural-to-urban, 22,
  44–45, 74, 88, 125, 176
military, U.S., 10, 12, 102
Milwaukee (Wisconsin), 50, 185
Minneapolis (Minnesota), 3
mobility: spatial, 92, 142, 184,
  194–95; upward, 131, 135
Montreal, 63, 70
morality: imagination, 6; immorality
  and cities, 74–75; moral indifference, 8, 188–89; moral tone, xiv;
  sense of, 74–75, 188–89
mortgages: debt, 110; insurance (*see*
  Federal Housing Administration);
  lending, 100, 119; residential,
  83, 110
Moscow, 167, 170
multiculturalism. *See* social diversity

Nagasaki, 103, 147
National Association of Real Estate
  Boards, 155
National Commission on Civil Dis-
  orders, 146
National Interstate and Defense
  Highway Act of 1956, 152
National Resources Board, 22
neighborhoods, ethnic, 134–35, 138;
  urban, 85, 133–35
neighboring, 129–30; *kaffeeklatsch,*
  129
neglect, urban, 6. *See also* decline,
  urban
Netherlands, the, 45
Newark (New Jersey), 22, 76, 193
New Deal, 12, 78, 80, 82, 90, 156
New Orleans (Louisiana), 184
new towns, 15, 64, 80
New York City, 2, 20, 26–27, 30, 45,

47–48, 61, 66, 70, 135, 148–49, 180, 187, 192–93

New Zealand, 66

Newsweek, 86

Nigeria, 67

Nixon, Richard M., 82, 166–69

Norfolk (Virginia), 30

nostalgia, 73, 137, 140–41, 194

Oakland (California), 50

obsolescence: of cities, 5, 175, 194

Office of War Information, 165

Omaha (Nebraska), 28, 31

open space, 88. *See also* land

Paris, 66, 73, 145, 180, 193

pastoralism, 73, 76

periphery, metropolitan. *See* suburbs

Philadelphia, 2, 20, 23, 26, 32, 38, 61, 66, 76, 96, 117, 174, 180

Phoenix (Arizona), 29, 30, 50, 132, 190

Pittsburgh, 2, 27, 31, 33, 47–48, 53, 63, 77, 96, 108, 176, 187, 190, 193

planning, city, 150–52

Plymouth Colony (Massachusetts), 31

policy: city, 78–79; federal, 78–80, 187; national urban, 4–5, 59, 70–71, 79–80, 91; pro-growth, 51, 91; state, 80; urban, 70–71, 78–87, 100

political economy, xii

political influence: of cities, 75, 82–83, 176

population: density (*see* density, population); growth, 29–32, 35, 37, 39; loss, 21–24, 26–27, 37–38, 201–2; loss in non-U.S. cities (*see* cities); Population Research Bureau, 151; rural areas, 23

Portland (Oregon), 26

Portsmouth (New Hampshire), 26

poverty, 15–16, 103

premarital sex, 159

President's Task Force on Suburban Problems, 190

productivity, 67, 105–7, 172

profits: and competition, 89–90; pursuit of, 89–90; and risk, 89

progress, 8, 9, 93

Progressive Era, 91

propaganda, 165–66; and cities, 170–71, 179–180; and popular culture, xii, 161, 164, 172; and Soviets, 145; and suburbs, 170

property, private, 92; wealth from, 110

property values, 110–11

prosperity, postwar, 1–2, 5, 10–11, 13, 17, 98, 101–21, 160, 173; and consumerism, 109–14, 131, 170; limits of, 120–21; and postwar urbanization, 116–20

Providence (Rhode Island), 27, 153, 185

public housing, 81–82; and anti-communism, 155–57

Puerto Ricans, 21; migration, 45

race, 4; anxiety, 17; discrimination, 15–17, 33, 84, 143, 188; relations, 2, 174, riots, 146

railroads, 32, 53

Randburg (South Africa), 65

real estate development, 54. *See also* development; cycles, building

recession: early 1970s, 1, 172, 190

redevelopment, urban, 88, 119, 176; investment in, 99, 101. *See also* resurgence, urban

redlining, 83

reform, social, 186

regional development, 5, 30

regional shifts, 5, 17, 30, 40, 45–50

regions, U.S.: East, 31; Midwest, 5,

Robert A. Beauregard is a professor in the Graduate School of Architecture, Planning, and Preservation at Columbia University. He is the author of *Voices of Decline: The Postwar Fate of U.S. Cities*, editor of *Atop the Urban Hierarchy*, and coeditor of *The Urban Moment: Cosmopolitan Essays on the Late Twentieth-Century City*.